Management Control Systems

Principles and Practices

Second Edition

Subhash Chandra Das

Management Consultant

Former Visiting Faculty
Indian Institute of Social Welfare and Business Management
University of Calcutta
and
Former Director (Finance), HPC Ltd.

PHI Learning Private Limited

Delhi-110092
2019

₹ 425.00

MANAGEMENT CONTROL SYSTEMS: Principles and Practices, Second Edition
Subhash Chandra Das

ISBN-978-93-87472-71-6 (Print Book)
ISBN-978-93-87472-72-3 (e-Book)

Second Printing (Second Edition) ... ... July, 2019

Published by Asoke K. Ghosh, PHI Learning Private Limited, Rimjhim House, 111, Patparganj Industrial Estate, Delhi-110092 and Printed by Mudrak, D-61, Sector 63, Noida, U.P.-201301.

To

My Respected Teacher and Mentor
Prof. S.K. Chakraborty,
who taught me the first lesson of Management

Contents

Preface

Enthused by the overwhelming response to the previous edition of this book and prodded by the suggestions received from my students and the readers, I have added the following new materials, texts and examples in the existing chapters as well as added a new chapter to enrich and update the book. The sections that are added are as follows:

- In Chapter 8: Budgeting and Budgetary Control, Objectives of Budgeting, Characteristics of Good Budgeting, Limitations of Budgetary Control.
- In Chapter 9: Standard Costing System and Variance Analysis for Control Actions, Standard Cost, Standard Costing, its advantages and limitations.
- In Chapter 11: Reward System, Performance Variables, its types (BSC).
- In Chapter 14: Marginal Costing, Profit–Volume Graph (P/V Graph) or Profit Chart, Multi-Product Break Even Chart and Comparison of Absorption Costing and Marginal Costing.

Chapter 14 has been re-titled as 'Marginal Costing' and revised. A new Chapter 15: 'Managerial Decision Making' has been included in this book to demonstrate with examples how managerial decisions are taken by the organisations as a part of management control exercise by the application of marginal costing techniques.

This book has the following special features:

- It contains glossary of terms to explain the core concepts.
- It explains concepts and theories in a cogent and lucid manner.
- It contains large number of illustrative examples in between the sections as well as numerous exercises for the benefit of students' analytical understanding on the subject.

- It discusses the topics along with Appendices at the back of the book enclosing related tables and figures.
- It discusses on current issues, and interrelations between these issues and management control systems.

Primarily intended for the postgraduate students of management, the new edition of the book can be equally beneficial for the commerce students, researchers, accounts professionals, and corporate policy and decision-makers.

Subhash Chandra Das

Preface to the First Edition

A control system is a set of formal and informal systems to assist the management in steering the organization towards its goals. Management Control System (MCS) is a set of interrelated communication structures that facilitates the processing of information to assist managers in coordinating the parts and attaining the purpose of an organization on a continuous basis. Therefore, management control system is an interdisciplinary subject as it requires contributions from all branches concerned with the management in achieving a high level of quality, productivity and innovation.

While writing my previous two books on the subject 'Corporate Governance', I searched for the reasons of big corporate failures in the world during the period of late 1990's and 2000, viz., Enron, WorldCom, AOL, and recently Lehman Brothers, Japan Airlines, etc. I noticed that there was either absence or deliberate malfunctioning of control systems, causing huge losses and ultimately bankruptcy. Besides, defective products and services, poor coordination between sections, departments, and subsidiaries also had contributed to lacunae in the control systems apart from governance failure. In fact, these corporate failures provoked me to work on the subject of management control system.

While going through the various works that have been done on this subject so far, I observed that except a few books written by foreign authors, the Indian books available on this subject are very few. Moreover, no attempt has been made from any quarter to make an in-depth study and bring all the principles, practices and various approaches of management control system comprehensively in one book for the benefit of the readers.

This book seeks to bring together, and critically examine the principles, practices and approaches of management control systems from various dimensions. It contains twenty two chapters, which are divided into seven parts. Part I, begins with an overview on the subject, followed by the approaches to MCS, its design and key success variables as control indicators. Part II, Environment and Management Control, describes goals, strategies and organization for adaptive control, divisional autonomy and responsibility. Part III, Management Control Tools and Processes, explains strategic planning and programming process, budgeting and budgetary control, standard costing and variance analysis, transfer pricing, reward system, and management control of operations. Part IV, Strategic Cost Management, examines various aspects of strategic cost management exercise and continuous process improvement methods, and cost analysis for managerial decision making. Part V, Auditing as a tool of Management Control System, deals with various kinds of auditing of management functions. Part VI, Management Control in Organizations, discusses on management control of multinational companies, service organizations, non-profit organizations, and project management control. Part VII, Current Issues and Management Control, explains the relationship between ethics and management control, and corporate governance and management control.

My gratitude is unlimited to the authors of books and various research publications whose works on management control have been consulted by me in course of my endeavour. I express my sincere thanks to my readers for their constant encouragement, and do hope that this book, primarily intended for the students of commerce, and management, can also be authoritatively used by researchers, professionals, corporate policy and decision-makers all over the world.

Subhash Chandra Das

Acknowledgements

A critical subject of varied nature, such as this, calls for intellectual nourishment, professional guidance and encouragement from many quarters. I would like to express my gratitude to the stalwarts in the field of management control system, who have shaped my understanding and conception through their rich and varied contributions. In particular, I am grateful to Dr. Jamshed J. Irani, Director, Tata Sons Limited for his valuable support.

I would also like to thank Dr. Achirangshu Acharya, Dr. Sekhar Chowdhury, Dr. S.N. Ray, Dr. Dipyendu K. Banerjee, Mr. Siddhartha Sen, Mr. S.R. Das, and Mr. C.R. Sen for their help, valuable advice and support.

My greatest gratitude, of course, is to my wife, Anjana, for her encouragement and sacrifice, and to my daughters, Aparajita and Animita, for their contribution.

Subhash Chandra Das

List of Abbreviations

ABC : Activity Based Costing
ARR : Accounting Rate of Return
B/C Ratio : Benefit–Cost Ratio
BEC : Break Even Chart
BSC : Balanced Score Card
BOD : Board Of Directors
CEO : Chief Executive Officer
CFO : Chief Finance Officer
CIMA (London) : Chartered Institute of Management Accountants (London)
CPI : Continuous Process Improvement
CPM : Critical Path Method
C-V-P : Cost-Volume-Profit
DCF : Discounted Cash Flow
DPB : Discounted Pay Back
DPR : Detail Project Report
EBDIT : Earning Before Depreciation, Interest and Tax
EBIT : Earning Before Interest and Tax
EDP : Electronic Data Processing
EOQ : Economic Order Quantity
EPS : Earning Per Share
FA : Financial Audit

FI	:	Financial Institution
FII	:	Foreign Institutional Investor
HRD	:	Human Resource Department
HQs	:	Head Quarters
IRR	:	Internal Rate of Return
IT	:	Information Technology
JIT	:	Just-In-Time
KRAs	:	Key Result Areas
L/C	:	Letter of Credit
MBO	:	Management By Objective
MCS	:	Management Control System
MIRR	:	Modified Internal Rate of Return
MIS	:	Management Information System
MNCs	:	Multinational Companies
M/S	:	Margin of Safety
MSSM	:	Mutually Supportive Systems Model
NFA	:	Non Financial Audit
NPV	:	Net Present Value
PAT	:	Profit After Tax
PB	:	Pay Back
PBT	:	Profit Before Tax
PERT	:	Project Evaluation and Review Technique
PI	:	Profitability Index
PVC	:	Present Value of Cost
P/V ratio	:	Profit-Volume ratio
R&D	:	Research and Development
ROE	:	Return On Equity
ROI	:	Return On Investment
SBU	:	Strategic Business Unit
SCM	:	Strategic Cost Management
SEBI	:	Securities and Exchange Board of India
TQC	:	Total Quality Control
TQM	:	Total Quality Management
TV	:	Terminal Value
WIP	:	Work In Progress
ZBB	:	Zero Based Budgeting

Part I

Management Control Systems

1

Management Control Systems
An Introduction

1.1 DEFINITION

A control system is a set of formal and informal systems to assist the management in steering the organization towards its goals. A Management Control System (MCS) is a set of interrelated communication structures that facilitates the processing of information to assist managers in coordinating the parts and attaining the purpose of an organization on a continuous basis. Therefore, management control system is an interdisciplinary subject as it requires contributions from all branches concerned with the management in achieving a high level of quality, productivity and innovation.

The word 'management control' has been defined differently by different authorities on the subject. According to Anthony, Dearden and Govindarajan, strategic planning, management control, and task control are the three interrelated processes of planning and control. William Newsman considers 'control' as an essential part of the management process. Katz, Kahn and Griesinger view the entire organization as a control system. Maciarello and Kirby opine that the control of strategy and operations is a part of management control.

If we go through the reasons of big corporate failures in the world during late 1990's and 2000, like Enron, WorldCom, AOL, and recently, Lehman Brothers, Japan Airlines, etc., we shall notice that there was either the absence or deliberate malfunctioning of control systems, causing huge losses and ultimately bankruptcy. Besides, defective products and services, poor coordination between sections, departments, and subsidiaries also have arisen due to lacunae in the control systems.

1.2 PURPOSE OF MANAGEMENT CONTROL SYSTEM (MCS)

The main purpose of a management control system is to assist management in coordinating the activities of the firm and in steering those activities towards achievement of the firm's overall purposes, goals and objectives.

The following functions are involved in the management control system:

(i) Planning the activities of the firm
(ii) Coordinating the activities of the firm
(iii) Communicating information to various levels of organization structure
(iv) Evaluating information and deciding the course of action
(v) Influencing people to change their style of functioning

The purpose of MCS is to compare the actual results with the set standards in order to ensure that the work of each section of the firm is harmoniously accomplished with the works of the other sections. Therefore, MCS bring about unity of purpose in an organization. A firm implements MCS to ensure that appropriate strategies are implemented to attain its goals. They also ensure that prompt actions are taken in case of emergency and uncertainty as well. They also help the management in decision-making process.

1.3 IMPORTANCE OF MANAGEMENT CONTROL SYSTEM (MCS)

The management control systems include the following areas of planning and control:

(i) Strategic planning
(ii) Management control
(iii) Task control
(iv) Strategic control
(iv) Operational control

The strategic planning and control deal with the issues pertaining to an organization's basic objectives and implementation followed by monitoring of its progress. The management deals with proper allocation and effective utilization of resources, sustenance in competition and transformation of the organization's objectives into reality. The task and operation controls deal with the factors of efficiency in operations of the firm.

Therefore, we can say that management control systems are the formal and informal systems which help the management in driving the organization towards its goals. They provide effective guidance to the employees of the organization for accomplishment of its objectives. Formal controls are laid down in writing by the management, whereas informal controls arise out of employees' behaviour.

1.4 ROLE OF MANAGEMENT CONTROL SYSTEMS

Organizations are divided into sub-units. Which are further based on the principles of specialization and division of labour. The control system plays a major role in coordinating the efforts of these sub-units. Control system designers try to design systems to minimize the transaction costs. Each sub-unit has an objective that is derived from the overall purpose of the firm.

The control systems assist the executives in meeting overall purpose of the organization and the requirements of its constituents. There are three essential managerial functions of an executive. These are as follows:

(i) Securing essential efforts from the employees as well as the stakeholders of the firm

(ii) Providing a good communication system to coordinate various activities of the firm

(iii) Setting up the purpose, goals and objectives for an organization and delegating responsibility to various sub-units to accomplish the goals

1.5 ELEMENTS OF MANAGEMENT CONTROL SYSTEMS

Anthony and Govindarajan have segregated MCS into four important elements as follows:

(i) A detector or sensor

(ii) An assessor

(iii) An effector

(iv) A communication network

The role of the 'detector' is to observe information as to what is happening, and accordingly analyze the situation to be controlled. The role of the 'assessor' is to compare the actual results with the standards set. An 'effector' is supposed to minimize the gap between the standard results and actual results. The responsibility of 'communication network' is to transmit information among the 'detector', the 'assessor' and the 'effector' (as shown in Figure 1.1).

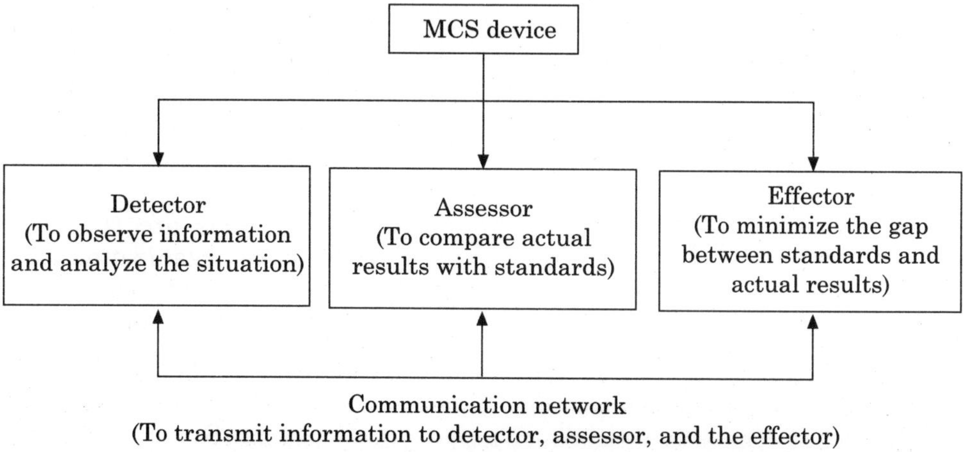

Figure 1.1 Elements of the Control Process.

1.6 FEATURES OF MANAGEMENT CONTROL SYSTEMS

We have seen so far that MCS is designed to assist managers in planning and controlling the activities of a firm. It is the tool by which the managers at senior level ensure that the subordinate managers attain the objectives of the organization effectively and efficiently. In fact, it is the process which ensures that resources are used in optimum manner in the accomplishment of the organization's objectives.

Management control decisions are based on the framework set up for strategy implementation by the organization. The resources in the organization may be scarce. Therefore, within the scarcity of the available resources, a company executive should be able to perform activities best-suited for his own development.

An effective MCS is an important tool for execution of management strategy. But the effective execution is possible only when there is an efficient HR management, excellent work culture as well as an efficient organization structure. All these tools can be provided by an effective MCS.

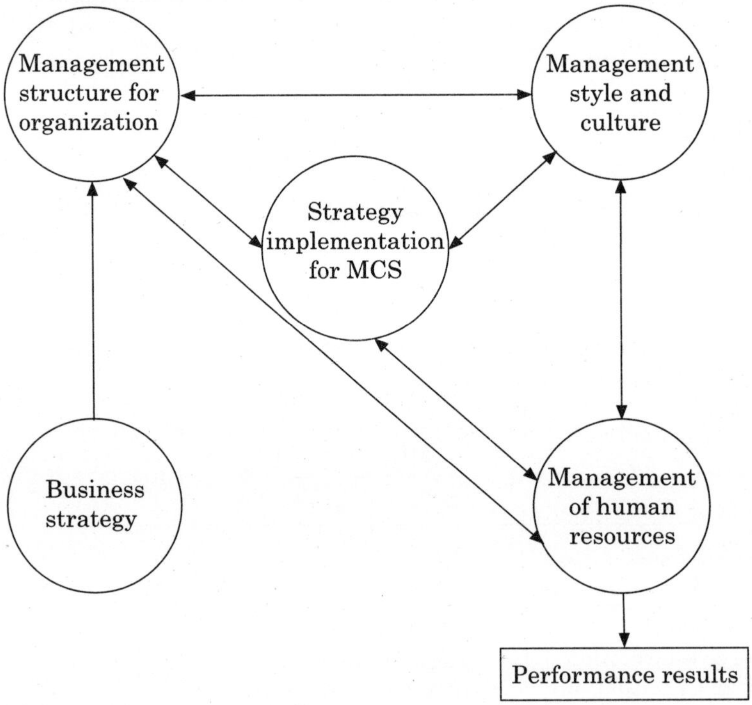

Figure 1.2 Strategy Implementation Framework.

A good MCS deals effectively with various problems of the employees in an organization such as lack of motivation, personal limitation, mismatch of individual goals with organizational goals, etc. An effective control system provides employees with the requisite support, motivation and direction to accomplish desired results as per their full potential and caliber. It balances nicely between the individual goals of the employees and organizational goals and strives to match them adequately. It also minimizes personal limitation by way of adequate training, sharing information and experience.

1.7 A GOOD MANAGEMENT CONTROL SYSTEM: THE PRE-REQUISITES

A good MCS must ensure the following:

(i) All round success for an organization
(ii) The goals and objectives of the organization are clearly defined and adequately communicated to all employees of the organization
(iii) Providing adequate and appropriate aid and opportunities to the employees for accomplishment of their tasks well
(iv) Putting in place adequate control devices for effective managerial control so as to minimize the control losses

1.8 STRATEGY FORMULATION VS. MANAGEMENT CONTROL VS. TASK CONTROL

It is important at this stage to spell out the differences between management control and strategy formulation, and task control and management control.

1.8.1 Management Control vs. Strategy Formulation

(i) Strategy formulation involves only the highest level of management, whereas management control involves managers and employees at all levels in the organization.
(ii) Strategy formulation involves formulation of various strategies by the highest level of management, whereas management control involves implementation of these strategies in a systematic manner.

1.8.2 Management Control vs. Task Control

Task control is concerned with the control of tasks of individual employees which are carried out as per rules and regulations laid down by the MCS, whereas management control is concerned with the behavioural aspects of the employees.

1.9 TYPES OF MANAGEMENT CONTROL SYSTEMS

MCS in an organization generally fall under two categories:

(i) Formal
(ii) Informal

We have mentioned before that formal controls are laid down in writing by the management, but the informal controls arise out of employees' behaviour. For example, work plans, rules and regulations, etc., which are laid down in writing are called **formal controls**, whereas group behaviour, work culture, organizational norms, etc., which are not in written form, are termed as **informal controls**. Therefore, we can say that formal controls are framed by the management and the informal controls arise from the behavioural aspects of the employees and greatly influenced by the prevalent socio-cultural factors.

Let us now discuss these controls in some details.

1.9.1 Formal Control Systems

Formal control systems make explicit the structure, policies and procedures to be followed by members of the firm. It helps management in planning and maintaining strategies in order to meet organizational goals.

Formal control systems are classified into the following:

(i) Controls on inputs or input controls
(ii) Controls on processes or process controls
(iii) Controls on outputs or output controls

Input controls involve taking actions by the management at the planning stage. They include resources availability and allocation, strategic planning, etc. Process controls involve monitoring of actual performance and taking corrective actions in case of deviations in the variables from the specified parameters. Output controls involve evaluating the actual results performed and comparing them with the standards set.

The formal control systems should be permanent, consistent and supportive of the informal systems of the organization. They help in managing the short-term goals and the innovations to meet the future challenges.

1.9.2 Informal Control Systems

Informal control systems promote greater compatibility of personnel, and encourage the 'willingness to serve' organizational purposes.

Informal control systems are of three types. They are as follows:

(i) Cultural controls
(ii) Social controls
(iii) Employee's self-control

Cultural controls can be exercised by the norms of social interaction, work culture and tradition of the organization. Social controls can be achieved by way of internalization of value system and mutual commitments between the employees and the organization towards achieving common goals. Benefits of the self-control to the organization can be achieved maximum when the organization's goals are in congruence with the employee's own goals.

Informal control systems increase a firm's ability to make adaptive responses. They support the management in adapting and maintaining the organization, environmental changes and technical innovation.

1.10 CONTROL SYSTEMS AND THEIR SUB-SYSTEMS AND COMPONENTS

The control systems consist of certain sub-systems which are interconnected. Each of these sub-systems has respective components. They are mentioned hereunder:

(i) Style and culture
(ii) Formal control process
(iii) Infrastructure
(iv) Rewards
(v) Co-ordination and integration
(vi) Informal control process

1.10.1 Style and Culture

Corporate culture

(a) Shared values and commitment of the people to shared values
(b) Common perceptions and the decision premises applied by the people to the activities and problems of the organization

Corporate culture as a control mechanism

(a) Developing a sense of group loyalty
(b) Reducing conflicts and friction

Management socialization and skill training

(a) Socializing members of the organization to its values, procedures and policies
(b) Training at the right time for the right people

Self-control through the acceptance of common values is the most effective control system, provided, the values are the right values for the environment that a firm faces at that time.

1.10.2 Formal Control Process

The formal control process has two dimensions as follows:

(a) Formal planning process
(b) Formal reporting process

A strategic planning system is necessary to assist the firm in planning and control of the projects. It helps the organization to decide its goals and objectives, and key strategies. An operational planning system undertakes activities that are short term in nature. Regular reports help the organization to analyze its performance periodically, and to decide on the next course of action.

1.10.3 Infrastructure

The infrastructure of an organization refers to the structure and the patterns of its autonomy that include delegation of responsibility and the methods of measuring accomplishment of tasks. The most common method of devolving responsibility for strategic business planning is to set up Strategic Business Units (SBUs). Each profit centre is a small business organization responsible for its own profit level.

1.10.4 Rewards

The best method of inducing individuals to participate in the various activities of the organization is to set up an appropriate incentive plan that may be monetary and/or non-monetary.

1.10.5 Co-ordination and Integration

Co-ordination and integration can be accomplished through committees and formal conferences of key managers. There are management committees, viz. strategic committees, operating committees, etc., for making decisions on allocation of resources. Similarly, various conferences are held among managers from time-to-time. Effective information and telecommunication systems help in co-ordination and integration.

1.10.6 Informal Control Process

Informal control process can be exercised in the following manner:

(a) Using adhoc teams to solve problems, improve productivity, and achieve organizational change
(b) Informal communication system used to develop work relationship
(c) Informal rewards and recognition

The informal control process helps in developing the new goals, and objectives.

1.11 CONCLUSION

Management control system is a set of interrelated communication structure that facilitates the processing of information to assist managers in coordinating the parts and attaining the purpose of an organization on a continuous basis. It is imperative for the successful attainment of corporate goals and objectives.

This introductory chapter has broadly dealt with the purpose, importance, roles and pre-requisites of a good MCS in an organization. Various elements of MCS and their features have also been discussed. It has provided the basic differences between management control, strategy formulation, and task control. The types of management control systems and their classifications into formal and informal controls and their sub-systems and components have been discussed in detail.

Review Questions

1.1 (a) Define management control system?
(b) Discuss the purpose and importance of management control system?

1.2 Explain with diagram various elements and features of management control system?

1.3 What according to you, should be the pre-requisites of a good management control system?

1.4 Differentiate between strategy formulation, management control and task control?

1.5 Discuss the various types of management control system?

1.6 What are the various sub-systems and components of management control system? How do they assist in establishing a good management control system in an organization?

2

Approaches to Management Control System

2.1 INTRODUCTION

Having discussed broadly the various aspects of MCS, we shall now discuss in this chapter the various approaches to the implementation of MCS. It is no denial of the fact that there is a need for designing control systems for an organization having complex structure, to function smoothly and efficiently. In this process, the various approaches, viz., cybernetic approach, contingency approach and business unit strategy help managers to understand the elements, design and variety of MCS in practice.

2.2 CYBERNETIC APPROACH TO MANAGEMENT CONTROL SYSTEM

Nobert Weiner, in 1940s, propounded the idea of cybernetics. He defined cybernetics as 'the study of entire field of control and communication theory, whether in the machine or the animal'. It involves self-regulatory principles in systems varying from the human biological system to mechanical system. It has wider applications in the areas of radar control, automatic machine tool control, language translation, artificial intelligence, robotics, etc., which make it popular as a unique self-regulation theory.

Due to its wide applicability, cybernetics has many characteristics which are mentioned as follows:

(i) Cybernetic system is complex as it has numerous interacting components which create multiple interactions within the sub-systems.

(ii) In this system, multiple interactions take place due to the multiple structures and processes.

(iii) This system generally does not apply in a planned and pre-designed manner, but grows and applies as and when required.

(iv) Cybernetic system increases in size and complexity according to its existing characteristics.

2.2.1 Cybernetic-Paradigm

Griesinger, in the 1970s, coined the idea of cybernetic paradigm. The cybernetic paradigm helps in capturing the essential elements of the repetitive control process economically.

The essential elements of the repetitive control process can be enumerated as follows:

(i) Establishing goals and performance standards

(ii) Measuring and assessing actual achievements

(iii) Comparing actual achievements with the goals

(iv) Computing variances

(v) Informing the variances by way of reporting

(vi) Identifying the reasons for variances

(vii) Taking appropriate action to stop adverse variances in future

(viii) Constant follow-up actions to ensure compliance of the goals or objectives

From the analysis of the essential elements we can say that the cybernetic paradigm starts with the assumption that decisions are made after the interaction between the managers (decision makers) and the external environment. The managers scan and observe the external environment from the data collected by the 'sensors' through reports and informal discussions with the members of the organization. The managers build up their perceptions based on the 'factual premises' drawn from the data collected.

In the next process, the factual premises are compared with the goals and objectives set by the organization. Every possible step is taken by the management to eliminate/minimize the gap between value premises of the managers and the factual premises drawn from the external environment, by analyzing the variances between the actual performance and the desired result. In case of adverse variance or shortfall in performance, the managers take appropriate course of action as the implementation process, to eliminate the variance.

In the implementation stage, the managers put in practice the desired control mechanisms. In the next stage which is called 'feedback stage', the required feedbacks are gathered to find out the reaction of the implementation action. If there is a positive feedback, same action is repeated again in similar situation in future.

2.3 CONTINGENCY APPROACH TO MANAGEMENT CONTROL SYSTEM (MCS)

Organizations are complex structures. Hence, there is a need to design controls for them to function effectively. The contingency approach to management control systems provides a potential explanation for the variety of management control systems actually practiced.

This approach is based on the premise that the design and use of control systems are contingent upon the particular context of the organizational setting in which the controls operate. It is an extension of theory of scientific management. It states that the appropriateness of different control systems depends on the setting of the business. The contingency theory focuses on the interaction between the organization and its environment. It is assumed that an organization receives energy and resources from the environment, converts them into goods, services and by-products, and then gives back to the environment, thus, changing the environmental circumstances in which the organization operates.

There are certain factors, viz., environment, organization structure, and technology, which have great influence on the contingency approach to MCS. The need for these factors and their influence in designing MCS in an organization are explained hereunder.

2.3.1 Environment

In order to survive and sustain in business, the organizations have to adapt to the demands of their environment. The contingency approach helps to develop a highly sophisticated control system, in line with the intensity and extent of competition the organization faces. It analyzes the components of the organization, its structure, cultural setting, and its ability to adapt to technological and structural changes.

Fisher (1998) identified five contingent control variables as:

(i) Uncertainty
(ii) Technology and interdependence
(iii) Industry, firm, and unit variables
(iv) Competitive strategy
(v) Mission and observability factors

All these factors can be either external or internal to the organization, and can affect organizational outcome, performance, resource allocation, and distribution of rewards.

2.3.2 Organizational Structure

An 'organic' organizational structure adapts easily to unstable conditions in rapidly changing environments. As the business grows, the work of the management increases and the organization structure becomes more complicated because new tasks or lines of production are added. The contingency approach helps in designing a control system that meets the demands of complex organization structures.

2.3.3 Technology

Technology influences the design of control systems. It helps managers to use resources more effectively, and to collect data for strategic and operational decision-making. The increased use of technology has brought in new control systems that can help managers to identify specific problems in administration or factory operations.

2.4 BUSINESS STRATEGY AND MANAGEMENT CONTROL SYSTEM

Management control systems are the tools which help in the effective implementation of strategy. Strategies can be considered at two levels in the organization as follows:

(i) Corporate strategy—Strategies for the company as a whole
(ii) Business unit strategy—Strategies for each business unit

2.4.1 Corporate Strategy

Corporate strategy relates to an organization as a whole. It involves making plans regarding where and how the organization can compete in an industry. Corporate strategy and controls should be integrated in order to keep employee behaviour in congruence with managerial goals. Since planning and control requirements are different for different corporate strategies, they need to be designed so that they are compatible with the corporate strategies. In companies, the corporate level managers need to have wide range of control across various departments.

Organizations can be classified into three categories:

(i) Single business firm operating in one line of business
(ii) Firm having diversification into businesses that are related to one another (i.e. related diversification)
(iii) Firm having diversification into businesses that are not related to one another (i.e. unrelated diversification)

Single business enterprise

This type of organization concentrates on a single business. For example, Apple Computers pursues a single business of manufacturing computers.

Business enterprise having related diversification

This type of organization diversifies into businesses which are related to one another and have common set of core competencies. For example, Infosys pursues various businesses relating IT and IT enabled services products.

Enterprise having unrelated diversification

This type of organization engages itself into different areas of business which are not related to the other. The only common link between them is that they are managed and financed by a common concern. For example, ITC Ltd. has various businesses not related to each other.

The characteristics of the control system vis-à-vis corporate strategy are given as follows:

(i) Control system will differ based on corporate strategy with diversification.
(ii) More diversification requires that the managers at the corporate level should have a wide range of expertise and knowledge relating to various activities of the organization.
(iii) Single business organization and the organizations having related diversification are based on company wide core competencies.

(iv) In the case of unrelated diversified firms, there is comparatively less interdependence among various units. As a company becomes more diversified, control systems should be changed to foster better cooperation among the diverse units, and to encourage their entrepreneurial spirit.

Activities in designing a control system for corporate strategy

There are various activities in designing a control system for corporate strategy.

(a) Strategic planning: Strategic planning systems for diversified business units are generally horizontal and vertical both. The horizontal process involves the preparation of a plan on behalf of each unit or group by an executive, with synergetic inputs from the different business units of the organization.

The strategic plans of the individual business units are circulated among the various business units as it helps in getting the feedback. In a single business firm, the CEO can control the budgeting operations through informal methods and personal intervention. In a conglomerate, it is difficult to rely on informal interpersonal relationship. Hence, the business unit managers have greater influence in developing their product/market environments.

(b) Compensation and incentives: The plan for employee compensation and incentives in companies varies as per the level of diversification of the companies. In the case of conglomerates, bonus is formula based.

In a single business firm, bonus is determined based on the subjective factors, viz., the performance of the business. In the case of single business firms and those with related diversification, the compensation is usually related to the performance of the unit and also the performance of the firm as a whole. Linking incentives to the overall performance of the organization helps to increase teamwork and interdependencies.

2.4.2 Business Unit Strategy

Diversified organizations segment themselves into business units and assign different strategies to the different business units. The business unit strategy deals with creating and maintaining competitive advantage in all the business operations.

Business unit strategy for an organization has two interrelated aspects—mission and competitive advantage.

Mission

A mission statement is a broad organizational goal, based on planning premises, which justifies the existence of an organization. There should be congruence between the mission statement and the use of controls. Management control systems help the managers to make decision on the trade-off between the short term and the long term. There are various planning models that help managers at the corporate level to allocate resources among different businesses and also help in identifying the missions of individual business units.

All planning decisions are based on certain factors which are as follows:

(i) Concentration on the internal and external factors of business
(ii) Competitive ability of the business unit
(iii) Attractiveness of the industry in which a unit operates

The planning models have a set of missions as follows:

(a) Build
(b) Hold
(c) Harvest
(d) Divest

(a) Build: It indicates that the business unit's goal is to increase its market share, even at the expense of short-term earning and cash flow. Business units with low market share in high growth industry typically pursue a 'build' mission.

(b) Hold: This mission aims to protect the business unit's market share and competitive position. Generally business units with high market share in high growth industries pursue a 'hold' mission.

(c) Harvest: It has the objective of optimising short-term profitability, cash flows etc. even at the cost of market share. Generally the business units with high market share in low growth industries pursue a harvest mission.

(d) Divest: It indicates a decision to withdraw from the business either through a process of slow liquidation or outright sale. Typically, business units with low market share in low growth industries are divested.

The process of strategic planning is more critical for 'build' business units than for 'harvest' business units. A 'build' mission is undertaken in the growth stage of the product life cycle, and the objective of the 'build' mission is to increase the market share.

Budgeting and budget revisions are more likely in the case of 'build' units than for 'harvest' units because of frequent changes in the market environment of 'build' units. 'Build' units managers usually have greater influence on the formulation of the budgets.

Managers have to decide on the size of incentive bonus payments, the measures of performance to be considered for incentive bonus (viz. sales volume, product development, ROI etc.), the criteria for subjective judgements, the frequency of payments, etc. The mission of the business units influences the type of incentives package to be formulated. Managers in 'build' units are likely to have higher incentive payments than managers in 'harvest' units.

Benefits of business unit strategy

To identify the competitive advantage, a business unit should analyze the competitive structure of the industry in which it plans to operate. Porter, in his 'five forces model' analyzes the competitive structure of an industry based on the following factors:

(i) Intensity of rivalry among the existing players
(ii) Bargaining power of the suppliers
(iii) Threat from substitutes
(iv) Threat from new entrants

An understanding of these factors can help a business unit to frame generic strategies defined as follows:

Low cost strategy

The primary focus of this strategy is to achieve low cost relative to competitors, through economies of scale, tight control of costs, and cost reduction.

Differentiation strategy

The goal of this strategy is to differentiate the product with that of competitors' products in terms of brand loyalty, customer service, dealer network, product design and features.

Focus strategy

This strategy requires the firm to focus on a particular buyer group, product segment, geographic market, etc. It helps the firm to achieve core competence.

Table 2.1 Recommended business strategy

High (strong)	Average	Low (weak)	Strategy
Invest/Grow/Build strategy (rapid)	Invest/Grow/Build (selective)	Protect (hold)	Strong
Invest/Grow/Build (selective)	Protect (hold)	Divest/Harvest	Average
Divest/Delay/Dominate	Divest/Harvest	Divest/Harvest	Weak

2.5 ESSENTIALS IN DESIGNING MANAGEMENT CONTROL SYSTEM

While designing a good and workable MCS, the following essential issues should be put in practice in an organization:

(i) All the employees of the organization should regard and support wholeheartedly the process of setting up MCS by the management as it will result in improving the performance of the employees.

(ii) The standard of performance set for the individual employee should be challenging, but attainable and measurable.

(iii) The controls must concentrate on the goals and objectives of an activity.

(iv) Adequate attention should be given to all the important factors in a balanced manner while setting up the objectives and key results of performance desired.

(v) Each individual employee shall be responsible for his areas of performance result.

(vi) The control mechanism must ensure comparison of actual performance with the desired result.

(vii) There should be a good feedback system to indicate the quality of control system in vogue.

(viii) There should be adequate control mechanism to analyze the causes of the adverse variances if any, and take immediate corrective action.

(ix) Adequate attention should be given in establishing prompt reporting system to show the variances between actual performance and desired performance for corrective actions.

(x) While implementing the corrective actions based on the reports, proper monitoring of the actions taken and feedback received should be paid due importance.

(xi) The managers must have the judgemental ability and insight while designing MCS.

2.6 HIERARCHY OF CONTROL PROCESS

In an organization, the control process hierarchy focuses on the relationship between the superior officers and the subordinates. As prerequisite of a good MCS, the goals of the subordinates should be congruent to the goals and objectives of the superiors, which can be achieved through negotiation and communication processes.

In a hierarchical organization with decentralized decision-making and authority, the control process begins with the superior officers meeting the subordinates, negotiating goals, objectives, and targets for the next year. After the goals are finalized, the performance is reviewed at periodical intervals. Both superior officers and subordinates review overall performance. In areas where performance is not satisfactory, they try to find out the reasons for the same. Thereafter, a plan of correction and modification is prepared based on the past corrective actions and the current performance. In this manner, the targets and the next year's course of actions are fixed.

Therefore, the goal-oriented control process follows cybernetic paradigm and involves planning, decision-making and controls. It operates through a hierarchy of control.

2.7 INDUSTRIAL DYNAMICS AND MANAGEMENT CONTROL

The industrial dynamics provide important insights into the management control through the key role of information in an organization. As the decisions of the management are in the best interest of the organization, management control systems should provide a framework that facilitates right decisions. The main aim of industrial dynamics is to arrive at right decisions with the help of information that flows through various levels of organization.

2.8 MANAGEMENT CONTROL AND ORGANIZATIONAL DISASTERS

The firms have to learn how to adapt to the changed circumstances due to factors–internal as well as external. Internal factors, like strike, resignation, etc., which may lead to disasters, are easy to deal with, but external factors due to change in environmental factors are not within the control of the management. An organization can avoid organizational disasters by developing a framework that should be able to forecast disaster and the organization should be prepared to face it (see Figure 2.1).

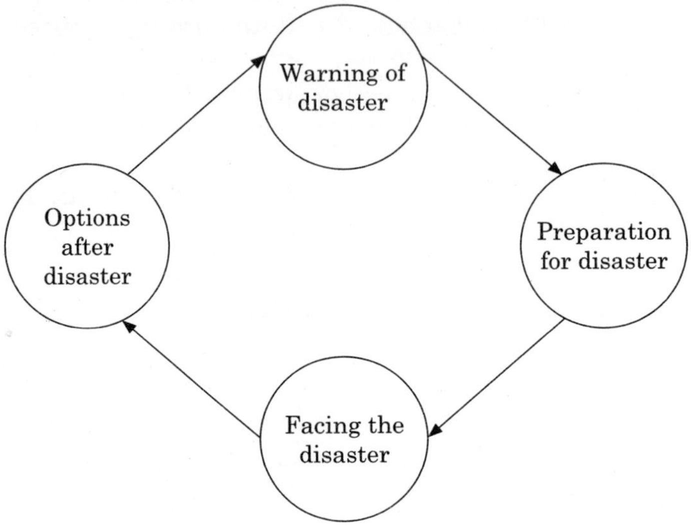

Figure 2.1 Management Control of Organizational Disasters.

2.9 CONCLUSION

This chapter examined the various approaches to MCS. The cybernetic approach helps the management in analyzing complex activities and managing the repetitive control process in an organization. The contingency approach to MCS provides a potential explanation for the variety of MCS observed in practice.

MCS are the tools that help in effective implementation of strategy. In this chapter the strategies have been dealt at two levels: the corporate level, and the business unit level. The corporate level strategy relates to the whole organization and can be differentiated based on the level and the extent of diversification undertaken by the organization. The business unit strategy deals with sustaining the business activities in the competition and has its own mission to develop the organization's competitive advantage.

The essentials for designing MCS and the hierarchy of control process have been adequately discussed in this chapter. The industrial dynamics provide important insights into the management control through the key role of information in an organization. The disasters in organization cannot be predicted, but can be prevented or minimized by the management by taking necessary steps.

REVIEW QUESTIONS

2.1 Discuss the various approaches to management control system?

2.2 Explain briefly the different factors and their influence in designing management control system in an organization?

2.3 What is business strategy? Explain the various levels of business strategy in an organization?

2.4 What is organizational disaster? How management control system can assist in avoiding organizational disaster?

2.5 Write short notes on:

(a) Industrial dynamics and management control

(b) Hierarchy of control process

(c) Essentials in designing management control system.

3

Design of Management Control System

3.1 INTRODUCTION

In chapter 2, we discussed about various approaches to MCS to analyze complexities in managing repetitive control process in an organization. We have stated in the preceding chapters that a MCS is a set of interrelated communication structures to facilitate processing of information and coordination between different segments of an organization. The sub-systems and components of MCS are so designed that they exhibit the goals and strategies of the organization and contribute to the effective implementation of the business strategies. In this chapter, we discuss about the steps in designing MCS, various factors influencing the design of MCS, implementation of Total Quality Management (TQM) and the influence of Information Technology (IT) in designing MCS.

3.2 STEPS IN DESIGNING MANAGEMENT CONTROL SYSTEM (MCS)

There are certain steps in designing MCS in an organization. They are as follows:

- (i) Identification of role of employees
- (ii) Identification of key actions
- (iii) Identification of role demands and KRAs
- (iv) Understanding likely results of role demands
- (v) Choice of controls
- (v) Use of mixed controls

3.2.1 Identification of Role of Employees

The role of each individual employee right from the chief executive to the lowest rank employee, is required to be identified.

3.2.2 Identification of Key Actions

Proper identification of the desired actions is imperative because the purpose of MCS is to influence and control actions of the employees. Therefore, identification of key actions is necessary though they differ from organization-to-organization as well as level to level of the organization in which the employees perform their tasks.

3.2.3 Identification of Role Demands and KRAs

Role demands are required to be identified from the Key Result Areas (KRAs). KRAs are the area of growth for an organization and they change as per the existing environment of an organization–internal as well as external.

3.2.4 Understanding Likely Results of Role Demands

The next step is to understand the likely results of the role demands. We can say that an organization has implemented MCS successfully when it is observed that there is no difference between the desired action and the likely action. In case of variation between the two, the causes of variance have to be found out and reported for corrective action.

3.2.5 Choice of Controls

Control mechanisms are selected from the various alternatives. A particular control mechanism can be selected based on the magnitude and depth of the problem. Therefore, the managers should initially consider and adopt personal or cultural control while choosing the alternatives.

Basically, two types of controls are adopted by the management of an organization. The types of controls are action controls, and result controls.

Action controls are the means for attaining work efficiency. They work on the standard set of procedures and are directly linked to the tasks to be performed. They can be adopted uniformly and in a coordinated manner throughout the organization. However, these controls do not encourage creativity and innovation among the employees since these controls are rigid, and are exercised for routine jobs.

Result controls are exercised to bring in control on the employees' behaviour. That is why these controls are also called as behavioural controls. By using these controls the managers advise the employees about what they are supposed to do in order to produce the desired results. Therefore, the managers define the dimensions and areas of work on which controls will be exercised by way of measuring actual performances against the set standards and providing sufficient incentives to encourage employees to perform efficiently. In fact, these controls increase motivation and improve commitments among employees to do effective jobs. However, any problem arising out of these controls is generally attributed to the mistakes of the employees.

3.2.6 Use of Mixed Controls

The controls can be exercised by the management tightly or loosely. The managers should be careful in exercising the extent of tightness or looseness of controls, which depend on how the organization understands the issues like, the advantages of tight or loose controls, cost incurred in exercising controls side-effects of tight or loose controls, etc. Therefore, the best advantage can be achieved by an organization if it uses mixed controls, i.e. a combination of tight and loose controls, by which the benefits of both types of controls in terms of creativity, innovation, and also rigidity can be achieved by the management.

3.3 FACTORS INFLUENCING THE DESIGN OF MANAGEMENT CONTROL SYSTEM (MCS)

There are number of factors which influence the design of MCS. They are:

(i) Management style
(ii) Corporate culture
(iii) Organization structure
(iv) Organizational slack
(v) Stakeholders' controls
(vi) Communication structures

Management style and corporate culture play an important role in designing the management control system. The style of a manager influences the style of other managers in the organization and the culture of an organization. Culture consists of shared values, and norms of the organization. It influences the prevailing style of management. Hence, management style and culture are interwoven.

3.3.1 Management Style

The different styles of management have an impact on the design of the control systems. If the control systems are designed with due regard to the management style, then future conflicts may not arise between organizational goals and objectives and managerial style of functioning.

The different managerial styles are as follows:

(i) External control style
(ii) Internal control style
(iii) Mixed control style

External control style

This style is authoritative and mechanical as the organizational goals are set by the top management. Various processes of this style are:

(a) Set difficult targets for the employees to stretch themselves
(b) Form strict regulations against manipulations of the tasks
(c) Introduce adequate incentives for employees' motivation to perform

The advantages of external control style are as follows:

(a) Subordinates are motivated to perform as rewards are directly linked to performance.

(b) Due to the high control executed by the top management, the senior officers are able to monitor subordinates' performance.

The disadvantages of external control style are as follows:

(a) There is no commitment for the employees towards their organization.

(b) Employees concentrate only on one aspect of their job ignoring the rest (for example: increase in sales volume but ignoring customer service).

(c) Only the positive outcomes are highlighted to the higher management.

Internal control style

This style assumes that the employees will experience a sense of achievement, recognition and self-esteem, if they are involved in the decision-making process. The strategies used here is:

(a) Participative management

(b) Joint problem-solving strategy without blaming each other

(c) Rewards based on accountability of the overall performance

The advantages of internal control style are as follows:

(a) High level commitment and motivation exist among employees

(b) It encourages accountability towards the work and an open work atmosphere

The disadvantages of internal control style are as follows:

(a) Loose managerial control is observed within the organization

(b) It does not work as an evaluation tool for rewarding employees

(c) There is an atmosphere of unwillingness on the part of some employees to participate

Mixed control style

We have discussed so far, two types of control styles and also their merits and demerits. Therefore, a manager has to carefully analyze the merits of each style and choose an appropriate one for the benefit of the organization.

While making use of the mixed control style in an organization, a manager has to consider the following issues and take appropriate action:

(i) Analytical problem solving and decision-making

(ii) Selection of best people and making sure of giving their dues

(iii) More frequent communication with the employees through meetings

(iv) Adequate control process through updated and regular reporting of performance

3.3.2 Corporate Culture

Corporate culture consists of shared values, common perceptions, and premises used by the members of the organization towards achieving goals. While designing management control systems, the CEO of a firm and his team of senior managers should take into account their culture. Values and beliefs are required to be conveyed to the employees at all levels, initially through recruitment and socialization process, and thereafter, by way of training and development.

Corporate culture helps in the overall coordination of all the works of a company, minimizes the problems and encourages a sense of loyalty within the organization.

Infosys has designed the following corporate culture for its employees. The guidelines of the same are as follows:

(i) Respect for the individual
(ii) Customer service
(iii) Dedication and commitment to work for excellence
(iv) Decentralized business
(v) Total quality management
(vi) Empowerment of people

The strength of corporate culture depends on the factors like the assumptions made by the firm, the clarity of the assumptions, and the degree and the extent of sharing the assumptions.

A control system should be so designed that it fits the existing culture of the organization. This can be achieved by way of emphasizing on the values to be followed by the employees as well as rewarding them for achieving goals based on these values.

3.3.3 Organization Structure

It is imperative for every organization to follow the path of decentralization in the decision-making authority. It is not important for an organization to decide whether it is decentralized or not but what really matters is to decide up to what extent it should be decentralized. Decentralization ensures that the decision-maker arrives at the right decision by making use of sufficient information. The decision-maker should find ways to deal with the complexity in the organizational environment even when the current information is limited.

3.3.4 Organizational Slack

Organizational slack occurs when a firm under-exploits its environment, resulting in higher salaries and perks than necessary, payment of high dividends, etc. The slack acts as a cushion against changing the business environment, and provides resources for innovation and adaptation in various areas.

3.3.5 Stakeholders' Controls

The stakeholders of a firm include investors, customers, employees, suppliers, and public at large. It is necessary for the firm to determine the goals and objectives, and performance measures of the stakeholders. A firm can exercise control over these stakeholders on the basis of their relationships with the organization. The analysis of stakeholders' relationships with the company involves the following steps:

(i) Identification of all stakeholders
(ii) Distinguishing the most important and influential stakeholders
(iii) Analysis of inducements to be offered to the stakeholders
(iv) Analysis of the contribution of a particular stakeholder
(v) Analysis of the competition of a particular shareholder

All these steps help the company in identifying crucial stakeholder variables that help in monitoring and influencing the control process.

3.3.6 Communication Structures

The communication system is crucial in understanding and improving the management control process. The communication structures support control process through the following steps:

(a) **Environmental scanning:** The information system scans the environment in which a firm operates.
(b) **Planning stage:** This stage is the most crucial of all, as it involves four sub-processes.
- Strategic planning
- Business planning
- Long range planning
- Operations planning

(c) Feedback through reporting at every stage
(d) Decision-making and implementation

3.4 TOTAL QUALITY MANAGEMENT (TQM)

TQM can be described as a system that emphasizes customer satisfaction and commitment to continuous improvement of its services and products to meet the needs of existing and potential customers, through empowerment and active involvement of all the staff.

TQM follows the steps as follows:

(i) The top management makes clear to the rest of the employees, the key philosophical principles of TQM.
(ii) The top management forms a company-wide quality improvement programme. A quality improvement team is set up with the main task of communicating various philosophies of TQM throughout the organization structure.
(iii) Each team is expected to come up with ideas about products and services to be launched. It also covers manufacturing the products according to the expectations of the customers.

Implementation of TQM is a long process which may take even several years. The top management should search for expert trainers and organize TQM training programmes for the different teams within the organization. They should be encouraged to work towards the improvement of TQM objectives. The sub-systems and components of a control system should be so designed as to help a TQM programme to achieve customer satisfaction. The importance of formal and informal systems necessary to support a TQM programme is shown in Appendix I.

3.5 INFORMATION TECHNOLOGY AND DESIGN OF MANAGEMENT CONTROL SYSTEM

The information technology provides significant help to the management in designing control systems in many ways as follows:

(i) Data can be managed more easily at a reasonable cost
(ii) Various departments of the organization can work on the same data
(iii) Data can be collected for strategic and operating decisions

The managers should take right decisions in choosing the right technology for operational needs. The decline in the cost of information processing has led to the increased use of activity-based costing system. It provides accurate cost data for the operational and strategic decisions in a firm. The introduction of an electronic equipment, i.e. optical scanning equipment has greatly improved the efficiency of inventory control system and market research.

3.6 CONCLUSION

This chapter examined the concept of designing of MCS. Designing of MCS involves several steps in achieving organizational goals. The managerial style and corporate culture of a firm should be clearly analyzed and defined while designing a control system. Three styles of MCS which are external control style, internal control style, and mixed control style have been adequately explained in this chapter. Decentralization of organization structure helps the managers to arrive at the right decision with sufficient information. Organization slack happens when a firm under-exploits its resources and incurs extra costs in its operations. It is the responsibility of the managers to identify key stakeholders and monitor their performance. While designing the control system, the management should coordinate various activities through proper communication structure.

Total Quality Management (TQM) ensures customer satisfaction and commitment towards all round improvement in the corporate activities. Information Technology (IT) benefits MCS in many ways.

REVIEW QUESTIONS

3.1 Discuss the various steps in designing management control system?

3.2 What are the factors that influence the design of management control system?

3.3 Define TQM and explain the various steps followed by TQM in designing management control?

3.4 How information technology can assist an organization in developing a good management control system?

4 Key Success Variables as Control Indicators

4.1 INTRODUCTION

A key success variable is a significant indicator of business activity, whose sudden and unpredictable change necessitates immediate action by the management. An important function of key variables is that they intimidate the need for the prompt action to the management. The top management should analyze the reasons for significant changes in key variables continuously. Some examples of the key success variables are as follows:

(i) Profitability
(ii) Productivity
(iii) Market share
(iv) Employee attitude

This chapter deals with various characteristics, sources and types of key variables, identification of the key variables, and key factors in selected industries.

4.2 CHARACTERISTICS OF KEY VARIABLES

Key variables differ from organization to organization depending on the nature of business activities. But the managers are supposed to identify key variables as they are the indicators of success or failure of any business. The selection of key variables requires a thorough understanding of the business, its operating conditions, goals and objectives of an organization.

The common characteristics of key variables are as follows:

(i) The key variables must be important in indicating the success or failure of the organization.
(ii) The managers should examine and evaluate these factors in detail.
(iii) These variables must be measurable either directly or indirectly.
(iv) These variables are not static as they can change rapidly.
(v) Changes of these variables may not be easily predictable to the managers.
(vi) Managers must take prompt action as soon as a significant change in a key variable occurs.

4.3 IDENTIFICATION OF KEY VARIABLES

The most common method of identification of key variables is the input–through–output model. They are related to raw materials, the input variables to production, processing and manufacturing, and the output variables to marketing.

4.3.1 Input Variables

The key variables related to inputs are as follows:

(i) Availability of raw materials, the absence of which leads to lower capacity utilization, difficulty in recovering fixed costs, and closure of the factory
(ii) Quality of raw materials, end products and profitability of the firm
(iii) Cost of raw materials as per cent of total costs

4.3.2 Product Variables

The key variables related to production are defined further.

(a) **Capacity utilization:** It is an important variable that is affected by either marketing variables or procurement variables. It reflects the ability of the production staff to schedule and plan, i.e. what to produce, how much to produce, and when to produce.
(b) **Production losses:** Production losses occur due to percentage of spoilage and wastage in manufacturing process and also due to percentage of yield.
(c) **Quality control:** It is necessary to identify the measures of quality from identifying number of complaints from customers, and through the quantity of goods returned.
(d) Maintenance of equipment for smooth production and better capacity utilization can be achieved by way of preventive maintenance and break-down maintenance.
(e) Cost of production
(f) Delivery of finished product systematically and on time.

4.3.3 Marketing Variables

The key marketing variables can be enumerated as follows:

(i) Order book position

(ii) Market share

  (a) Company's performance and its competitive strength

(iii) Institutional sales

  (a) Number of orders received from institutional buyers

  (b) Percentage of institutional sales on total sales

4.3.4 Asset-management Variables

The management of fixed assets and current assets is important for an organization. The managers should look into the following asset-management variables:

(i) Asset-turnover

  (a) Ratio between the total assets and sales volume

(ii) Working capital turnover

  (a) Ratio between total inventory and turnover

  (b) Ratio between credit sales and accounts receivable

4.3.5 Steps in Identification of Key Variables

Following steps are important while identifying the key variables:

(i) Identification of decision variables

(ii) Interactions with the environment

(iii) Implications for the control structure

(iv) Key success variables and the control paradigm

Decision variables

Decision variables are those key success factors which help the management to choose a particular course of action and execute it promptly. The identification of decision variables is crucial for a firm as they influence the goals and strategies of an organization.

Environment variables

Environment variables are identified in order to find out the key success factors. The most important environment factors influencing an organization are:

(a) The economy

(b) Political climate

Control structures

Control structures can be chosen based on the following important parameters:

(a) Efficiency and effectiveness

(b) Economies of scale

(c) Coordination
(d) Assignment of profit responsibility
(e) Conflict of profit responsibility

The control system designers set up the critical success factors that help managers to achieve their goals. Each unit and sub-units of the organization structure should coordinate and control the various key success factors in pursuit of the overall goals of the organization.

4.4 SOURCES OF KEY VARIABLES

Basically, there are five sources of key variables that the managers come across in an organization. They are as follows:

(i) Industry characteristics, like occupancy rate in hotel industry
(ii) Environmental factors, like economic factor, and political climate
(iii) Competitive strategy, viz. low cost strategy
(iv) Stakeholders, e.g., customers, employees, suppliers, creditors, etc.
(v) Special functions, viz. quality of raw materials purchased by a purchase manager

4.5 TYPES OF KEY VARIABLES

Key variables are classified broadly into the following categories (as shown in Figure 4.1):

(i) Strategy variables
(ii) Structural variables
(iii) Process variables
(iv) Environmental variables

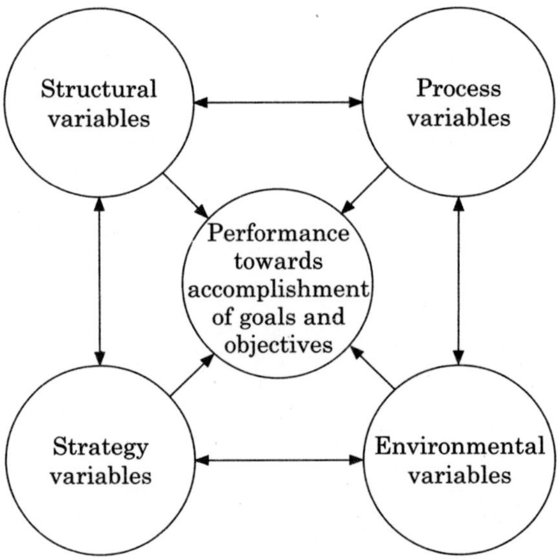

Figure 4.1 Interaction and Integration of Key Variables.

Strategy variables

Strategy variables refer to the long-term choices in regard to the programmes, goals, policies and action plans that are formulated by a firm.

Structural variables

Structural variables can be studied in terms of the structure of the organization—centralized or decentralized, and the organizational autonomy.

Process variables

Process variables refer to the processes that influence the behaviour of the employees towards achievement of organizational goal.

Environmental variables

Environmental variables help in understanding the scope, diversity, and uncertainty in regard to a firm. There is a positive relationship between the key variables and the organizational performance as the performance of a firm improves if there is congruence between these variables.

4.6 KEY SUCCESS VARIABLES AND MULTIVARIATE OR FACTOR ANALYSIS

This analysis is useful in identifying the key factors that influence the organizational variables. It helps in identifying the critical control variables and latent factors. Factor analysis is helpful in identifying the organizational variables and contributing to the success of the firm. The rating scales and graphic representations make the work of factor analysis easier through the systematic classification and graphic representation of data.

4.7 PERFORMANCE INDICATORS AND CONTROL SYSTEM

The main objective of monitoring the performance of key variables at each layer of the organization is to push them to the desired level, and if that is not possible, to react to the performance of key variables in order to balance their impact or influence. However, a number of precautions have to be taken with regard to the measurement of performance in a responsibility area. The precautions are as follows:

(i) The variables that are measured should correspond with the goals and objectives of the firm.

(ii) The crucial factors or variables should be measured.

(iii) The factors should be measured in such a way that the measures take account of both short-term objectives as well as long-term goals.

However, there are certain limitations of performance indicators. The limitations are described below:

(i) Absence of consensus among managers on the use of indicators

(ii) Problems encountered during the measurement of indicators

(iii) Lack of clear specification of the unit of measurement
(iv) Lack of consistent information resulting in incorrect conclusions

However, these limitations can be overcome by developing systematic and scientific methods to improve quality of the data for decision-making.

Example of Tata Steel

Tata Steel divided the task of measuring key success factors in the company into three sub-groups for measurement of each of the company's divisions. The divisions are as follows:

(i) Measuring the whole department as an economic entity
(ii) Measuring the functional departments, viz. finance, marketing, etc.
(iii) Measuring the performance of the management of the divisions:

Tata Steel developed the following performance measures for each of its divisions:

(i) Profitability
(ii) Market share
(iii) Productivity
(iv) Product leadership
(v) Personnel development
(vi) Employee attitude
(vii) Social responsibility of business
(viii) Balancing short-range objectives and long-term goals

4.8 EXAMPLES OF KEY VARIABLES IN INDUSTRIES

Industry in power sector

(i) Quantity and quality of coal
(ii) Availability of wagons for transportation of coal
(iii) Availability of water
(iv) Capacity utilization
(v) Preventive and breakdown maintenance
(vi) Power transmission losses

Hospitality industry

(i) Room occupancy rate
(ii) Number of complaints by the customers
(iii) Value of food wasted in the restaurant
(iv) Percentage of total revenue contributed by the restaurant
(v) Percentage of absenteeism among the employees

Industry in service sector, viz. Insurance company

(i) Number of claims settled in a given period of time
(ii) Number of claims outstanding against policies

(iii) Number of policies processed in a given period
(iv) Growth rate in insurance business

Agro-based Industry, viz. Sugar mill

(i) Price of sugar sold in the open market
(ii) Transportation cost per tonne of sugar cane
(iii) Fuel cost per kilogram of sugar
(iv) Number of production days lost
(v) Support price by the government

4.9 CONCLUSION

Key variables are the significant indicators of business activity. Every organization should identify the key variables for the fulfillment of its goals and objectives and business strategies. This chapter dealt with the concept, types, sources, characteristics of key variables. It discussed the identification of key variables by input-throughput-output analysis. Various steps involved in identification of key variables and some examples of key variables in different industries have also been given here.

Review Questions

4.1 What is meant by key success variables? Give some examples of key success variables?

4.2 Enumerate the characteristics of key variables?

4.3 What are the various steps in identifying the key variables? Discuss the various aspects of key variables in an organization?

4.4 "Basically there are five sources of key variables that the managers come across in an organization". What are they?

4.5 Discuss with diagram the various types of key variables?

4.6 Give some examples of key variables in the following industrial sectors:

(i) Industry in steel sector
(ii) Industry in power sector
(iii) Industry in hospitality sector
(iv) Industry in service sector
(v) Agro-based industry

Part II

Environment and Management Control

5

Goals, Strategies and Organization for Adaptive Control

5.1 INTRODUCTION

A management control system is designed to suit the particular goals and strategies of a firm. In order to carry-out the management control process, the managers must know what the company's goals and strategies are, and they must understand how these goals influence the process. In this chapter we discuss the goals, objectives and strategies as part of MCS. This chapter also deals with the organization structures as well as the need and importance of adaptive organization for adaptive control.

5.2 GOALS AND OBJECTIVES AS PART OF MANAGEMENT CONTROL SYSTEM (MCS)

Goals are defined as broad statements of what the organizations aim to achieve in the long run or on a permanent basis. Hence, goals are fairly timeless statements, not affected by the passage of time.

Objectives, on the other hand, are more specific statements and indicate what the organizations want to achieve within a specified time period. Objectives are, hence, time and activity specific, and can be used to measure the extent to which the firms have achieved them.

Measurement of the performance of an organization may not be possible if the goals and objectives are vague or ill-defined. Different key managers perceive the goals and objectives differently. This has led the organizations to insist on proper induction of new entrants to the organizational philosophy. The management of a firm also attempts to achieve super-ordinate goals, in addition to achieving the broad goals and objectives. Super-ordinate goals serve as guiding concepts, and reflect the shared values of the employees within the organization. These have a spiritual or inspirational overtone. They consist of values that genuinely seek congruence between the individual and the firm's purposes. They also include concepts of service to the society.

5.3 STRATEGIES AND MANAGEMENT CONTROL SYSTEM (MCS)

As defined by the Stanford Research Institute, 'strategy' is a way in which a firm reacts to its environment, deploys its principal resources, and marshals its main efforts in pursuit of its purpose.

Strategy pertains to the interface between a firm and its environment. The important determinants of strategy in relation to its environment are: competition, technology, political stability, socio-economic factors, government controls and policies. The objectives of a company are described broadly in the Memorandum of Association, wherein the boundaries of its activities are specified, indicating the primary objectives as well as incidental or ancillary objectives.

An organizational strategy may be elimination of competition, and enabling mutual co-operation of the various sub-units of a firm. Generally, the companies, capable of viewing problems as opportunities are able to respond properly to the environment by way of evolving appropriate strategies through the continuous re-appraisal and re-examination.

5.3.1 Criteria for Evaluation of Strategy

The strategy of a firm can be evaluated by posing certain key questions as follows:

(i) Is the strategy internally consistent?
(ii) Is the strategy consistent with the environment?
(iii) Is the strategy appropriate in view of the available resources?
(iv) Does the strategy involve an acceptable degree of risk?
(v) Does the strategy have an appropriate time horizon?
(vi) Is the strategy workable?

It is important that a strategy be consistent not only with the environment but also with the organizational goals and objectives. Moreover, resource availability, and the risk taking ability of the management should be kept in view while formulating a strategy.

5.3.2 Strategies and Policies

After formulating the strategy as a whole and for each of its Strategic Business Units (SBUs), the firm must elaborate in details the strategies into policies to facilitate the achievement of goals and objectives. The policies must be consistent with the strategies. The management must coordinate the strategy of each SBU, through the process of policy formulation. Prices, products, personnel, finance, R&D, etc. are all taken into account for the formulation of policies.

5.3.3 Strategy, Structure and Control

The business organizations follow different strategies in adopting various structures due to the rapid changes in business environment. In multidivisional structures, the divisional managers enjoy autonomy in decision-making. Of course, they have accountability for the performance of their divisions.

5.4 CENTRALIZATION AND DECENTRALIZATION

In a centralized organization structure, the overall decision-making power is vested with the top management. When the organization is small and a few homogeneous markets exit, it is easy to exercise management control and obtain the advantage of centralized organization structure. However, centralization restricts delegation of decision-making authority.

Decentralization means delegation of authority to the lowest feasible level of decision-making within the framework of predetermined responsibilities and clearly set goals.

Evaluation of decentralization

(i) It allows close control and supervision on subordinates in the department.
(ii) It motivates the managers to perform better by providing right environment and autonomy.
(iii) It evaluates overall performance of various organizational units.

5.5 MATRIX ORGANIZATION STRUCTURE

A matrix organization structure is a mixed form of organization structure, generally adopted by the large organizations that handle various complex projects or pursue high technology products to maintain high degree of technical excellence in various disciplines. In this type of organization, two channels of command exist, one along the functional lines, and the other along the project lines. This structure requires high division of labour and specialization.

In the matrix organization structure, the managers can achieve the goals and objectives of each of the complex projects by sharing the resources economically among these projects. However, there are problems in implementing the matrix structure in an organization due to the difference in orientation and priorities fixed by the managers themselves as well as unclear and undefined boundary of responsibility for the activities. Conflicts may arise in resolving problems on technical and finance issues and assigning priorities to various programmes. The matrix structure may be useful for the product organizations, service organizations, project organizations and multinational companies.

5.5.1 Product Organizations

A matrix organization structure can be adapted to a product organization when the organization has many complex products to handle, and when it requires closer coordination among various functional departments. The matrix structure helps a product organization to achieve economies of scale in each department, and ensures high level of effectiveness in business activities. A format of the product matrix organization is shown in Appendix II.

5.5.2 Service Organizations

A matrix structure can be usefully applied to service organizations (for example, Tourism Industry) which require close cooperation among various units and better control of numerous activities. It helps to provide close coordination between the various departments of the organization and help management in meeting the desired satisfactions of the customers.

5.5.3 Project Organizations

A matrix structure can be beneficially adapted to a project organization. It helps the project organization to achieve desired performance with respect to cost, quality and time management.

5.5.4 Multinational Companies (MNCs)

A multinational company designs its organization structure on the basis of combination of the product and the market area. The matrix structure helps the management in providing a dual structure to manage both the product and the market place. However, it is necessary for an MNC matrix organization to ensure behavioural adjustments among the managers and inculcate team approach for attaining its goals and objectives.

5.6 ORGANIZATIONAL DESIGN AND CONTROL FACTORS

In some organizations decentralization is sometimes associated with dysfunctional performance, resulting in incremental costs. If the incremental benefits are more than the incremental costs involved, the organization maintains a decentralized structure. In a centralized structure, the overall decision-making power is vested with the top management. Organizations have to choose the design that is likely to benefit them the most. The evaluation of each design is done on a qualitative measure based on the efficiency and coordination.

A centralized organization faces the problems of coordination and loss of effectiveness. These problems lead to cost overruns, bottlenecks and financial losses. The matrix organization avoids coordination problems that arise during the handling of complex programmes because it places total responsibility in the hands of manager to devise plans, and coordinate and integrate the activities of the organization for achieving a balance among performance.

The function of control systems in the evaluation of organizational design is to calculate the net benefits of each of the three designs on a qualitative basis, and help the organization to adopt the best one. The design selected should promote communication, co-operation, teamwork, motivation and performance as qualitative measures.

5.7 ORGANIZATION FOR MCS DESIGNER

An MCS designer is an executive who is responsible for designing and implementing the MCS in his organization. He plays a crucial role in the design and operation of the control system. He has to advice management on the implications of decisions under management consideration. He analyzes various programmes, and budget proposals, and unites various segments of the organization together. He has to create awareness among employees on the benefits being derived by the organization because of effective implementation of MCS.

Therefore, it is imperative for an organization to select an able MCS designer who should possess adequate qualification and qualities, viz., personal integrity, professional commitment to his responsibilities, adequate knowledge, analytical skill, ability to judge information, effective interpersonal relationship, etc.

5.8 ADAPTIVE ORGANIZATION

In order to face the challenges in the rapid changing environment, the firms need to develop adaptability and modify their structure at regular intervals. An organization which is not adaptive to environmental changes will become inefficient in due course of time.

5.8.1 Factors for Managing Adaptive Organization

There are certain factors which create the need for managing an adaptive organization. They are basically environmental factors. As the organization is influenced by the environmental changes, these changes are also influenced by the following factors:

(i) Environmental uncertainty
(ii) Environmental complexity
(iii) Environmental diversity
(iv) Environmental hostility

The control system designer analyzes the above factors before taking a decision for redesigning of the organization structure in order to implement control measures.

5.8.2 Adaptive Organization and Adaptive Controls

In an adaptive organization, the control mechanism is more implicit. An adaptive organization needs high levels of awareness, skill, commitment, and integrity within the employees' group. The culture of an organization should provide opportunities to the employees to receive global awareness, continuous learning and training, and flexibility towards adjustment and acceptance of new assignments and responsibilities.

In a formal control system, the infrastructure of the organization structure can be easily formed and dissolved. The planning and control processes should concentrate on the organization's vision, strategy, information system, etc. The reward system should motivate the employees to achieve the goals and objectives of the organization.

The formal and informal controls for adaptive organization are shown in Appendix III and Appendix IV, respectively.

5.9 CONCLUSION

This chapter examined the goals, strategies, and organizations for adaptive control. It examined in detail, the various types of organization structures—centralized, decentralized and matrix. Among these structures, the matrix has proved to be useful for product organizations, service organizations, project organizations and MNCs.

The role and importance of MCS designer for designing and implementation of MCS has been discussed. An adaptive organization adapts itself rapidly to the environmental changes. In this respect, the role of control systems to facilitate the adaption has also been dealt in this chapter.

REVIEW QUESTIONS

5.1 What do you mean by goal? How does it differ from 'objective'?

5.2 Define strategy? discuss the various criteria for evaluation of strategy?

5.3 What is an organizational policy? How is it related to the strategy of a firm?

5.4 What is meant by centralized organization structure and how does it differ from decentralized structure?

5.5 The matrix organization structure may be useful for the product organizations, service organizations, project organizations, and multinational companies". Discuss.

5.6 Who is a MCS designer? Why is it necessary for a firm to appoint an able MCS designer?

5.7 Enumerate the factors for managing adaptive organization? What is the relationship between adaptive organization and adaptive control?

6

Divisional Autonomy and Responsibility

6.1 INTRODUCTION

A business organization uses a number of structural elements that play an important role in influencing the autonomy of managers at divisional level. These elements also influence considerably in measuring and evaluating the managerial performance. This chapter deals with the managerial autonomy at divisional level, its determinant factors, and the concepts of responsibility centres.

6.2 AUTONOMY AT DIVISIONAL CONTROL LEVEL

Nowadays, almost all organizations are operating in dynamic, volatile and highly competitive markets. Therefore, it is important for the top management to decide on the right kind of autonomy to be given to the managers. The top management must decide upon the level of decentralization of decision making.

Prof. R.F. Vancil has developed a theory of decentralized management shown in Figure 6.1.

According to this theory the variables that determine the levels of autonomy in a firm can be classified as:

(i) Management philosophy, style, processes, policies and procedures
(ii) Diversification strategy
(iii) Business strategy
(iv) Responsibility structure
(v) Reward systems
(vi) Measurement of costs and assets assigned

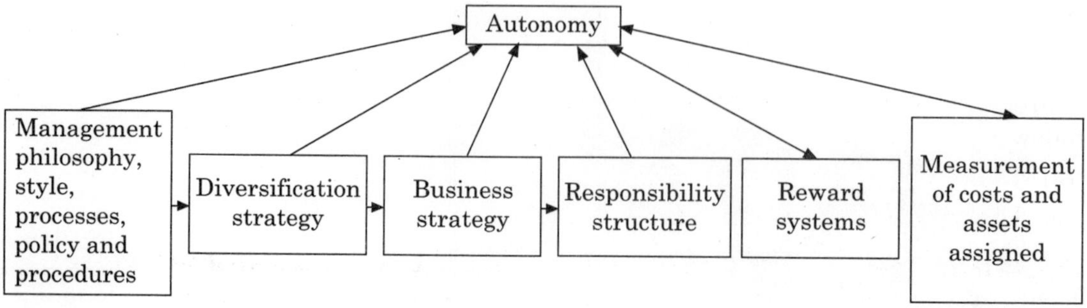

Figure 6.1 Vancil's Theory of Decentralized Management.

6.2.1 Management Philosophy, Style, Processes, Policies and Procedures

They play an important role in influencing the behaviour of the employees in an organization. The managers need to decide whether the organization should be run in a centralized manner or by striking a balance between centralized control and decentralized action. The personal factors that influence the level of autonomy are as follows:

(a) The level of involvement of the corporate managers in the business
(b) The interactions of the corporate managers with other managers
(c) The level of trust and confidence of the managers in the ability of their subordinates

The management style reflects the process of decentralization in a firm. Similarly, the management policies and procedures show the path where the management decisions are to be taken in a uniform manner.

6.2.2 Diversification Strategy

According to Vancil, autonomy of a manager may be restricted in an organization, which deals with single product business, or is diversified in related business. But the extent of managerial autonomy is definitely high in an organization, which handles multiproduct business or is diversified in various unrelated business ventures.

6.2.3 Business Strategy

Various business strategies undertaken by an organization have great influence on the autonomy of its divisional managers.

6.2.4 Responsibility Structure

It represents the physical, human and financial resources which are entrusted to the managers of the profit centre. A responsibility accounting system helps managers to record the plans and performance of the centre for which the manager is accountable.

The measurement of the performance of a responsibility centre is done through cost, profit, revenue, investment, and the quality of goals set by the firm.

Three different methods of measuring the performance of a responsibility centre are as follows:

(a) The measure of efficiency
(b) The measure of process
(c) The measure of effectiveness

'Efficiency' can be measured in terms of inputs received for a stated level of output within a specified period. 'Process' can be measured in terms of production process and 'effectiveness' can be measured in terms of the output achieved by the organization in relation to its goals and objectives.

6.2.5 Reward Systems

They are determined on the performance of a particular centre. The amount and method of allocation of bonuses depends on the manager's autonomy. Rewards to the managers are financial and/or non-financial in nature. Financial rewards include higher salaries and perks, and non-financial rewards include higher position in the management, improved status, more authority, etc.

6.2.6 Measurement of Costs and Assets Assigned

The costs and assets assigned to the divisional managers need to be measured to show them how much they should be careful about optimum utilization of assets and minimization of costs at the desired level. Generally, the measurement methods are proration, negotiation and metering. Proration relates to allocation of resources, and negotiation and metering relate to the level of autonomy given to the managers in decision making as to the quality and quantity of inputs used by them.

As a measure of overall effectiveness of an organization, Return On Investment (ROI) principle is a good indicator. It helps management in measuring the control systems and overall financial performance of a responsibility centre.

$$\text{ROI} = \frac{\text{Net profit}}{\text{Total capital invested}}$$

$$\text{ROI} = \left(\frac{\text{Net profit}}{\text{Sales revenue}}\right) \times \left(\frac{\text{Sales revenue}}{\text{Total capital invested}}\right)$$

6.3 RESPONSIBILITY CENTRE

It is a unit or function of a firm headed by a manager who is directly responsible for its performance. It generates information and allows them to be used directly in motivating and controlling the action of each manager in charge of the responsibility centre.

A responsibility centre of a manufacturing organization uses inputs, viz., raw materials, labour, overheads, working capital, plant and machinery, etc., in its production process to produce outputs. These outputs are measurable. But the outputs of service departments like, HRD, Finance and Accounts department, Administrative office, etc., cannot be measured.

6.3.1 Classification of Responsibility Centres

Responsibility centres are classified as follows:

(i) Revenue centre
(ii) Expense centre or cost centre
(iii) Profit centre
(iv) Investment centre

Revenue centre

In this centre, the manager is responsible for the level of revenue or output of a centre, measured in monitory terms, but he is not responsible for the cost of goods produced or services. For example, a marketing department.

A marketing department manager's responsibility is to maximize revenues, but he assumes no responsibility for the cost of goods or services.

Expense centre or Cost centre

In expense centre, input costs or expenses are measured in monitory terms, but the outputs are not measured in monitory terms. Two types of expense or cost centres are:

(i) Engineered expense centre
(ii) Discretionary expense centre

Engineered costs can be estimated by the management. For example, direct material costs, direct labour costs, etc. But discretionary costs cannot be estimated by the management.

In engineered cost centre, input costs or expenses are measured in monitory terms and outputs are measured in physical terms. For example, a manufacturing unit using standard costing system. The efficiency of a manufacturing unit is measured by comparing the standard cost with the actual cost of production.

In discretionary cost centre, the outputs cannot be measured in monitory terms. For e.g., legal expenses, administrative expenses, etc. The management decides on certain policies, based on which these expenses are incurred in this centre.

Profit centre

This centre is given the responsibility of earning profits. It is involved in manufacturing and sale of outputs, and in determining the efficiency of the head of the centre. Performance of this centre is measured in terms of contribution margin, EBDIT, EBIT, PBT, and PAT.

The contribution margin, EBDIT, EBIT, PBT, and PAT can be calculated as follows:

Contribution margin/Gross Margin = Sales revenue – All direct costs
= Sales revenue – (Direct material cost + Direct labour cost + Direct expenses)

Earning before depreciation, interest and tax (EBDIT)

= Contribution – All operating expenses

= Contribution – (Production overhead + Administrative overhead + Selling and Distribution overhead)

Earning before interest and tax (EBIT) = EBDIT – Depreciation

Profit before tax (PBT) = EBIT – Interest on borrowed capital

Profit after tax (PAT) = PBT – Taxes

A profit centre helps the organization to make the best use of specialized market knowledge of divisional managers. It improves the motivation of managers to show good results by way of taking more initiatives and using their own perceptions. However, the top management of the organization does not have significant control over the profit centres. It has to depend on control reports sent by the divisional managers.

Investment centre

This centre has control over sales revenues, operating costs, and the investments made to generate profit. It analyses all elements of profit and investment. Given the amount of investment required, the main objective of this centre is to maximize profit of the organization.

6.4 RESPONSIBILITY ACCOUNTING

Responsibility accounting is defined as a system of accounting that recognizes various responsibility centres throughout the organization and that reflects the plans and actions of each such centre, by assigning particular revenues and costs to one having pertinent responsibility.

It is a management control system which identifies the specific responsibilities of functional managers and departmental supervisors in terms of their performance. The following conditions must exist for successful operation of responsibility accounting:

(i) Costs and revenues should be directly associated with the specific level of management responsibility.
(ii) Costs and revenues should be controllable at the responsibility level.
(iii) Budget data should be developed to assess the managerial effectiveness in controlling costs and revenues.

6.4.1 Purposes of Responsibility Accounting

The purposes of responsibility accounting are as follows:

(i) To improve managerial effectiveness in controlling costs and revenues
(ii) To enhance the business performance
(iii) To evaluate a manager's performance in terms of authority and responsibility

6.4.2 Steps in the Introduction of Responsibility Accounting

Following steps are required to be taken while introducing responsibility accounting:

(i) Setting up of an organization structure clearly defining the lines of authorities and responsibilities;
(ii) Fixation of targets or budgets as per responsibility;
(iii) Evaluation of performance, i.e. comparison of actual figures with budgeted ones to ascertain variances;
(iv) Analysis of variances according to controllable and uncontrollable groups to pinpoint responsibilities and reporting to appropriate management; and
(v) Taking corrective action and reporting to the person responsible.

6.4.3 Controllability

Controllability is the degree of influence that a specific manager has over costs, revenues, profits, or other items. Controllable costs are those costs which may be directly regulated at a given level of managerial authority.

There are two aspects of controllability. They are

(i) The distinction between controllables and uncontrollables can be made with reference to a given level and scope of the management authority.
(ii) The span of time is vital because given a sufficiently long period, virtually all costs are controllable.

Another way of fixing the responsibility of managers is to identify the person in the organization structure with the most decision-making power over the item.

Most advocates of responsibility accounting favour the exclusion of the uncontrollable items from the 'performance report'. Generally, only financial measures of performance are emphasized. Now the effort is being made to stress on the non-financial performance measures as well viz. material yield, labour productivity, market growth, etc.

6.5 CONCLUSION

This chapter examined the autonomy and the responsibility of the managers at divisional level in an organization. Divisional autonomy refers to the freedom that a divisional manager enjoys in decision making. The variables that influence autonomy have been discussed in this chapter.

Responsibility centre is a unit or function of a firm headed by a manager who is directly responsible for its performance. Various classifications of responsibility centre, viz., revenue centre, expense centre, profit centre and investment centre, and their concepts and implications have also been discussed. The main objective of such classification is to ensure integration of the various activities of an organization as control process towards fulfillment of its goals and objectives.

Responsibility accounting is defined as a system of accounting that recognizes various responsibility centres throughout the organization and that reflects the plans and actions of each such centre, by assigning particular revenues and costs to one having pertinent responsibility. It is a management control system which identifies the specific responsibilities of functional managers and departmental supervisors in terms of their performance.

Review Questions

6.1 What is meant by divisional autonomy? Discuss the various factors that determine the levels of autonomy in a firm?

6.2 Define responsibility centre? Explain the various classifications of responsibility centres?

6.3 What do you mean by responsibility accounting? Discuss the purposes of responsibility accounting in an organization?

6.4 What steps must be taken by a company in introducing responsibility accounting?

Part III

Management Control Tools and Processes

7

Strategic Planning and Programming Process

7.1 INTRODUCTION

Strategic planning involves long-term planning of an organization. It is usually undertaken by the top management. It is the process of deciding on the programmes that the firm will undertake and the resources that will be allocated to each programme in next few years. In order to make strategic planning effective, the strategic planning should be accompanied by an appropriate organization structure, an effective management information system, a budgetary control system and a reward system. Programming is an organizational process for making managerial decisions in regard to allocation of resources on long-term basis.

This chapter examines the concept of strategic planning, its characteristics, importance and various processes. It also deals with the aspects of programming process, and explains briefly, the Bower's model of decision-making and Kover's model of capital investment approval process.

7.2 STRATEGIC PLANNING AND ITS CHARACTERISTICS

As mentioned earlier, the strategic planning involves a long term planning undertaken by the top management in an organization. It deals with various important issues relating to the changes in business environment—external and internal, business competition, customers' need and perception about the company's products, etc. It helps the management to identify the strengths and weaknesses of the organization so that its strength can be increased and weaknesses can be overcome.

Strategic planning consists of two aspects—one, the setting of goals, and the other, formulation of strategy by the top management.

The characteristics of strategic planning can be enumerated as follows:

(i) Strategic planning is irregular in nature. It is dealt with whenever perceived.

(ii) The process of strategic planning requires a number of estimates and variables to show the expected results of the plan. It is a complex process.

(iii) The information required for strategic planning is derived from the external environment.

(iv) It essentially involves the process of goal setting. It requires the communication of objectives, policies, guidelines, decisions and results throughout the organization.

(v) It is a creative and analytical process. It is more of an analytical process because goal setting is done only after analyzing the strengths, weaknesses, opportunities and threats faced by the organization. It is a creative process since it involves evaluation of new opportunities and ideas from time-to-time.

(vi) It is a long-term process and its end result is the formulation of policies and goals for the organization.

(vii) The process of strategic planning is greatly affected by the turbulence in external environments.

(viii) It is difficult to appraise the performance of strategic planning as there are no prescribed standards.

(ix) It relates to some parts of the organization and not the entire organization.

7.3 IMPORTANCE OF STRATEGIC PLANNING

The importance of strategic planning can be emphasized in the following manner:

(i) It takes into account the changing business environment before organizational change.

(ii) It identifies and analyzes the internal business culture and evaluates its impact on the company's performance.

(iii) It analyzes available opportunities and potential threats.

(iv) It allocates resources to the most beneficial activities.

(v) It helps managers to set realistic objectives that are demanding and yet attainable.

(vi) It identifies poor performance areas and eliminates them.

(vii) It helps in obtaining better information for decision-making.

(viii) It develops a framework of reference for budgets and short-range operating plans.

(ix) It brings coordination of internal activities, and thereby enhances the organization's growth.

The strategic planning, therefore, provides a roadmap of the company's target and how to reach it. It enables managers to prepare for and deal with rapidly changing environment in which their organizations operate.

7.4 PROCESSES OF STRATEGIC PLANNING

There are six steps involved in the process of strategic planning in an organization. They are:

(i) Review and updating of strategic plan
(ii) Decision on assumptions and guidelines for the strategic plan
(iii) Initial iteration of the strategic plan
(iv) Analysis of the strategic plan by the corporate office
(v) Second iteration of the strategic plan
(vi) Final review and approval of the strategic plan

Let us discuss each of these processes below.

7.4.1 Review and Updating of Strategic Plan

Review and updating take place every year when the strategic plan is prepared, depending on the decisions of the management. There is no fixed time limit set for the review. The updating of these plans is done with the help of a computer program in incorporating the decisions on revenues, expenses, capital expenditures and cash flow.

7.4.2 Decision on Assumptions and Guidelines for the Strategic Plan

It involves making broad assumptions about growth in the gross domestic product, cyclical movements, general inflation, labour rates, price of raw materials, selling price, market conditions, government legislations in each country in which the company operates. The process of updating has implications on revenues, expenses, and cash flows of the existing operating facilities. It provides estimation for the senior management to decide about the key guidelines to be observed in planning and for designing of the methods for achieving the objectives. The objectives are presented separately for each product line, and expressed as sales revenue, or as percentage of profit or return on capital employed. Most companies hold meetings between the corporate and business unit managers, which continue for several days.

7.4.3 Initial Iteration of the Strategic Plan

After framing the assumptions and guidelines, the business units prepare the first iteration of the strategic plan. Thereafter, a final decision is taken by the business unit managers. During the preparatory stage, employees from the corporate office visit the concerned business unit to find out whether the guidelines, assumptions and instructions are being followed. The completed strategic plan consists of income statements and other balance sheet items. They are presented for the next two years, with summary information for the later years. Then these are submitted to the corporate office.

7.4.4 Analysis of Strategic Plan by Corporate Office

On receipt of the plan prepared by the business unit, it is integrated into the overall corporate strategic plan. Employees from functional areas and the planning staff take care of the analysis. If any slack is detected, then it gets resolved through discussions between corporate office and their counterpart-staffs in the business units. The corporate office should also ensure that there is coordination between different departments.

7.4.5 Second Iteration of Strategic Plan

The analysis of the first plan may lead to the revision of the plans of the business units. In some companies, changes in the business unit plans are negotiated informally, and the results incorporated into the plan by the corporate office.

7.4.6 Final Review and Approval of Strategic Plan

The revised plan is discussed with the senior corporate officials. It is presented in the board meetings and final approvals obtained from the CEO. The approval process should be completed before beginning the budget preparation process.

7.5 PROCESS OF PROGRAMMING

The programming process deals with allocation of long term resources of the organization. The important aspect of the programming process is that the firms make decisions about resource allocations which require expenditure now in anticipation of the 'returns' in future. It includes defining, evaluating, and implementing new programmes to achieve long-term goals. The decisions which are important and made during the programming process are as follows:

(i) Replacement of worn-out machine to remain in competition
(ii) Expansion of the firm's capacity to produce quality goods and offer better services
(iii) Effective adaptation to the changing environmental conditions
(iv) Adoption of merger and acquisition policy

The programming process depends on the size and diversity of the company. The decisions made in this process have a significant impact on the ability of the firm to survive and achieve its goals and objectives.

7.6 BOWER'S MODEL OF INVESTMENT DECISION-MAKING

Bower's model of investment decision-making examines the discrepancy between actual results and desired results of key variables. The model suggests that ideas, proposals and recommendations of projects come from the lower levels of management. The middle level management approves the projects and allocates resources to these projects. The final decision regarding investment is made by the top management, which approves the projects and determines the reward.

7.7 KOVER'S MODEL OF CAPITAL INVESTMENT APPROVAL

Prof. D.G. Kover propounded a model on the capital investment approval process. According to Kover, there are three stages of investment process in the different levels of the organization. They are:

(i) Initial stage
(ii) Integration stage
(iii) Corporate stage

In the first two stages of investment process, the managers prepare the plans which help in identification of new investment opportunities. The corporate stage identifies and evaluates the opportunities for growth of the organization. Accordingly, steps are taken for implementation of the opportunities for growth.

The mutually supportive management systems help in designing the programming process. The organizations adopt the formal programming processes to define, evaluate and implement the investment projects.

7.8 CONCLUSION

Strategic planning is the process of deciding on the programmes that a firm undertakes and the resources that are allocated to each programme in the future years. This chapter examined the concepts, characteristics and importance of strategic planning. Various processes of strategic planning have also been dealt in this chapter. Programming is an organizational process which deals with allocation of long term resources of an organization. Programming process depends on the size and diversity of a company.

Bower's model of investment decision making examines the difference between actual results and the desired results of key variables. Kover's model of capital investment approval process defines three stages of investment process in the various levels of the organization, viz. initial stage, integration stage, and the corporate stage. The mutually supportive management systems help in designing the programming process.

REVIEW QUESTIONS

7.1 What is strategic planning? Enumerate the characteristics of strategic planning?

7.2 Discuss the importance of strategic planning?

7.3 Explain fully the various steps involved in the process of strategic planning in an organization?

7.4 Write short notes on:

(a) Process of programming
(b) Bower's model of investment decision-making
(c) Kover's model of capital investment approval

8

Budgeting and Budgetary Control

8.1 INTRODUCTION

Every organization prepares budgets for its functional activities and exercises control over them. Such managerial control is exercised by adoption of budgetary control process in an organization. This chapter deals in depth, the definitions, concepts, processes and practical approach for budgeting and budgetary control.

8.2 DEFINITION OF BUDGET

Budgets are formal quantitative statements of resources for carrying out planned activities over a given period of time. The CIMA-London Terminology defines a budget as "a plan quantified in monetary terms, prepared and approved prior to a defined period of time, usually showing planned income to be generated and/or expenditure to be incurred during that period and the capital to be employed to attain a given objective".

The National Association of Accountants (USA) defines budgeting as "the process of planning all flows of financial resources into, within, and from an entity during some specified future period".

Budget has a very wide application in different areas of life, in government sector, in industry and commerce and even in family life. For a manufacturer or business organisation a budget not only contains the target for a given period viz. profits or sales but also the details of all the coordinated activities required for achieving that target, viz. production, purchase, employment of labour and capital, capacity utilisation, etc. The budget is a blue print of business activities expressed in measurable units.

8.2.1 Purpose for Budgeting

The purposes or the needs for budgeting can be realized from the following points:

(i) It reduces uncertainty by allowing executives to make out future course of action.

(ii) It increases coordination among different departments which tend to function in a well-coordinated manner in an attempt to implement the planned courses of action systematically.

(iii) It identifies weakness by finding out the reasons for inefficient performance.

(iv) It helps managers to analyze the expenditure and keep it under check, thereby preventing wastage.

(v) It helps in the establishment of performance standards for operational activities and the adoption of standard costing technique.

(vi) It identifies deviations from pre-planned courses of action and implements remedial measures.

(vii) It helps to establish standards of performance. Evaluation of performance against standards enables employees to analyze their strengths and weaknesses.

8.2.2 Objectives of Budgeting

(a) **Planning:** Through budget a manager prepares his plan for future in specific and objective manner. He pinpoints the responsibilities of his own and his subordinates. He prepares for combating the future uncertainties through budget.

(b) **Performance criterion:** Through budget, a manager sets the target of performance level. Based on the budgeted level, the actual performance is appraised and incentives are provided. Thus, budget serves as a standard for promoting performance.

(c) **Coordination:** Commencing from key budget and ending at master budget, all budgets are set in such a manner that the multi-dimensional activities of an organisation are coordinated and synchronised to serve the objective of the organisation. Thus, budget is an effective tool for coordinating diverse activities.

(d) **Control:** As budgets are the plans for specified future period of activities expressed in quantitative terms, they are measurable with respect to each responsibility centre and the control aspect is served in the process.

8.2.3 Characteristics of Good Budgeting

Certain characteristics of good budgeting are as follows:

(a) **Forecasting:** Reliable forecasting essentially supports good budgeting.

(b) **Clear and realistic goal:** A good budget should set a clear and realistic goal in quantitative term.

(c) **Cohesiveness:** A good budget should promote cohesiveness among sectional objectives to serve the overall goal.

(d) **Coordination:** A good budget should coordinate diverse departmental places into an integrated plan.

(e) **Communication:** Budgeting is good when budgets are well-communicated to all the persons responsible for implementing them.

(f) **Flexibility:** The element of flexibility adds dynamism in the budgeting process that is important for its success.

(g) **Framework:** Budget should provide framework for evaluation of performance.

8.3 DEFINITION OF BUDGETARY CONTROL

As per CIMA-London Terminology, "Budgetary control is the establishment of budgets, relating the responsibilities of executives to the requirements of a policy, and the continuous comparison of actual with budgeted results, either to secure by individual action the objective of that policy or to provide a basis for its revision".

Therefore, a budget is a 'means', while budgetary control is the 'end results'.

8.3.1 Advantages of Budgetary Control

Budgetary control offers several benefits to the management of an organization. They are:

(i) It offers an overall picture of the various functions in an organization, and presents a managerial view of all the activities within an organization structure.

(ii) It bridges the gap between planning and performance by anticipating the results of courses of action, by comparing the actual results with the anticipated results, and setting up proper standards for performance.

(iii) It promotes division of work and specialization. These help in the allocation of responsibility and accountability for performance to each member of the organization.

(iv) It fosters coordination and integration. These help managers to coordinate the activities of the organization, and bring about integration of plans, policies, and actions of different departments.

8.3.2 Limitations of Budgetary Control

As we have observed that budgetary control is a system wherefrom a number of advantages flow in, provided, it is applied in an appropriate manner. On the contrary, if the system is interpreted in a wrong way, misused, or approached with negative attitude certain ill-effects may arise for which the budgetary control system should not be blamed. Some negative outcomes are mentioned hereunder:

(i) Budget may be taken as a rigid plan for future for which the firm may lose its flexibilities to meet the contingencies in future.

(ii) Budget, being an estimate there remain scope for bias.

(iii) Lazy participants often set budget as a standard at the low level. This practice, however, allows for inefficiency.

(iv) It allows more authority to previous plan than to the present need.

(v) Workers and management are often unwilling to exceed budgeted level of performance in apprehension that instead of rewarding their efficiency in the long-term, the budget may be revised to set new standards.

8.3.3 Steps for Organization of Budgetary Control

In order to organize an effective budgetary control system, following steps are taken by an organization:

(i) Organization for budgeting
  (a) Budget centres
  (b) Budget manual

(ii) Responsibility for budgeting
  (a) Budget controller
  (b) Budget committee

(iii) Budget period

(iv) Level of activity

(v) Principal budget factors or key factors

(vi) Budget report

(a) Budget centre: A budget centre is a section of an organization developed for the purpose of budgetary control, and is intended to facilitate formulation of various budgets with the help of head of the department.

(b) Budget manual: It is a written document which contains standing instructions regarding the procedures to be followed at the time of budget preparation. A budget manual contains the following guidelines:

- Functions of various concerned officials for formulation of budgets
- Steps in the preparation of budgets
- Schedule date and time of submission of budgets
- Review and approval of various budgets
- Final adoption of budgets
- Time table for budget operations
- Records, reports, format, etc., to be used and maintained for budgeting

Therefore, budget manual is a document where the entire system of budgeting is stated in chronological manner. It contains the role, authority and responsibility of different persons in the budgetary control system. It contains the procedure and flow of decisions and creation of records in connection with preparation of budget. Thus, the entire budgeting process is stated, explained, clarified, and documented through budget manual.

(c) Budget controller: The entire process of budgetary control is supervised by the budget controller who advises the management on important issues, viz., budget preparation, revision of budgets, approval of budgets, etc. The budget controller is accountable to the chairman of the company.

(d) **Budget committee:** The budget committee consists of heads of various departments of the firm. The committee works under the budget controller and assists him. Since budget is an all encompassing plan, the makers of the budget shall consist of a group of persons representing all the major functions of the firm. This group is formally known as budget committee, which comprises heads of various departments of the firm, and is headed by one of them as budget controller.

Budget committee is the authority for preparation of budget, and is responsible for all decisions and actions taken for preparation of budget. The committee is directly responsible to the top management.

(e) **Budget period:** It is the period for which a budget is prepared and used. The budget period usually covers one year. However, it depends on the nature of the business, production period, and control aspects. This period should be determined in such a way that short period budgets are integrated with long period budgets.

(f) **Level of activity:** It is essential to establish a normal level of activity since it forms the basis of the budget. Three levels of activity are considered as follows:

- Level of activity that past results suggest which may be attained
- Level of activity that can be attained by highest possible efficiency
- Level of activity that can be attained by efficient working under existing conditions

(g) **Principal Budget Factor or Key Factor:** CIMA-London Terminology defines a key factor as "a factor which at a particular time or over a period will limit the activities of an organization and which is therefore, taken into account in preparing budgets". In other words, key factor is the resource or activity or condition, which limits all other activities of the firm. Let us assume that the firm operates in a very competitive market where demand at a given selling price is the limiting factor. Accordingly, sales budget would be prepared first on the basis of limited sales. All other budgets viz. production, purchase, etc. would be prepared based on the key factors budget.
Examples of key factors are given below:

❑ **Sales activity**

- Low demand for product
- Shortage of efficient salesman
- Inadequate warehouse facilities
- Inefficient advertising, etc.

❑ **Plant capacity**

- Shortage due to fund constraint
- Shortage due to import restriction
- Shortage due to lack of shop floor space
- Bottlenecks in key process

- **Raw materials**
  - Shortage of raw materials due to non-availability of supply
  - Shortage due to restriction imposed by licenses, quotas, etc.
- **Labour**
  - General shortage of labour in industrial area
  - Shortage of skilled labour
- **Management**
  - Shortage of efficient executives
- **Working capital**
  - Shortage due to lack of liquidity
  - Inefficient use of working capital

The key factors are 'temporary' in nature, and in the long run they may be overcome by suitable management actions. In preparation of the budgets, the principal budget factor or key factor is the starting point, and all the budgets must be centered around it.

(h) Budget report: Budget reports should furnish details about the responsibility of each department in budget preparation, and give reasons for variances from the actuals as compared to budgets so that corrective actions can be initiated.

8.4 STEPS IN FORMULATION OF BUDGETS

Budget preparation starts with the top management of the organization. But the information or input data needed for budget preparation starts at the lower hierarchical levels. Managerial forecasts provide data on the anticipated level of activity while accounting reports provide data on the financial magnitude of past and current operations.

There are various steps in formulation of budgets. They are described as follows:

Step 1: Organization

(i) Budget department: The budget department administers the information flow during the budget preparation. The functions of this department are:

(a) To publish the procedures and forms for preparation of the budget

(b) To ensure that the information is communicated in the right manner between different departments

(c) To analyze the proposed budgets and make suitable corrections and recommendations

(d) To administer the process of budget revision at regular intervals

(e) To coordinate the work of the business units

(ii) Budget committee: The function of the budget committee is to review budgets, approve them and make necessary and make necessary adjustments.

Step 2: Issue of guidelines

The budget guidelines are developed by the staff of the budget department and these guidelines are approved by the senior management. The guidelines issued by the budget department are to be followed by the responsibility centres.

Step 3: Initial budget proposal

The managers of the responsibility centres develop a budget request which may be modified as per guidelines issued to the responsibility centres. Following changes call for modifications of budget request:

(i) Changes in external forces
 (a) Changes in general level of economic activity
 (b) Changes in labour rates, raw materials, etc.
 (c) Changes in selling prices

(ii) Changes in internal policies and practices
 (a) Changes in market share and product mix
 (b) Changes in production costs
 (c) Changes in discretionary costs, etc.

Step 4: Negotiation

The budget planner discusses the budget proposal with his superior. There should be an improvement in the performance in the budget year over the performance in the previous year.

(a) **Slack:** The difference between the budget amount and the best estimate is known as 'slack'. It is the duty of the superior to discover and eliminate slack.

Step 5: Review and approval

The budget committee presents the fully developed and reworked budget to the CEO who approves the final budget, and then submits the same to the board of directors.

Step 6: Budget revision

In order to check discrepancies if any, the budgets are revised from time to time, by following any of the two procedures:

(i) Systematic updating of the budgets
(ii) Revision of budgets under special circumstances

8.5 ADMINISTRATION AND REVIEW OF BUDGETS

The administration and review of budget and budgetary control is done through the following steps:

(i) Determining the objectives
(ii) Establishing the budget centres
(iii) Introducing adequate accounting records and assigning verifiable codes to them

(iv) Preparing a budget organization chart
(v) Establishing budget committees
(vi) Preparing the budget manual
(vii) Selecting the budget period
(viii) Fixing up the level of activity
(ix) Locating the key or principal budget factors
(x) Determining the budget cost allowance
(xi) Budget reporting

8.6 BEHAVIOURAL ASPECTS OF BUDGETING

It is no denying the fact that budgeting and budgetary control can be most effective in an organization when there is a full support and involvement of all employees in the control exercise. Therefore, the behavioural aspects of budgeting cannot be ignored as the individuals are involved in the budgeting process.

Behavioural aspects of budgeting exercise can be discussed under the following heads:

(i) Participation in budgeting process
(ii) Degree of budget goal
(iii) Involvement of senior management
(iv) Budget department

8.6.1 Participation in Budgeting Process

A budget can either be set by the senior management for the lower levels or the lower level managers may participate in setting the budgets. However, the actual process of budgeting is a blend of two approaches. The lower level managers first prepare the budget proposal and submit the first draft to senior management (bottom-up). The senior management reviews the budget and suggests certain guidelines for improving the budget (top-down). Bottom-up or participative budgeting is considered to be more effective budgeting approach because it results in greater acceptance of budget goals and leads to personal commitment towards achieving these goals. It also leads to information exchange between the staffs and superiors.

8.6.2 Degree of Budget Goal

Budget goals should be challenging but attainable. If they are achievable, then managers do not engage in data manipulation to meet the budget. An attainable budget ensures allocation of resources to gear up the budget activities.

8.6.3 Involvement of Senior Management

Senior management should actively participate, review and approve the budgets to make the budgetary control system effective.

8.6.4 Budget Department

Budget department collects the input data for preparation of budgets, prepares them and analyzes and ensures that no excessive allowances are contained in the budgets. The members of the budget department should be fair and objective in their approach. They should have the skill to deal effectively with people.

8.7 FUNCTIONAL BUDGETS

A functional budget is a budget of income and/or expenditure applicable to a particular function. Functional budgets include the following:

(i) Sales budget
(ii) Selling and distribution cost budget
(iii) Production budget
(iv) Production cost budget
(v) Personnel budget
(vi) Purchase budget
(vii) Plant utilization budget
(viii) Capital expenditure budget
(ix) Repairs and maintenance budget
(x) Administration cost budget
(xi) Research and development cost budget

As we have observed that budgets are the final product of the budgeting process. In a business firm, a number of budgets, as stated above, are prepared for different functions of business. Each of these functional budgets is well-coordinated and harmonised to serve the overall objective of the business.

Key factor budget is prepared first, and on the basis thereon, other budgets are prepared. Generally, market stands the key or limiting factor for most of the business and therefore, sales budget is prepared first, based on sales forecast made by the market survey. In a normal situation, next comes the production budget because production should be planned according to the sales volume keeping the inventory policy in consideration. Production cost budget, purchase budget, etc. follow from the production quantity budget.

Ultimately, when all the revenues and expenditures are planned through different functional budgets and capital expenditures budget, cash budget can be prepared specifying the time and volume of cash inflows and outflows. Therefore, after preparation of all the budgets, it is possible to summarize them for preparation of:

(a) Cash budget
(b) Budgeted profit and loss account, and
(c) Budgeted balance sheet.

Both budgeted profit & loss account and balance sheet are called Master Budget.

8.7.1 Sales Budget

Sales budget is a forecast of total sales expressed in monetary and/or quantitative terms. In practice, quantitative budget is prepared first, and then it is translated into monetary terms. A sales budget may be prepared on the basis of the following:

(i) Product or group of product
(ii) Area, territories or town or location
(iii) Salesman or agent
(iv) Types of customer
 (a) Central Government
 (b) State Government
 (c) Export
 (d) Wholesalers
 (e) Retailers
(v) Period wise, e.g., week, month, quarter, year, etc.

The sales budget is important because planning of other functional budgets rests primarily on activities of the sales department.

Preparation of sales budget

The preparation of sales budget is the responsibility of sales manager. Following aspects are considered for preparation of sales budget:

(i) Analysis of past sales to indicate trends and seasonal fluctuations
(ii) Market analysis to ascertain potential market demand, product design, expected competition, prices, etc.
(iii) Salesman's reports as to expected sales, customers' habits, expected competition, etc.
(iv) General business conditions, viz. national and international economic affairs, political influences, government policies, etc.
(v) Change in company's policy, viz. introduction of new product, new design, change in distribution methods, market research
(vi) Special conditions, e.g., development of new township leading to demand for the products, etc.
(vii) Plant capacity.

Example 1

ABC Limited produces two products, A and B, and operates three sales divisions for sale of their products. Prepare a sales budget for six months ending 30/06/2006 from the following information:

Budgeted sales for six months ended 31/12/2005:

	Div. I	Div. II	Div. III
Product A	1600 @ ₹ 10	2400 @ ₹ 10	2400 @ ₹ 10
Product B	800 @ ₹ 9	4800 @ ₹ 9	2000 @ ₹ 9

Actual sales during the same period:

Product A	2000 @ ₹ 10	3200 @ ₹ 10	2800 @ ₹ 10
Product B	400 @ ₹ 9	4000 @ ₹ 9	1600 @ ₹ 9

In the management meeting, following decisions have been taken:

(i) The price of product A should be increased by ₹ 1 as there is a high demand for product A.

(ii) Product B is not selling at the expected rate as this product has been over-priced. However, if the selling price is reduced by ₹ 1, it is expected that the market would pick up. Therefore, the divisional sales managers have made the following estimates:

Percentage increase over previous budget (%)

Product	Div. I	Div. II	Div. III
A	20%	30%	10%
B	5%	10%	8%

Solution:

The sales budget is as follows:

Sales Budget
6 months ended 30/06/2006

		Budget 30/06/06			Budget 31/12/05			Actual 31/12/05		
Div.	Product	Qty.	Price (₹)	Value (₹)	Qty.	Price (₹)	Value (₹)	Qty.	Price (₹)	Value (₹)
I	A	1920	11	21120	1600	10	16000	2000	10	20000
	B	840	8	6720	800	9	7200	400	9	3600
Total		**2760**		**27840**	**2400**		**23200**	**2400**		**23600**
II	A	3120	11	34320	2400	10	24000	3200	10	32000
	B	5280	8	42240	4800	9	43200	4000	9	36000
Total		**8400**		**76560**	**7200**		**67200**	**7200**		**68000**
III	A	2640	11	29040	2400	10	24000	2800	10	28000
	B	2160	8	17280	2000	9	18000	1600	9	14400
Total		**4800**		**46320**	**4400**		**42000**	**4400**		**42400**
Grand Total:		**15960**		**150720**	**14000**		**132400**	**14000**		**134000**

8.7.2 Selling and Distribution Cost Budget

It is a forecast of the cost of selling and distribution of the goods during the budget period. This budget is based on:

(i) Sales budget

(ii) Selling and distribution cost budget for the current period

(iii) Actual selling and distribution cost for the current period
(iv) Expected change of method of distribution, advertisement policy, etc.

Selling and distribution cost budget may be prepared division wise.

Selling and Distribution Cost Budget
Period

Elements of cost	Budget (₹)			Prev. Budget (₹)			Actual expenses		
	Div. I	Div. II	Total	Div. I	Div. II	Total	Div. I	Div. II	Total
1. Direct selling expenses									
Salesmen's salaries									
Salesmen's commission									
Salesmen's expenses									
Car expenses									
2. Sales office expenses									
Salaries									
Rent and rates									
Depreciation									
Postage and stationery									
General expenses									
3. Distribution expenses:									
Warehouse wages									
Driver's wages									
Warehouse rent, rates, etc.									
Lorry expenses									
Depreciation									
General expenses									
4. Advertisement expenses									
Press, cinema, and TV.									
Road side and shop window									
Coupon									
Total									

8.7.3 Production Budget

It is a forecast of production for the budget period expressed in units, and/or standard hours. Preparation of this budget is based on:

(i) Sales budget
(ii) Production capacity of the plant
(iii) Estimated changes in stock position

(iv) Inherent loss in production
(v) Company's production policy

It is the duty of production manager to prepare this budget. When the production capacity exceeds sales forecast/budget, then compilation of production budget poses no problem. But if production capacity is the limiting factor, then various other alternatives, e.g., overtime working, shift-working, acquiring new plant, etc., should be considered.

A production budget may be prepared:

(i) Products or group of product wise
(ii) Manufacturing departments/process wise
(iii) Period wise–weekly, monthly, etc.
(iv) A combination of above

Example 2

From the following information, prepare a production budget for ABC Ltd. assuming that:

(i) There is no loss of production,
(ii) Normal loss of production is 2% and 5% for product A and B.

Sales budget (units)	Product A	Product B
Div. I	1920	840
Div. II	3120	5280
Div. III	2640	2160
Total (units)	7680	8280

Stock as on 30th June:

A = 1200 units
B = 2200 units.

Stock as on 31st December is estimated to be more by 10% in quantity.

Solution:

Production Budget
Budget period

Particulars	Product A	Product B	Total (units)
Sales requirements (units) as per sales budget	7680	8280	15960
Add: Estimated increase in stock (10% of 1200 units and 2200 units)	120	220	340
Minimum production required:	7800	8500	16300

Production requirement (considering normal loss):

$$2\% \text{ for A} = \frac{7800}{98} \times 100 = 7960$$

$$5\% \text{ for B} = \frac{8500}{95} \times 100 = 8948$$

$$\text{Total} \qquad = 16908$$

8.7.4 Production Cost Budget

It is a forecast of the cost of production estimates in the production budget. The cost of production includes direct material, direct labour, direct expenses, and factory overheads.

This budget will be based on the following:

(i) Production budget
(ii) Estimated increase or decrease in the price of materials and supplies
(iii) Estimated increase or decrease in the rates of wages and salaries and expenses

This budget may be prepared under the following classifications:

(i) Elements of cost wise
(ii) Products or group of product wise
(iii) Manufacturing department wise/process wise

Example 3

Prepare a production budget for each month and a summarized production cost budget for the six months period ending 31st December, 2010 from the following data of product X:

The units to be sold for different months are:

July, 2010	1100
August	1100
September	1700
October	1900
November	2500
December	2300
January, 2011	2000

There will be no work-in-progress at the end of any month.

Finished units equal to half the sales for the next month will be in stock at the end of each month (including June, 2010).

Budgeted production and production cost for the year ending 31st December, 2010 are as follows:

Production (in units)	22000
Direct material per unit	₹ 10
Direct wages per unit	₹ 4
Total factory overhead apportioned to product	₹ 88000

Solution:

Production Budget (in units)

For six months ended 31st December, 2010

	July	August	September	October	November	December	Total
Sales	1100	1100	1700	1900	2500	2300	10600
Closing stock	550	850	950	1250	1150	1000	1000
	1650	1950	2650	3150	3650	3300	11600
Opening stock	(550)	(550)	(850)	(950)	(1250)	(1150)	(550)
Production	1100	1400	1800	2200	2400	2150	11050

Summarized Production Cost Budget
For six months ended 31st December, 2010

Production (units)		11050
	Unit cost (₹)	Total cost (₹)
Direct material	10	110500
Direct wages	4	44200
Factory overhead	4	44200
	18	198900

Note: In absence any further information, factory overhead has been treated as variable expense, i.e. it relates to production and not to time. Hence, rate per unit = ₹ 88000/22000 = ₹ 4.

8.7.5 Personnel Budget

It is a forecast of planned outlay on direct and indirect labour of a company during the budget period. This budget is based on the following:

(i) Production budget
(ii) Sales budget
(iii) Capital expenditure budget
(iv) R&D cost budget
(v) Possibility of new wage agreements

The main purposes of this budget are:

(i) To help in the efficient labour management
(ii) To show the planned outlay on direct and indirect wages

8.7.6 Purchase Budget

It is a forecast of purchases to be made during the budget period. This will include direct and indirect materials and services. Purchase budget may be expressed in terms of quantity or money. The budget is based on:

(i) Sales budget
(ii) Production cost budget
(iii) Capital expenditure budget
(iv) R&D budget
(v) Estimated increase or decrease in raw materials, supplies, or bought out finished goods stock
(vi) Purchase orders already placed
(vii) Materials to be manufactured
(viii) Maximum and minimum stock levels
(ix) Economic Order Quantity (EOQ), etc.

The main purposes of this budget are as follows:

(i) To indicate cash requirements in respect of purchases to be made during the budget period;
(ii) To enable the purchase department to plan its operations in time in respect of purchases so that long-term forward contract may be arranged.

Example 4

The marketing director of a manufacturing company reports that next year he expects to sell 54000 units of a product. The production manager consults the storekeeper and casts his figures as follows:

Two kinds of raw materials, A and B are required for manufacturing the product. Each unit of the product requires 2 units of A and 3 units of B. The estimated opening balances at the beginning of the next year are:

Finished product: 10000 units, A: 12000 units, B: 15000 units.

The desirable closing balances at the end of the next year:

Finished product: 14000 units, A: 13000 units, B: 16000 units.

Prepare the materials purchases budget for the next year.

Solution:

Materials Purchases Budget
For the year

	Material A (Units)	Material B (Units)
Materials required:		
A (58000 × 2)	116000	
B (58000 × 3)		174000
Closing stock	13000	16000
	129000	190000
Less: Opening stock	(12000)	(15000)
Budgeted purchases	117000	175000

Working:

Budgeted production for the year:

	Units
Sales	54000
Closing stock	14000
	68000
Opening stock	(10000)
Budgeted production	58000

8.7.7 Plant Utilization Budget

This budget shows the estimated plant facilities required to meet the budget production as set out in the production budget. This budget is expressed in 'working hours'. The main purpose of this budget is to show the budgeted machine load on departments, machines or group of machines.

8.7.8 Capital Expenditure Budget

It is the planned outlay on fixed assets during the budget period. This budget is usually prepared for a long period say 5/10 years. It is discussed in detail in the later sections.

8.7.9 Repairs and Maintenance Budget (R&M Budget)

This budget may be set in four parts, viz.,

(i) Budget for the cost of preventive maintenance
(ii) Budget for the cost of emergency maintenance
(iii) Budget for the cost of major maintenance
(iv) Budget for the cost of maintenance department

Budgets for preventive maintenance are easy to prepare. As such, maintenance would be pre-planned, and the materials and supplies required for maintenance work are pre-determined. Budgeting for emergency repairs is comparatively difficult as no standard for such work can be fixed. However, past figures may be adopted for this purpose. Periodic major maintenance costs may be capitalized as these would increase the useful life of the asset concerned. Past figures may be suitably modified in light of anticipated change in conditions and a budget may be accordingly prepared. The general costs of maintenance department, e.g., depreciation, rent, lighting, general expenses, etc., would be fixed nature and therefore, may be easily budgeted.

The maintenance cost budget may be prepared for the factory as a whole or separately for each operational department, which utilizes the services of maintenance department.

8.7.10 Administration Cost Budget

This budget shows the total estimated cost of administration, i.e. cost of formulating the policy, directing the organization and controlling the operations. Most of the expenses relating to administration are of 'fixed' nature within defined limits. So, this budget is easy to prepare. Formally, each budget centre or department prepares its own budget which gets incorporated in this budget afterwards.

8.7.11 Research and Development Cost Budget

Research costs are the costs incurred by an organisation for

(i) Fundamental research for basic knowledge
(ii) Invention of new products, processes, equipments, formula, etc.
(iii) Improvement of existing processes, products, equipments, etc. and
(iv) Searching for better layout, and better organisation, etc.

Development costs are the costs of the processes, which start with the implementation of the decision to produce a new product, or improved product, or to employ a new or improved method, and finishes with the beginning of commercial production or formal method. Therefore, development costs include the cost of initial patterns, tools, moulds, dies, indirect expenses of designers, drafting, purchase of patents and payment for royalties, preliminary expenses for regular production, etc.

Research and development cost budget is a planned outlay on R&D activities of a company. The budget covers materials, equipment and supplies, salaries, expenses, and other costs relating to design, development, and technical research projects.

8.7.12 Cash Budget

It is a detailed budget of cash income and cash expenses incorporating both revenue and capital items. This budget is prepared after all functional budgets are prepared. It extends over the budget period. However, for control purposes, it is necessary to analyze cash budget to show monthly or weekly requirements of cash.

A cash budget can be prepared in three ways:

(i) Receipt and payment method–for detailed short and long-term cash budget
(ii) Adjusted profit and loss method–for making long-term cash budget
(iii) Balance sheet method–for making long-term cash budget

Reviewing the budgeted liquidities position, different financial plans and policies are chalked out, and their impact on liquidities are also incorporated within the cash budget. For example, let us assume that the cash budget reveals a negative cash position in the month of July. The management would immediately plan for filling the financial, gap say, through issue of debenture. The cash inflow from such planned issue of debenture also would be incorporated in the cash budget.

There are enormous advantages in preparing a cash budget:

(i) It aids in securing optimum working capital needed for smooth running of the operation and planning for payments to the shareholders
(ii) It eases strains of a cash shortage
(iii) It facilitates temporary cash investment whenever, and to whatever extent, found in excess
(iv) It provides for normal growth

A better planning is necessary to ensure that only an optimum balance of cash/bank is held, and that the surplus cash is invested in more profitable opportunities elsewhere, if investment in the business is not possible or desirable at once. This will help in improving the rate of return of a firm. Such surplus cash is often invested temporarily in short term securities.

Cash budgeting by months, weeks, or even days will enable a firm to determine with reasonable degree of accuracy, what proportion of cash balance, and for how long, is available for investment outside the business.

When a company needs additional long-term capital, it is usually possible to obtain such capital on favourable terms, if the need is known well in advance. Cash budgeting makes it possible to choose an advantageous time to tap the market for equity capital or long-term debt capital.

Cash budgeting—Short term and long term

The principal method of short-term cash forecasting is the receipt and payment method. Cash budget prepared under this method shows the timing and magnitude of expected cash receipts and payments over the budget period, not usually exceeding one year. Items of cash receipts and payments and the basis of their estimation are as follows:

Items	Basis of estimation
Cash sales	Sales budget and its division into cash and credit sales
Collection of accounts receivables	Sales budget and its division into cash and credit sales as well as collection pattern
Interest and dividend receipts	Firm's portfolio securities and returns expected of them
Increase in loan/deposits and issue of securities	Financial plan
Sale of assets	Proposed disposal of assets
Cash purchase	Purchase budget and its division into cash and credit purchase
Payment for purchase	Purchase budget and its division into cash and credit purchase terms
Wages and salaries	Manpower employed and wages and salaries structure
Manufacturing expenses	Production budget
General administration and selling expenses	Administration and sales personnel, and proposed sales promotion and distribution expenditure
Capital equipment purchase	Capital expenditure budget, and payment pattern associated with capital equipment purchase
Repayment of loans and retirement of securities	Financing plan

Example 5

From the following information, prepare a monthly cash budget for 3 months ending 31st December, 2005.

Month	Sales (₹)	Materials (₹)	Wages (₹)	Prod. overhead (₹)	Admn. Selling and Distr. overhead (₹)
June	6000	3600	1300	450	320
July	6500	4000	1500	450	320
Aug	7000	4800	1500	500	350
Sept	7500	4500	1500	600	350
Oct	8000	4600	1600	600	400
Nov	8500	5000	1800	700	400
Dec	9000	5200	2000	700	450

Credit terms are:

(i) Sales—3 months to S/Debtors. 10% of sales are on cash. On average, 50% credit sales are paid on due date, whereas the other 50% are paid in the month following.

(ii) Creditors (materials)—2 months.

(iii) Lag in payment: Wages—1/4 month, Overheads—1/2 month.

Cash and bank balances on 1st October is expected to be ₹ 3000. Other relevant information are:

(i) Plant and machinery to be installed in August at a cost of ₹ 48,000 will be paid by monthly installment of ₹ 1000 from October, 1st.

(ii) Preference share dividend of 5% on capital of ₹ 100,000, are to be paid on 1st December.

(iii) Calls on 500 equity shares @ ₹ 2 per share are expected on 1st November.

(iv) Dividends from investment amounting to ₹ 500 are expected on 31st December.

(v) Income tax is to be paid in December ₹ 1000.

Solution:

Cash Budget

Budget period: Ending 31st December, 2005

Details	October (₹)	November (₹)	December (₹)
Balance b/d	3000	1075	700
Receipts:			
Sales	6425	6925	7425
Capital		1000	
Dividends			500
Total (a)	**9425**	**9000**	**8625**
Payments:			
Creditors	4800	4500	4600
Wages	1575	1750	1950
Prodn. Overhead	600	650	700

Admn.sel and dist.o/h	375	400	425
Pref. dividend			5000
Income tax			1000
Plant and machinery	1000	1000	1000
Total (b)	**8350**	**8300**	**14675**
Balance (a) – (b)	**1075**	**700**	**(–) 6050**

Workings:
Receipts from sales (₹)

Months	Sales	October	November	December
June	6000	2700		
July	6500	2925	2925	
Aug	7000		3150	3150
Sept	7500			3375
Oct	8000	800		
Nov	8500		850	
Dec	9000			900
Total		**6425**	**6925**	**7425**

Calculation of Wages

October: 1/4th of September + 3/4th of October wages

November: 1/4th of October + 3/4th of November wages

December: 1/4th of November + 3/4th of December wages

Example 6

Make out a cash budget for the period April–June 2011 from the following information:
Actual and Budgeted sales:

Months	Actual (₹)	Months	Budgeted (₹)
January	90000	April	100000
February	90000	May	90000
March	80000	June	85000

Actual and Budgeted purchases:

Months	Actual (₹)	Months	Budgeted (₹)
January	50000	April	60000
February	45000	May	55000
March	40000	June	40000

Actual and Budgeted wages and expenses:

Months	Actual (₹)		Months	Budgeted (₹)	
	Wages	Expenses		Wages	Expenses
January	25000	7000	April	30000	10000
February	20000	8000	May	25000	8000
March	28000	8000	June	22000	7000

Advance income tax to be paid in May ₹ 5000
Plant to be purchased in April ₹ 15000
Rent ₹ 400 payable each month, not included in expenses
10% purchases and sales are on cash basis.
Credit purchases are paid after one month and credit sales are collected after two months.
Time lag in wages and expenses half-month
Cash and bank balances on 1st April 2011 ₹ 15000.

Solution:

Cash Budget
For the period April–June, 2011

	April (₹)	May (₹)	June (₹)
Opening balance	15000	10600	(9800)
Receipts:			
Cash sales (10% of total for the month)	10000	9000	8500
Debtors (2 months' previous) 90%	81000	72000	90000
	106000	91600	88700
Payments:			
Cash purchases (10% of total for the month)	6000	5500	4000
Creditors (previous month) 90%	36000	54000	49500
Wages (1/2 of previous month + 1/2 of current month)	29000	27500	23500
Expenses (–do–)	9000	9000	7500
Advance income tax	–	5000	–
Plant	15000	–	–
Rent	400	400	400
	95400	101400	84900
Closing balance	10600	(9800)	3800
	106000	91600	88700

Evaluation of Receipt and Payment method

Advantages

(i) It provides a complete picture of expected cash flows.
(ii) It is a sound vehicle for exercising control over day-to-day transactions.

Disadvantages

(i) Its reliability is impaired by delays in collection or sudden demand for large payments.
(ii) It fails to provide a clear picture of important changes in the company's working capital movement, relating to inventories and receivables.

Long-term cash forecasts

Long-term cash forecasts are generally prepared for a period ranging from 2 to 5 years, and serve to provide a broad picture of a firm's financing needs and availability of investable surplus in future. Such forecasts are helpful in planning capital investment outlays and long term financing. The method used for this purpose is the 'adjusted net income method'. A format of the same is given in Box 8.1.

Box 8.1 Adjusted Net Income Method

Years	2005	2006	2007	2008	2009
Sources					
Net income (after tax)					
Non-cash charges (depreciation etc.)					
Increase in borrowings					
Sale of equity shares					
Miscellaneous					
Uses					
Capital expenditure					
Increase in current assets					
Repayment of borrowings					
Dividend payment					
Miscellaneous					
Surplus/deficit					
Opening cash balance					
Closing cash balance					

This method of long-term cash forecasting resembles the fund flow statement.

Under the balance sheet method, a budgeted balance sheet for the budgeted period showing all items excluding cash is prepared. The balancing figure in the balance sheet is represented by cash. If the liability side of the balance sheet is larger than the asset side, it would mean a cash or bank balance. If the asset side is greater than the liability side, the difference would mean bank overdraft.

Cash reports for management control

Cash reports provide a comparison of actual developments with forecast figures. These are helpful to the management in controlling and revising cash forecasts on a continuous basis. The important cash reports are:

(i) Daily cash report
(ii) Daily treasury report
(ii) Monthly cash report

8.7.13 Master Budget

It is defined as a budget which is prepared from the functional budgets in summary form. When all functional budgets are prepared, they are summarized to produce budgeted profit and loss account, and budgeted balance sheet.

So, a master budget takes the form of a budgeted profit and loss account and a budgeted balance sheet. Budgeted 'fund flow' may also form part of a master budget. Therefore, this budget is an overall business plan of a company. When it is approved by the budget committee, it becomes the target for the company during the budget period.

Example 7

The operating results of XYZ Ltd. for the year ending 31st December, 2002, are summarized below:

	₹ (in lakhs)
Sales (40000 units)	48.00
Less: Trade discount	2.40
Net sales	45.60
Cost of sales:	
Direct materials	14.40
Direct labour	12.60
Factory overheads	6.30
Administration overheads	3.60
Selling and distribution overheads	4.50

The following changes are to be incorporated in the budget for the year 2003:
Sales (units) to be increased by 25%
Material price to increase by 15%
Direct wages to go up by 12%
Factory overheads to increase by 15%
A new facility to be added to the factory laboratory at a recurring cost of ₹ 12500 per year
Administration overheads to increase by 10%
Selling and distribution overheads to increase by 14%
No change in inventory
Profit target for the year to be fixed at ₹ 6 lakh
No change in the rate of trade discount

Calculate the unit selling price and present the budget for 2003 in a meaningful manner.

Solution:

Computation of Estimated Figures for 2003

Sales (units)	= 40000 × 125/100 = 50000 units	
Materials	= 14.40 × (125/100 × 115/100)	= ₹ 20.70 lakh
Labour	= 12.60 × (125/100 × 112/100)	= ₹ 17.64 lakh
Factory overheads	= 6.30 × 115/100 = ₹ 7.245 lakh	
Add: Cost of new facility	= ₹ 0.125 lakh	= ₹ 7.370 lakh
Administration overheads	= 3.60 × 110/100	= ₹ 3.96 lakh
Selling and distribution overheads	= 4.50 × 114/100	= ₹ 5.13 lakh
Total estimated cost		= ₹ 54.80 lakh

Net sales value to cover costs and profit = ₹ 54.80 + 6.00 = ₹ 60.80 lakh
As trade discount is 5%, gross sales value would be = 100/95 × 60.80 = ₹ 64 lakh
Therefore, selling price per unit = ₹ 6400000/50000 units = ₹ 128

Operating Budget

For the year 2003

	2003 (Budgeted)	2002 (Actual)
(a) Sales:		
In units	50000	40000
Unit selling price	₹ 128	₹ 120
	₹ (in lakh)	₹ (in lakh)
Gross sales value	64.00	48.00
Less: Trade discount	3.20	2.40
Net sales value	60.80	45.60
(b) Costs:		
Direct materials	20.70	14.40
Direct labour	17.64	12.60
Factory overheads	7.37	6.30
Administration overheads	3.96	3.60
Selling and distribution overheads	5.13	4.50
Total cost	54.80	41.40
Profit (a) – (b)	6.00	4.20

8.8 FIXED BUDGET AND FLEXIBLE BUDGET

A fixed budget is a budget which is designed to remain unchanged irrespective of the volume of output.

A flexible budget is a budget which, by recognizing the difference in behaviour between fixed and variable costs in relation to fluctuations in output, turnover, or other variable factors, is designed to change appropriately with such fluctuations.

In this type of budget, the costs are analyzed according to behaviour, e.g., variable, fixed, and semi-variable. When flexible budgetary control is exercised by the management in conjunction with standard costing, the variable and fixed portion of semi-variable expenses are to be segregated. The flexible budget shows the budgeted expenses against each item of cost corresponding to different levels of activity. Thus, cost ascertainment at different levels of activity, price fixation, tendering quotations, etc., are facilitated.

8.8.1 Preparation of Flexible Budget

There are three methods applied by the management in preparation of flexible budget in an organization. They are as follows:

(i) Tabular method
(ii) Charting method
(iii) Ratio method

Tabular method

Under this method, a table is prepared showing different capacity levels in horizontal columns. The budget expenses against different capacity levels are written in the vertical columns. The expenses are recorded under major groups–variable, semi-variable, and fixed.

Charting method

Under this method, expenses or group of expenses are analyzed as per their behaviour–variable, semi-variable, and fixed. Then an estimate of expenses is made against different levels of activity and plotted on a graph paper. The budgeted cost corresponding to the level of activity attained can be read out from the chart.

Ratio method

Here the normal costs are estimated for normal production or level of activity, so that a number of ratios can be worked out showing relationship of each expense or group of expenses with each, say, 10% movement in the level of activity. Therefore, the budgeted costs for any desired level of activity can be ascertained with the help of these ratios.

Example 8

(i) A Ltd. produces a standard product. The estimated costs per unit are given below:

Raw material	₹ 10
Direct wages	₹ 8
Direct expenses	₹ 2
Variable expenses	₹ 3
	₹ 23

Semi-variable overhead at 100% activity level (10000 units) are expected to be ₹ 40000, and these overheads vary in steps of ₹ 2000 for each change in output of 1000 units. Fixed overheads are estimated at ₹ 50000. Selling price per unit is expected to be ₹ 40.

Prepare a flexible budget at 50%, 70%, and 90% level of activity.

(ii) During the same period, the following expenses were incurred for producing 7000 units. Present the cost figures to the management in a suitable form:

Raw material	₹ 69500
Direct wages	₹ 56600
Direct expenses	₹ 14100
Variable overheads	₹ 35100
Fixed overheads	₹ 70000
Total	₹ 245300

Solution:

(i)

Flexible Budget
Period

	Normal level of activity		
Capacity	50%	70%	90%
Units	5000	7000	9000

Flexible Budget
Period

	Normal level of activity		
	(₹)	(₹)	(₹)
Materials	50000	70000	90000
Direct wages	40000	56000	72000
Direct expenses	10000	14000	18000
Prime cost	100000	140000	180000
Variable overhead	25000	35000	45000
Marginal cost	125000	175000	225000
Sales	200000	280000	360000
Contribution	75000	105000	135000
Fixed overhead	70000	70000	70000
Profit	5000	35000	65000

Note: Semi-variable overheads are segregated into variable and fixed elements as follows:

$$\text{Variable cost/Unit} = \frac{₹\ 2000}{1000 \text{ units}} = ₹\ 2$$

Fixed cost = ₹ 40000 – (10000 units @ ₹ 2) = ₹ 20000.

Total variable overhead/Unit = ₹ 3 + ₹ 2 = ₹ 5.

Total fixed overhead for the period = ₹ 50000 + ₹ 20000 = ₹ 70000.

(ii)

Budget Report

Production: 70000 units — Budgeted profit = ₹ 35000

Variances		Favourable (₹)	Unfavourable (₹)	
Materials—Budgeted	₹ 70000			
Actual	₹ 69500	500		
Direct wages—Budgeted	₹ 56000			
Actual	₹ 56600		600	
Direct expense—Budgeted	₹ 14000			
Actual	₹ 14100		100	
Variable o/h—Budgeted	₹ 35000			
Actual	₹ 35100		100	
Fixed o/h—Budgeted	₹ 70000			
Actual	₹ 70000	Nil	Nil	
		500	(800)	(300)
Actual profit				= 34700

Example 9

The following data are available in a manufacturing company for the year 2011:

	₹ (in lakhs)
Fixed expenses:	
Wages and salaries	9.50
Rent, rates, and taxes	6.60
Depreciation	7.40
Sundry administrative expenses	6.50
Semi-variable expenses (at 50% capacity):	
Repairs and maintenance	3.50
Indirect labour	7.90
Sales department salaries	3.80
Sundry administrative expenses	2.80
Variable expenses (at 50% capacity):	
Materials	21.70
Labour	20.40
Other expenses	7.90
	98.00

Assume that the fixed expenses remain constant for all levels of production, semi-variable expenses remain constant between 45% and 65% of capacity, increasing by 10% between 65% and 80% capacity and by 20% between 80% and 100% capacity.

Sales at various levels are:

	₹ (in lakh)
50% capacity	100
60% capacity	120
75% capacity	150
90% capacity	180
100% capacity	200

Prepare a flexible budget for the year and forecast the profit at 60%, 75%, 90%, and 100% of capacity?

Solution:

Flexible Budget

For the year 2011

₹ (in lakh)

Activity level	50%	60%	75%	90%	100%
Fixed expenses:					
Wages and salaries	9.50	9.50	9.50	9.50	9.50
Rent, rates and taxes	6.60	6.60	6.60	6.60	6.60
Depreciation	7.40	7.40	7.40	7.40	7.40
Sundry administrative expenses	6.50	6.50	6.50	6.50	6.50
Semi-variable expenses:					
Repairs and maintenance	3.50	3.50	3.85	4.20	4.20
Indirect wages	7.90	7.90	8.69	9.48	9.48
Sales department salaries	3.80	3.80	4.18	4.56	4.56
Sundry administrative expenses	2.80	2.80	3.08	3.36	3.36
Variable expenses:					
Materials	21.70	26.04	32.55	39.06	43.40
Labour	20.40	24.48	30.60	36.72	40.80
Other expenses	7.90	9.48	11.85	14.22	15.80
Total cost of production	98.00	108.00	124.80	141.60	151.60
Profit	2.00	12.00	25.20	38.40	48.40
Sales	100.00	120.00	150.00	180.00	200.00

8.9 CAPITAL EXPENDITURE BUDGET

Capital expenditure budgeting decision is the firm's decision to invest its current funds most efficiently in the long-term assets in anticipation of an expected inflow of benefits over a period of years. The firm's investment decisions would generally include expansion, acquisition, modernization and replacement of the long-term assets.

The features of capital investment decisions are enumerated as follows:

(i) It is the exchange of current funds for future benefits.

(ii) The funds are invested in the long term assets.

(iii) Future benefits will occur to the firm over a series of years.

(iv) Investment decisions affect the firm's value as profitable investments add to the shareholders' wealth.

8.9.1 Importance of Capital Budgeting Decisions

(i) Capital budgeting decisions influence the firm's growth in the long run.
(ii) They affect the risk of the firm as a long-term commitment of funds may change the risk propensity of the firm.
(iii) They involve commitment of large amount of funds.
(iv) Capital investment decisions are irreversible.
(v) They are among the most difficult decisions to make as it is a complex problem to correctly estimate the future cash flow of an investment.

8.9.2 Control for Capital Expenditure

Capital expenditures are inevitably reflected in the company's operations—either in sales or in costs. Thus capital budget is integrated with the operating budgets. The control for capital expenditures involves the following steps:

(i) A creative search for investment opportunities
(ii) Long range plans and projections for the company's future development
(iii) A short range budget of supply of funds and required capital
(iv) A correct yardstick of economic growth
(v) Realistic estimation of economic worth of individual projects
(vi) Standards for screening investment proposals
(vii) Expenditure control of outlays for facilities by comparison of authorizations and specifications
(viii) Post-completion audit of project earnings or post-completion project review
(ix) Investment analysis of facilities available
(x) Forms and procedures to ensuring smooth working of the system

8.9.3 Capital Budgeting Process

Capital budgeting process is a complex process which involves planning the availability and controlling allocation and expenditure of long term investment funds. Three essential questions are to be answered in the capital budgeting process. They are as follows:

(i) How much is needed for capital expenditure in the coming plan period?
(ii) How much money will be available in totality for such proposed investment?
(iii) How are available funds going to be allocated to the projects under consideration?

Capital budgeting process may be divided into the following phases:

(i) Identification of potential investment opportunities
(ii) Assembling of proposed investments

(iii) Decision-making
(iv) Preparation of capital budget and appropriations
(v) Implementation involving—
  (a) Adequate formulation of projects
  (b) Use of the principle of responsibility accounting
  (c) Use of network techniques viz. PERT, CPM, etc.
(vi) Performance review or post-completion projects review

Control of capital expenditure is difficult without capital budgeting. Capital budgeting helps the management in forecasting requirements for funds and planning in advance to secure additional funds. A capital budget is an effective way of adjusting demand for funds and selecting and assigning priorities to projects within the framework of corporate goals and objectives. This is accomplished by setting evaluation tests for projects and establishing minimum consideration for acceptance.

8.9.4 Types of Capital Investment Decisions

(i) Expansion of existing business
(ii) Expansion of new business, viz. diversification
(iii) Replacement and modernization of capital assets to improve operating efficiency, and reduce costs
(iv) Mandatory capital investments
(v) Research and development projects

8.9.5 Classification of Capital Assets Investment

Basically, the capital assets investments fall into three categories. They are as follows:

(i) Mutually exclusive investments
(ii) Independent investments
(iii) Contingent investments

Mutually exclusive investments serve the same purpose and compete with each other. If one investment is undertaken, others will have to be excluded. Independent investments serve different purposes and do not compete with each other. Contingent investments are dependent projects which mean the choice of one investment necessitates undertaking of one or more other investments, viz. housing/road construction in a remote project.

8.9.6 Criteria for Evaluation of Capital Assets Investment

There are four criteria for evaluation of capital assets investment. They are as follows:

(i) Estimation of cash flows—both inflow and outflow
(ii) Estimation of required rate of return
(iii) Application of a decision rule for making the choice

(iv) A sound appraisal technique to measure the economic worth of the investment project

8.9.7 Characteristics of a Sound Investment Evaluation Criterion

(i) It should consider all cash flows to determine the true profitability of the project

(ii) It should provide for an objective and unambiguous way of separating good projects from the bad projects.

(iii) It should help ranking of projects according to their true profitability.

(iv) It should recognize the fact that bigger cash flows are preferable to smaller ones and early cash flows are preferable to later ones.

(v) It should help to choose, among mutually exclusive projects, that project which would maximize the shareholders' wealth.

(vi) It should be applicable to any conceivable investment project independent of others.

8.9.8 Planning Capital Expenditure

The capital budget is made up of outlays on plant and equipment to be incurred by the several division of a company. General manager of each division submits requests for authority to make such outlays. The requests are forwarded to the budget controller who and his team consolidate the requests and review them prior to presentation to higher authority or managing director. The managing director in turn, presents the capital budget to the Board Of Directors (BODs) for final approval.

Selection of projects

To keep capital outlay within reasonable limit, capital budget control procedure should be designed to ensure that more desirable projects get priority over others. The proposals submitted by the operating divisions can be classified under the following categories:

(i) Urgent or essential towards satisfactory operations

(ii) Replacement resulting from wear and tear or obsolescence

(iii) Desirable on an earnings basis

(iv) Desirable from the standpoint of logical expansion and development

Review of projects

Minor projects may be approved at the lower level of management. Major projects must pass the scrutiny of top management. The better managed organizations have evolved standard forms which should be filled in for each proposed expenditure above a certain limit. These forms describe the proposal and its purpose, estimated cost of the project, its impact on operating costs and profits, any equipment to be replaced, etc., which are necessary for its approval.

Some companies set up a review committee called capex committee for this purpose, whose duty is to review the consolidated estimate from the overall view point as to necessity, profitability, justification and urgency of projects. Final approval is given by the board, after which detailed engineering studies, economic and technical analysis take place.

The appropriation requests submitted for management approval usually contain the following basic information:

(i) Date of the request
(ii) Project identification number
(iii) Description of the project
(iv) Purpose of and risk of the project
(v) Estimated total cost
(vi) Estimated starting and completion date
(vii) Timing of expenditure
(viii) Estimated cost savings and other justifications
(ix) Estimate of the income and its timing from the project approval

8.9.9 Capital Budgeting Techniques

Generally there are two basic techniques for capital budgeting. They are discounted cash flow and non-discounted cash flow.

Discounted Cash Flow criterion (DCF)

(i) Net Present Value (NPV)
(ii) Internal Rate of Return (IRR)
(iii) Modified Internal Rate of Return (MIRR)
(iv) Profitability Index (PI)
(v) Discounted Payback (DPB) Period

Non-discounted cash flow criterion

(i) Payback (PB) Period
(ii) Accounting Rate of Return (ARR)

Net Present Value (NPV) method

It is a process of calculating the present value of a project's cash flows, using the opportunity cost of capital as the discount rate, and finding out the net present value by subtracting the initial investment from the present value of cash flows.

Under the NPV method, the investment project is accepted if its NPV is positive (NPV > 0). The market value of the firm's share is expected to increase by the positive NPV of the project. Between the mutually exclusive projects, the one with the highest positive NPV will be chosen.

Acceptance rules under NPV

(i) Accept the project if its NPV > 0

(ii) Reject the project if its NPV < 0

(iii) May accept the project if its NPV = 0.

Formula

$$\text{NPV} = \left[\frac{C_1}{(1+K)} + \frac{C_2}{(1+K)^2} + \frac{C_3}{(1+K)^3} + \cdots + \frac{C_n}{(1+K)^n}\right] - C_0$$

or

$$\text{NPV} = \frac{\sum C_t}{(1+k)^t} - C_0$$

where,

C_1, C_2, C_3 = Net cash inflows in the years 1, 2, 3, etc.

K = Opportunity cost of capital

C_0 = Initial cost of investment

n = Expected life of the project

Example 10

The project X costs ₹ 2500 now, and is expected to generate yearend cash inflows of ₹ 900, ₹ 800, ₹ 700, ₹ 600, and ₹ 500 in years 1 to 5. The opportunity cost of capital is assumed to be 10%. Find out the NPV of the project taking the discounting rate of ₹ 1 as follows:

1st year = ₹ 1 = 0.909

2nd year = ₹ 1 = 0.826

3rd year = ₹ 1 = 0.751

4th year = ₹ 1 = 0.683

5th year = ₹ 1 = 0.620

Solution:

$$\text{NPV} = \left[\frac{900}{(1.10)} + \frac{800}{(1.10)^2} + \frac{700}{(1.10)^3} + \frac{600}{(1.10)^4} + \frac{500}{(1.10)^5}\right] - 2500$$

$$= [(900 \times 0.909) + (800 \times 0.826) + (700 \times 0.751) + (600 \times 0.683) + (500 \times 0.620)] - 2500$$

$$= 2725 - 2500$$

= (+) ₹ 225

Thus, the project should be accepted as its NPV is positive.

Evaluation of NPV method

The merits of evaluation of NPV method are as follows:

(i) It recognizes the time value of money.

(ii) It uses all cash flows occurring over the entire life of the project.

(iii) It satisfies the value-additive principle. It means that the NPVs of 2 or more projects can be added.

(iv) It is consistent with the objective of maximizing the shareholders' wealth.

(v) It is the true measure of profitability.

The demerits of evaluation of NPV method are as follows:

(i) It is difficult to estimate the cash flows due to various uncertainties.

(ii) It requires computation of opportunity cost of capital which poses practical difficulties.

(iii) Caution needs to be taken in using NPV method when alternative projects with unequal lives or under funds constraint are evaluated.

Internal Rate of Return (IRR) method

It is another discounted cash flow technique which takes account of the magnitude and timing of cash flows. The IRR is that discount rate at which the project's NPV is 0. In other words, it is the rate which equates investment outlay with the present value of inflows received after a period of time. Under the IRR rule, the project will be accepted when its IRR is higher than the opportunity cost of capital (IRR > K).

Formula

$$\text{IRR} = \frac{C_1}{(1+r)} + \frac{C_2}{(1+r)^2} + \frac{C_3}{(1+r)^3} + \cdots + \frac{C_n}{(1+r)^n} = C_0$$

or,

$$\text{NPV} = \frac{\sum C_t}{(1+r)^t} - C_0 = 0$$

It can be observed that IRR is the same as the one used for NPV method but with the difference that under the NPV method, the required rate of return '*K*' is known, whereas in the IRR method the value of '*r*' has to be found out at which the NPV is 0.

Acceptance rules under IRR

(i) Accept the project if its IRR > K

(ii) Reject the project if its IRR < K

(iii) May accept the project if its IRR = K.

Evaluation of IRR

The advantages of IRR method are as follows:

(i) Like NPV method, the IRR method recognizes the time value of money.

(ii) It considers all cash flows occurring over the entire life of the project to calculate its rate of return.

(iii) It is the true measure of profitability.

(iv) It is consistent with the shareholders' wealth maximization objective.

The disadvantages of IRR method are as follows:

(i) It is a tedious task to estimate the cash flows.

(ii) At times it fails to indicate correct choice between mutually exclusive projects.

(iii) It is relatively difficult to compute IRR of a project.

(iv) At times, it yields multiple rates.

(v) It does not hold the value-additive principle which means that IRRs of 2 or more projects do not add.

Example 11

From the following data find out the IRR of a project:
Investment = ₹ 100000
Cash flows for:
1st year = ₹ 30000
2nd year = ₹ 30000
3rd year = ₹ 40000, and
4th year = ₹ 45000.

Solution:

The IRR is the value of r, which satisfies the following equation:

$$100000 = \left[\frac{30000}{(1+r)} + \frac{30000}{(1+r)^2} + \frac{40000}{(1+r)^3} + \frac{45000}{(1+r)^4}\right]$$

The calculation of r involves a process of trial and error. Let us see the annuity table and try r = 15%. Applying the value of r in the above equation we get:

$$\frac{30000}{(1.15)} + \frac{30000}{(1.15)^2} + \frac{40000}{(1.15)^3} + \frac{45000}{(1.15)^4} = 100802.$$

Since 100802 is slightly higher than 100000, we may increase the value of r to 16%, and apply on the equation.

$$\frac{30000}{(1.16)} + \frac{30000}{(1.16)^2} + \frac{40000}{(1.16)^3} + \frac{45000}{(1.16)^4} = 98641.$$

We can conclude that the value of r is in between 15% and 16%.

Now, we can do the interpolation exercise by the following procedure:

Step I Determine the NPV of the two close rate of return.

Here, NPV at 15% = 100000 – 100802 = (+) 802.

NPV at 16% = 100000 – 98641 = (–) 1359.

Step II Find the sum of the absolute values of the NPVs obtained in Step I.

Here, 802 + 1359 = 2161.

Step III Calculate the ratio of NPV of the smaller discount rate identified in step

Here, $\frac{802}{2161} = 0.37.$

Step IV Add the number obtained in Step III, to the following discount rate.

Here, 15 + 0.37 = 15.37%.

Therefore, the decision rule for IRR is as follows:
Accept the project if the IRR is greater than the cost of capital.
Reject the project if the IRR is less than the cost of capital.

Modified Internal Rate of Return (MIRR) method

The shortcomings of the regular IRR can be overcome by the modified IRR or MIRR. The procedure for calculating MIRR is as follows:

Step I Calculate the Present Value of the Costs (PVC) (investments) associated with the project, using cost of capital r as the discount rate.

$$PVC = \frac{\sum \text{Cash outflows}}{(1+r)^t}$$

Step II Calculate the Terminal Value (TV) of the cash inflows expected from the project. So, TV = Σ Cash inflows $(1 + r)^{n-t}$

Step III Obtain MIRR by solving the following equation:

$$PVC = \frac{TV}{(1 + MIRR)^n}$$

Example 12

PQR Ltd. is evaluating a project that has the following cash flow stream associated with it.

Year	Cash flows (in lakhs)
0	(–) 120
1	(–) 80
2	20
3	60
4	80
5	100
6	120

The cost of capital for the company is 15%. Find out the Present Value of Cost (PVC)? Find out also the Terminal Value (TV) of the cash inflows? Show the MIRR?

Solution:

The Present Value of Costs (PVC) = $\frac{120 + 80}{(1.15)} = 189.6$

The Terminal Value (TV) of cash inflows can be calculated as follows:

$$TV = 20(1.15)^4 + 60(1.15)^3 + 80(1.15)^2 + 100(1.15) + 120$$
$$= 34.98 + 91.26 + 105.76 + 115 + 120$$
$$= 467$$

MIRR can be calculated as follows:

$$189.6 = \frac{467}{(1 + \text{MIRR})^6}$$

or, $$(1+\text{MIRR})^6 = \frac{467}{189.6} = 2.463$$

or, $$1+\text{MIRR} = (2.463)^{1/6} = 1.162$$

or, $$\text{MIRR} = 1.162 - 1 = 0.162$$

or, $$\text{MIRR} = 16.2\%.$$

MIRR is superior to the regular IRR in two ways:

(a) MIRR assumes that project cash flows are reinvested at the cost of capital, whereas the regular IRR assumes that project cash flows are reinvested at the project's own IRR. Since the reinvestment at cost of capital is more realistic than reinvestment at IRR, MIRR reflects better the true profitability of a project.

(b) The problem of multiple rates does not exist with MIRR.

Profitability Index (PI) or Benefit-Cost (B/C) ratio method

It is the ratio of the present value of cash inflows, at the required rate of return, to the initial cash outflow of the investment.

Formula

PI = Present value of cash inflows/Initial cash outlay

$$= \frac{\sum C_t}{(1+K)^t / C_0}$$

Acceptance Rules of PI

(i) Accept the project if PI > 1

(ii) Reject the project if PI < 1

(iii) Project may be accepted if PI = 1.

Example 13

The initial cash outlay of a project is ₹ 100000. It can generate cash inflow of ₹ 40000, ₹ 30000, ₹ 50000, and ₹ 20000 in 1 through 4 years. Assuming a 10% rate of discount, find out the PI of the project? The discount rate of ₹ 1 is as follows:

1st year = ₹ 1 = 0.909
2nd year = ₹ 1 = 0.826
3rd year = ₹ 1 = 0.751
4th year = ₹ 1 = 0.683

Solution:

$$\text{Present Value of Cash Inflow} = (40000 \times 0.909) + (30000 \times 0.826) + (50000 \times 0.751) + (20000 \times 0.683) = ₹\ 112350.$$

$$\text{NPV} = ₹\ 112350 - ₹\ 100000 = ₹\ 12350.$$

So,

$$\text{PI} = \frac{112350}{100000} = 1.1235.$$

The project should be accepted as PI > 1.

Evaluation of PI method

The advantages of evaluation of PI method are as follows:

(i) It considers all cash flows in calculation.
(ii) It recognizes time value of money.
(iii) It is the true measure of profitability and is a conceptually sound method of appraising investment projects.
(iv) It is generally consistent with the wealth maximization principle.

The disadvantages of evaluation of PI method are as follows:

(i) It is a tedious task to estimate the cash flows.
(ii) At times, it fails to indicate correct choice between mutually exclusive projects.

Pay Back (PB) method

It is the most popular and widely recognized traditional method of evaluating investment proposals. It is defined as the number of years required to recover the original cash outlay invested in a project.
Formula

$$\text{Pay Back} = \frac{\text{Initial investment}}{\text{Annual cash inflow}} = \frac{C_0}{C}$$

Example 14

A project requires an outlay of ₹ 50000 and yields an annual cash inflow of ₹ 12500 for 7 years. Find out the payback period?

Solution:

$$\text{Payback period} = \frac{₹\ 50000}{₹\ 12500} = 4 \text{ years}$$

In the case of unequal cash inflows, the payback can be found out by adding up the cash inflows until the total is equal to the initial cash outlay.

Example 15

A project requires a cash outlay of ₹ 20000, and generates cash inflows of ₹ 8000, ₹ 7000, ₹ 4000, and ₹ 3000 during the next 4 years. Find out the payback period of the project?

Solution:

Let us add up the cash inflows:

1st year =	8000
2nd year =	7000
3rd year =	4000
Total =	19000

We find that in the first 3 years ₹ 19000 of original cash outlay is recovered. In the 4th year, cash inflow generated is ₹ 3000, whereas only ₹ 1000 (20000 – 19000) of the original outlay remains to be recovered. So the time required to recover ₹ 1000 = (₹ 1000 × 12 months)/₹ 3000 = 4 months.

Therefore, payback period = 3 years + 4 months = 3 years 4 months.

Acceptance Rules of Payback Period

(i) Accept the project if PB < Standard payback period

(ii) Reject the project if PB > Standard payback period

Evaluation of payback method

The merits of evaluation of payback method are as follows:

(i) It is simple to understand and easy to calculate.

(ii) It is less costly as compared to other sophisticated technique requiring lot of time and use of computers.

(iii) It emphasizes the liquidity.

(iv) It is an easy and crude method to cope with risk.

(v) It uses cash flow information.

The demerits of evaluation of payback method are as follows:

(i) It fails to take account of the cash inflows earned after the payback period.

(ii) It ignores the time value of money.

(iii) It is not an appropriate method of measuring the profitability of an investment project as it does not consider all cash inflows earned by the project.

(iv) It fails to consider the pattern of cash inflows, i.e. magnitude and timing of all cash inflows. In other words, it gives equal weightage to the returns of equal amount even though they occur in different periods of time.

(v) This method cannot show an objective way to determine the standard payback.

(vi) It has no relationship with the wealth maximization principle.

Discounted Pay Back (DPB) method

It is defined as the number of years required in recovering the cash outlay of the project on the present value basis. Except using the discounted cash flow in calculating payback, this method has all the demerits of payback method.

Accounting Rate of Return (ARR) method or Return On Investment (ROI) method

This method uses accounting information as revealed by the financial statements, to measure the profitability of an investment project. The ARR is found out by dividing the average post-tax profit by the average investment.

The average investment would be equal to half of the original investment if it is depreciated constantly. Alternatively, it can be found out dividing the total of the investment's book values after depreciation by the life of the project.

Formula

$$\text{ARR} = \frac{\text{Average post-tax profit}}{\text{Average investment}}$$

$$= \frac{\left[\sum \text{EBIT}\,(1-T)/n\right]}{(I_0 + I_n)/2}$$

where,

EBIT = Earnings before interest and tax

T = Tax rate

I_0 = Book value of investment in the beginning

I_n = Book value of investment at the end of nth years.

Example 16

A project will cost ₹ 40000. Its stream of Earnings Before Depreciation, Interest and Taxes (EBDIT) during the 1st year through 5 years is expected to be ₹ 10000, ₹ 12000, ₹ 14000, ₹ 16000, and ₹ 20000. Assuming a tax rate of 50% and depreciation @ 20% on straight line basis, find out the project's ARR?

Solution:

Period	1st year	2nd year	3rd year	4th year	5th year	Average
EBDIT	10000	12000	14000	16000	20000	14400
Less: depreciation @ 20%	8000	8000	8000	8000	8000	8000
EBIT	2000	4000	6000	8000	12000	6400
Less: taxes @ 50%	1000	2000	3000	4000	6000	3200
Earning before interest	1000	2000	3000	4000	6000	3200
Book value of investment						
Beginning	40000	32000	24000	16000	8000	
Ending	32000	24000	16000	8000	—	
Total	72000	56000	40000	24000	8000	
Average investment	36000	28000	20000	12000	4000	20000

$$\text{ARR} = \frac{(3200 \times 100)}{20000} = 16\%$$

By applying the formula we can solve this example:

$$\text{ARR} = \frac{\left[\sum \text{EBIT}(1-T)/n\right]}{(I_0 + I_n)/2}$$

$$= \frac{[32000\,(1-0.5)/5]}{(40000+0)/2}$$

$$= \frac{[16000/5]}{20000}$$

$$= \frac{3200 \times 100}{20000}$$

$$= 16\%.$$

Acceptance Rules of ARR

(i) Accept the project if ARR > Minimum rate of return

(ii) Reject the project if ARR < Minimum rate of return

(iii) Project may be accepted if ARR = Minimum rate of return

Evaluation of ARR

The advantages of evaluation of ARR are as follows:

(i) It is simple to understand and use.

(ii) It can be readily calculated from the accounting data. Therefore, no adjustments are required to arrive at the cash flows of the project.

(iii) This method incorporates the entire stream of income in calculating the project's profitability.

The disadvantages of evaluation of ARR are as follows:

(i) It uses the accounting profits, but not cash flows in appraising the project. Accounting profits are based on arbitrary assumption and also include non-cash items. So the ARR is not an appropriate method for measuring the acceptability of the investment project.

(ii) This method ignores the time value of money.

(iii) There is no objective way to determine the minimum acceptable rate of return.

8.9.10 Methods of Appraisal and their Rationale

(i) A wide variety of measures are used for evaluating investments.

(ii) The most commonly used method for evaluating investments of small size is the Payback (PB) period method.

(iii) For investments of large size, the Average Rate of Return (ARR) is commonly used as the principal criterion and the Payback period is used as a supplementary criterion.

(iv) Discounted Cash Flow (DCF) techniques are gaining in importance particularly in the evaluation of large investments.

(v) Several other criteria are used for evaluating investments, viz.,
   (a) Profit per rupee invested
   (b) Cost saving/reduction per unit of product
   (c) Investment required to replace a worker, etc.

8.9.11 Size of Capital Budget

There are three main approaches to the size of capital budget. They are as follows:

The fixed or 'rationing' type of capital budget

Under this approach, budgeted amount is determined by the available cash flow and the projects are selected within this established limit. The rationing approach is concerned with how to pick the best projects to fill out a fixed amount of planned spending. The amount of capital budget is set first and then 'rationed' among the most desirable projects proposed.

The open end or 'financing' type capital budget

Under this method, budgeted amount is established by funds requirements of desirable projects and additional financing is planned to take advantage of favourable opportunities. This approach is more flexible because the size of the capital budget is determined by the number of the investment opportunities rather than the availability of funds as such. The theory underlying this approach is that a company will maximize the level of profits if it selects a level of capital expenditure for which the marginal return on projects is equal to the marginal cost of capital.

A 'one-at-a-time' approach

Under this method, each capital expenditure project is decided on its own merit as proposals are made during the year.

8.9.12 New Analytical Techniques Used in Capital Budgeting

There has been a steady development of techniques designed to help the capital expenditure decision process. Some of these new techniques used are as follows:

(i) Sensitivity analysis
(ii) Risk analysis
(iii) Simulation models
(iv) Linear programming
(v) Cost estimates using Critical Path Method (CPM) and Project Evaluation and Review Techniques (PERT).

Sensitivity analysis

A sensitivity analysis displays in graphical or tabular form how much project income and rate of return will differ from the project estimate if sales, labour cost, or some other factor does not come out as expected. This analysis presents a variety of outcomes so that the analysis and the decision-maker can look at the impact of the range of possibilities.

Risk analysis

Risk analysis in project evaluation involves attaching of probability factors to revenue, cost or other elements of the proposal. Calculations are then made for the likelihood of the possible project results.

Simulation models

The process of simulation has wide variety of uses in financial analysis and in capital budgeting. Simulation basically consists of one or more trial runs of a process to know that its possible outcomes are as representative as is necessary for the simulation to be realistic. It is helpful where the key factors in a business problem are expected to take on various patterns of variation and it is impossible to settle on single values for estimating purposes.

Linear programming

Linear programming can be related to capital expenditure analysis in the same way as any analytical method of determining relative profitability or a least cost combination. While a decision to invest in a given project is usually based on its prospective rate of return or present value, the choice of equipment or the profit contribution of the proposed project may well be based on linear programming analysis.

Critical Path Method (CPM) and Project Evaluation and Review Techniques (PERT)

The basic principle involved in both these techniques is the development of a network of project tasks for turning the critical path which identifies those events most crucial to completing the project in time. Nowadays, the computers are widely used in project analysis. Detailed discussion on CPM and PERT has been made in Chapter 19.

8.10 ZERO-BASED BUDGETING (ZBB)

It refers to the 'nil' budget as the starting point. This budget starts with the premise that the budget for the next period is 'zero' so long as the demand for a function, process, project or activity is not justified for each rupee. The assumption of the top management is that without such justification no spending will be allowed. Therefore, the onus lies with each divisional manager of the organization to justify why the money should be spent at all and to indicate what would happen if the proposed activity is not carried out and no money is spent.

ZBB is a planning, allocation, and control tool of management.

8.10.1 Pre-condition for ZBB Implementation

(i) There should be an efficient budgeting and budgetary control system in the organization.

(ii) The managers should develop quantitative measures for use in performance evaluation.

Generally, ZBB is more suitable for application in service or support type activities of an organization.

8.10.2 Steps in ZBB

The various steps followed in the process of ZBB are as follows:

(i) Identification of 'decision unit' and development of 'decision packages'
(ii) Evaluation and ranking of all 'decision packages' in order of importance by way of cost/benefit analysis
(iii) Allocation of resources

A decision unit is a tangible activity or group of activities for which a single manager is responsible for successful performance. A decision package is a budget request which should contain the following:

(i) A description of activity
(ii) The goals/objectives of the activity
(iii) Specific measures of performance
(iv) Benefits to be derived from financing the activity
(v) Consequence of its non-funding
(vi) Projected costs of the package
(vii) Alternative ways of performing the same activity

8.10.3 Advantages of ZBB

(i) It ensures more careful management planning before the budget itself is prepared.
(ii) It provides increased involvement of lower and middle level personnel in the budgeting process.
(iii) It provides better information for the decision-makers.
(iv) Resources are allocated as per needs and the benefits derived.

8.10.4 Criticisms of ZBB

(i) Time and effort required for ZBB preparation may prove to be costly, thereby vitiating the very purpose of ZBB.
(ii) ZBB has limited application.

8.11 MANAGEMENT BY OBJECTIVES (MBO) AND BUDGETING AS AN AID TO CONTROL

MBO is a process of joint setting of goals/objectives by the superior and the subordinate, and clarifying on the objectives itself. It is proved to be a powerful tool for management control. MBO is a much broader concept as compared to budgeting and budgetary control, though the process of control is similar.

The major focus in the budgetary control system is on economic performance, but MBO involves both economic performance and human performance. Budgeting is a technique refined by the accountants while MBO approach has its roots in behavioural science. In budgetary control quantitative information is emphasized for monitoring physical/monetary performance. But MBO emphasizes quantitative as also qualitative performance.

However, both budgeting and MBO are likely to provide better results in improving the effectiveness of the organization.

8.12 CONCLUSION

A budget as a plan quantified in monetary terms, prepared and approved prior to a defined period of time, usually showing planned income to be generated and/or expenditure to be incurred during that period and the capital to be employed to attain a given objective. Budgetary Control is the establishment of budgets, relating the responsibilities of executives to the requirements of a policy, and the continuous comparison of actual with budgeted results, either to secure by individual action the objective of that policy or to provide a basis for its revision. Therefore, a budget is a means, while budgetary control is the end results.

Budgeting and budgetary control are the powerful and effective tools for management control. This chapter dealt with the meaning, concept, and advantages of budgeting process and budgetary control in detail. Various steps in formulation of budgets, administration and review of budgets, and behavioural dimensions of budgeting have been explained in this chapter. It has explained in details, the various functional budgets and showed with examples, how to prepare them. Capital budget and its various dimensions, and techniques have been explained with examples. The concepts of fixed and flexible budgets, zero based budgeting, and MBO as management control tools have been discussed in this chapter.

REVIEW QUESTIONS

8.1 What is a budget? What are the purposes for budgeting in an organization?

8.2 What is budgetary control? What are the advantages of budgetary control for an organization?

8.3 Explain the various steps followed by a company in organizing budgetary control system?

8.4 Define principal budget factor or key factor? Explain with examples?

8.5 Explain the various steps followed by a firm in formulating the budgets?

8.6 How the budgets are administered and reviewed by a company?

8.7 "The behavioural aspects of budgeting cannot be ignored as the individuals are involved in the budgeting process". Discuss.

8.8 Enumerate the functional budgets and explain their utilities in an organization?

8.9 What is a cash budget? How many ways the cash budget can be prepared? Explain the benefits of cash budgeting in an organization?

8.10 What is a master budget? When is it prepared by a company?

8.11 What do you mean by flexible budget? How does it differ from fixed budget?

8.12 What is meant by capital expenditure budget? Explain the importance of capital budgeting decisions and control for capital expenditure?

8.13 What are the various phases of capital budgeting process?

8.14 Classify the capital assets investment and explain the criteria for evaluation of capital assets investment?

8.15 You are appointed as budget controller of a company. Explain how do you propose to plan capital expenditure for the projects?

8.16 Explain the various techniques adopted by a company for capital budgeting of its projects?

8.17 What is Zero-Based Budgeting (ZBB)? Explain the various steps followed in the process of ZBB?

8.18 What is MBO? How does it help as an aid to budgetary control exercise?

8.19 Prepare a cash budget for three months ended 30th June 2003, from the information given below:

Months	Sales ₹	Materials ₹	Wages ₹	Overheads ₹
February	14000	9600	3000	1700
March	15000	9000	3000	1900
April	16000	9200	3200	2000
May	17000	10000	3600	2200
June	18000	10400	4000	2300

Credit terms are:

Sales/Debtors – 10% sales are on cash, 50% of the credit sales are collected next month and the balance in the following month.

Creditors – Materials 2 months
Wages 1/4 month
Overheads 1/2 month

Cash and bank balance on 1st April 2003, is expected to be ₹ 6000.

Other relevant information are:

(i) Plant and machinery will be installed in February 2003, at a cost of ₹ 96000. The monthly installment of ₹ 2000 is payable from April onwards.
(ii) Dividend @ 5% on preference share capital of ₹ 200000 will be paid on 1st June.
(iii) ₹ 9000 will be received for sale of vehicles in June.
(iv) Dividends from investments ₹ 1000 are expected to be received in June.
(v) Advance income tax of ₹ 2000 is to be paid in June.

9

Standard Costing System and Variance Analysis for Control Actions

9.1 INTRODUCTION

We know that historical costing is used to ascertain the costs after they have been incurred. But costs in two periods or at two different levels of activity may fluctuate widely, and adversely affect the profit figure. Historical costing does not help management to detect mistakes and inefficiencies leading to variation in profit. The reasons for the cost fluctuation may be detected by the use of standard costing. Its usefulness has been widely accepted in recent years by the corporate management all over the world.

One of the most important aspects of management control system is to find out and report the variances between actual performance and standard performance. The analysis of variations in performance is imperative for immediate control actions to be taken by the management. This chapter therefore, deals with the system of standard costing and shows the different techniques of analysis of variances on performance for managerial control actions. Let us begin with the definition and concepts of standard costing. Variance analysis will follow thereafter.

9.2 NEEDS FOR STANDARDS

The purpose or the need for standards can be enumerated as follows:

(i) Cost control
(ii) Pricing decisions
(iii) Performance appraisal
(iv) Cost awareness

9.3 STANDARD COST

What is standard cost? In simple language, we can define standard cost as a predetermined amount of what cost ought to be incurred for a given level of activity under specified condition.

9.4 STANDARD COSTING

What is meant by standard costing? Standard costing, according to CIMA, is "a technique which uses standards for costs and revenues for the purpose of control through variance analysis". It involves:

(i) Ascertainment and use of standard costs
(ii) Measurement of actual costs
(iii) Comparison of standard costs and actual costs
(iv) Analysis of variances and taking appropriate actions

9.4.1 Advantages of Standard Costing

There are enormous advantages of standard costing, some of which can be enumerated hereunder:

(i) Standard costing promotes the principle of 'management by exception' since the variances from standard constitutes exceptions.
(ii) It serves as a check on wastage and booster of efficiency.
(iii) Variance analysis locates the cause of variance. The diagnosis contributes to cure the system of the adverse elements.
(iv) The variance analysis not only identifies the weak activities but also recognises the areas of strength from the mix-up of aggregate result.
(v) It is a management control technique, which in turn assists in modifying the plans.
(vi) It raises consciousness on the relevant areas of cost, price, usage, and productivity.

9.4.2 Limitations of Standard Costing

There are certain limitations of standard costing too, which can be as follows:

(i) If standards are not properly set, standard costing system will fail.
(ii) The standards are not easy to develop.
(iii) Even if standards are set with due care and diligence, they need to be regularly revised and updated.
(iv) Unless uniform and repetitive production system is carried on, standard costing system cannot be applied usefully.
(v) As quantitative differences are measured in standard costing, qualitative difference may not get due weightage from management.
(vi) Variance analysis cannot explain all the variables contributing to the differences.

9.5 DIFFERENCE BETWEEN STANDARD COSTING AND BUDGETARY CONTROL

(i) Budgetary control deals with the operation of departments or business as a whole, while standard costing is applied to manufacturing of a product or providing a service. Budgetary control is extensive, but standard costing is intensive in its application.

(ii) In standard costing variances are analyzed according to their originating causes. But such analysis of variances is not possible in budgetary control.

(iii) Budgetary control can be applied in part, which is not done in the application of standard costing.

However, both standard costing and budgetary control are complementary to each other and both should be in operation for optimum benefit of an organization.

9.6 PREREQUISITES TO THE ESTABLISHMENT OF STANDARD COSTS

There are certain preliminaries to be taken into consideration before setting up the standard costs. They are as follows:

(i) Establishment of cost centres

(ii) Classification of accounts

(iii) Type of standards

9.6.1 Establishment of Cost Centres

A cost centre is a location, function or items of equipment in respect of which costs may be ascertained and related to cost units for control purposes. The cost centre should be set up for fixing responsibility and defining the line of authority.

9.6.2 Classification of Accounts

Accounts are to be classified in order to facilitate collection and analysis of costs. So, the costs should be used for each item of costs.

9.6.3 Types of Standards

There are three types of standards as follows:

(i) Current standard

(ii) Basic standard

(iii) Normal standard

Current standard

It is a standard which is established for use over a short period of time and is related to current conditions. Current standards may again be based on ideal standard, or expected standard.

An ideal standard is that standard which can be attained under the most favourable conditions. This standard is fixed with very high degree of efficiency which is almost impossible to attain.

Expected standard is that standard which is anticipated to be attained during a future-specified budget period. All the expected conditions are given due weightage. This is more realistic than the ideal standard.

Basic standard

It is the standard established for use over a long period from which a current standard can be developed. But this standard is unsuitable from the standpoint of cost ascertainment and cost control.

Normal standard

It is the average standard which is anticipated, can be attained over a future period of time, preferably long enough to cover a trade cycle.

For example, a period of say 5 years is taken and forecast made of expected production and sales for 5 years. Then the standard costs are assessed on an average basis and used for 5 years.

9.7 ESTABLISHMENT OF STANDARD COSTS

Normally, in large organisation there is a standards committee which is vested with the work of setting standard costs. The committee consists of production manager, purchase manager, personnel manager, production engineer, sales manager, and cost & management accountant. The cost & management accountant plays a vital role as he has to supply necessary cost figures and has to coordinate the activities of the committee so as to ensure that standards are set accurately.

Standards should be set for each of the elements of cost as follows:

(i) *Direct material*
  - (a) Determination of standard quantity of materials
  - (b) Determination of standard price per unit of materials

(ii) *Direct labour*
  - (a) Determination of standard time
  - (b) Determination of standard rate

(iii) *Variable overhead*

It is necessary to calculate standard variable overhead per unit or per hour so that per unit cost can be multiplied by budgeted production during the period.

(iv) *Fixed overhead*
  - (a) Determination of total fixed overhead
  - (b) Determination of budgeted production

9.8 REASONS FOR VARIANCE

There are plenty of reasons for variances between the actual costs and sales revenues vis-à-vis standard costs and revenues. They are shown in Figure 9.1.

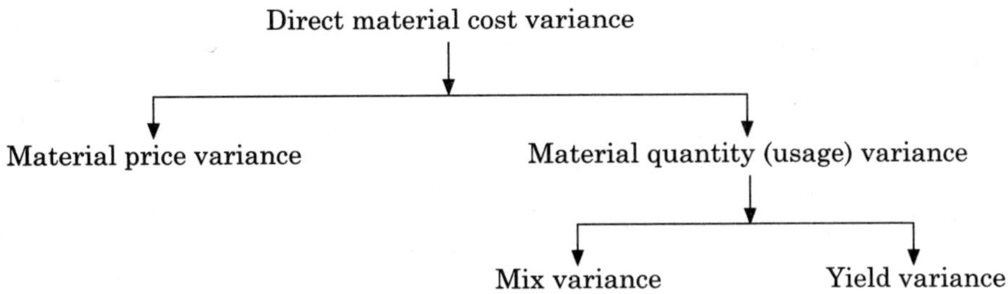

Figure 9.1 Direct Material Cost Variance.

9.8.1 Direct Material Cost Variance

Direct material price variance—Causes

(i) Change in price
(ii) Quantity of materials being different from the standard
(iii Failure to obtain quantity discounts resulting in higher prices
(iv) Changes in the inward transport charges, handling and store-keeping

Direct material quantity or usage variance—Causes

(i) Use of different grades of materials
(ii) Change in product design
(iii Change in labour performance
(iv) Carelessness in handling of materials
(v) Pilferage
(vi) Use of non-standard material mix
(vii) Defective production requiring further materials for rectification

9.8.2 Direct Labour Cost Variance

The direct labour cost variance is depicted in Figure 9.2.

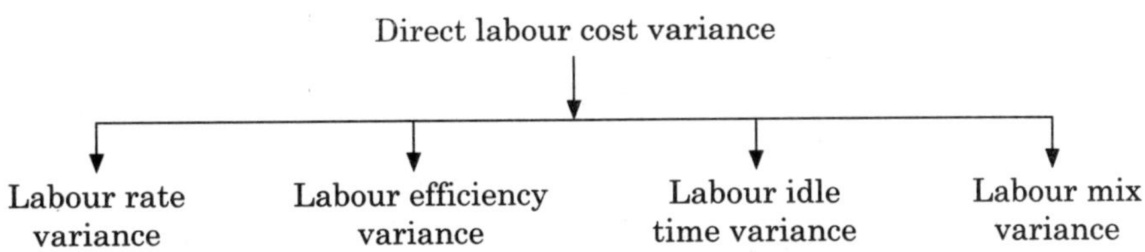

Figure 9.2 Direct Labour Cost Variance.

Direct labour rate variance—Causes

(i) Payment at a rate higher or lower than the standard rate
(ii) Change in the grades of the employees

(iii) Inclusion of new workers
(iv) Change in the method of payment of remuneration

Direct labour efficiency variance

Gains—Causes

(i) Employment of more efficient workers
(ii) Strict supervision
(iii) Improved method of production
(iv) Introduction of new and improved tools
(v) High quality of materials
(vi) Good working condition

Losses—Causes

(i) Employment of less efficient workers
(ii) Improper supervision
(iii) Inferior quality of materials
(iv) Old and inferior machine tools
(v) Unsatisfactory working condition
(vi) Wrong material specification causing difficulty in operation

Direct labour idle time variance—Causes

(i) Break down of machines
(ii) Power failure, etc.

Labour mix variance—Cause

(i) Change in actual mix of labour against the standard mix.

9.8.3 Variable Production Overhead Cost Variance

Causes

(i) Change in actual variable overhead compared to standard variable overhead.

9.8.4 Fixed Production Overhead Cost Variance

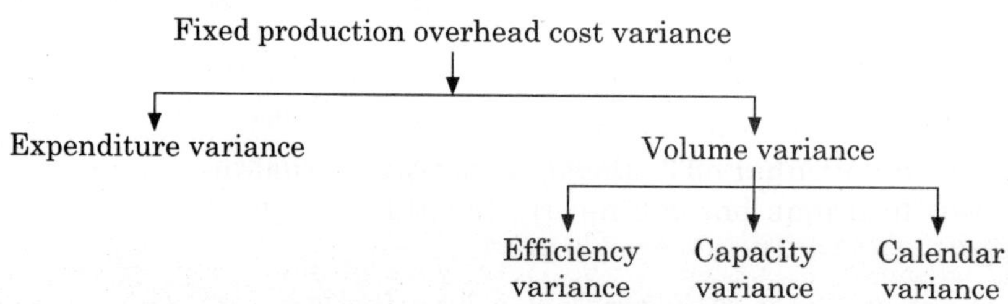

Figure 9.3 Fixed Production Overhead Cost Variance.

Fixed overhead expenditure variance—Causes

(i) A change in overhead costs, e.g., a price increase

(ii) A change in output, e.g., loss of production due to machine breakdown, etc.

Fixed overhead volume variance—Causes

(i) Change in demand

(ii) Interruption or stoppage of work due to:

   (a) Defective planning

   (b) Shortage of materials

   (c) Lack of proper tools

   (d) Absence of, or faulty instructions

(iii) Absence of workers

(iv) Breakdown of machine

(v) Power failure

(vi) Labour trouble, etc.

9.8.5 Sales Variance

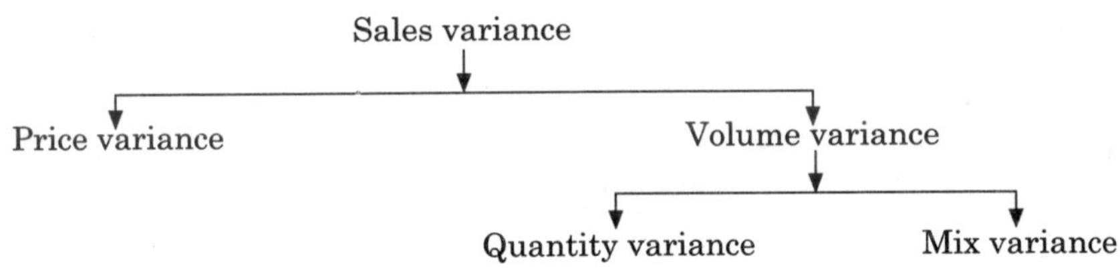

Figure 9.4 Sales Variance.

Sales Variance—Causes

1. Change in selling price
2. Change in volume of sales
3. Change in sales mix

9.8.6 Profit Variance Due to Sales

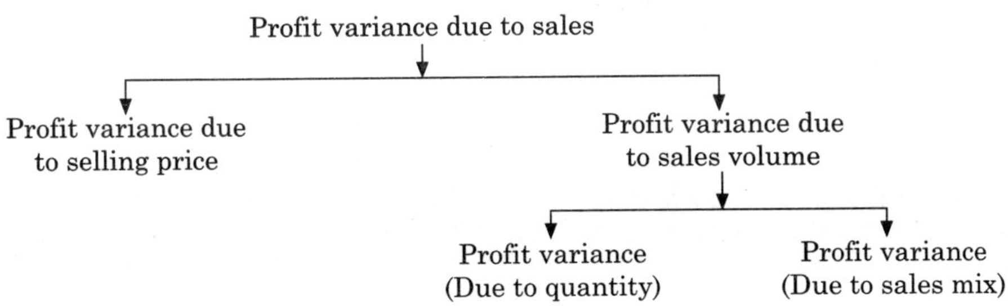

Figure 9.5 Profit Variance due to Sales.

9.9 VARIANCE ANALYSIS

The deviation of actual from standard is called 'variance'. When actual cost is less than the standard cost, it is known as 'favourable variance (fav.)'. When actual cost is more than the standard costs, it is known as 'unfavourable or adverse variance (adv)'. In standard costing, greatest emphasis is given on cost control and cost reduction by means of variance analysis, and for fixing managerial responsibilities.

The objectives of the variance analysis are:

(i) To locate the causes of variances
(ii) To initiate corrective actions to the activities that deviated from the standard
(iii) To identify the functions running effectively and running inefficiently
(iv) To reveal objectively the factors external or internal responsible for the variances

Formulae

Material Cost Variance

Direct material cost variance = (Standard quantity of actual output × Standard price per unit) – (Actual quantity consumed × Actual price)

Direct material price variance = (Standard unit price – Actual unit price) × Actual quantity of material used

Direct material usage variance = (Standard quantity specified for actual production – Actual quantity used) × Standard price per unit

Direct material mix variance = (Quantity in standard mix proportion – Quantity in actual mix) × Standard price

Direct material yield variance = (Standard yield of actual input – Actual yield of input) × Standard material cost

Labour Cost Variance

Direct labour cost variance = Standard labour cost – Actual labour cost

= (Standard hours × Standard rate per hour of actual production) – (Actual hours × Actual rate per hour)

Direct labour rate variance = (Standard rate – Actual rate) × Actual hours of production

Direct labour efficiency variance = (Standard hours for actual production – Actual hours) × Standard rate per hour

Direct labour idle time variance = Abnormal idle hours × Standard hourly rate.

Direct labour mix variance = Standard cost of standard mix – Standard cost of actual mix

Variable Production Overhead Variance

Variable production overhead variance = Standard variable o/h – Actual variable o/h

= (Actual production × Standard rate) – Actual variable o/h

Note: $$\text{Standard rate} = \frac{\text{Budgeted variable o/h}}{\text{Budgeted production}}$$

Fixed Production Overhead Variance

Fixed production overhead variance = Standard fixed o/h – Actual fixed o/h

= (Actual production × Standard recovery rate) – Actual fixed o/h

Fixed overhead expenditure variance = (Standard fixed o/h recovery rate × budgeted production) – Actual fixed o/h

Fixed overhead volume variance = Standard fixed o/h – Budgeted fixed o/h

= (Actual production × Standard recovery rate) – Budgeted fixed o/h

Note: $$\text{Standard fixed o/h recovery rate} = \frac{\text{Budgeted fixed o/h}}{\text{Budgeted production}}$$

Fixed overhead efficiency variance = (Standard production – Actual production) × Standard rate per unit

Fixed overhead capacity variance = (Standard production – Budgeted production) × Standard rate per unit

Fixed overhead calendar variance = (Standard working days – Actual working days) $\times \dfrac{\text{Total fixed o/h in budget period}}{\text{Standard days in budget period}}$

Sales Value Variance

Sales value variance = Actual sales – Budgeted sales

Sales price variance = Actual sales – Standard sales

= Actual sales – (Standard price × Actual quantity sold)

Sales volume variance = Standard sales – Budgeted sales

Sales quantity variance = Revised standard sales – Budgeted sales

= (Budgeted sales for each product × Total standard sales/total budgeted sales) – Budgeted sales

Sales mix variance = Standard sales – Revised standard sales

Profit Variance due to Sales

Profit variance due to sales = Actual profit – Budgeted profit

Profit variance due to selling price = Actual profit – Standard profit

Profit variance due to sales volume = Standard profit – Budgeted profit

Profit variance (due to quantity) = Revised standard profit – Budgeted profit

Profit variance (due to sales mix) = Standard profit – Revised standard profit

Example 1 Material cost variance

It is estimated that for producing 1(one) unit of product X, 10 kg of materials are consumed. The standard price per kg of raw material is ₹ 0.50. In June, 30000 kg of raw materials were consumed to produce 2900 units of X. The actual price of materials was ₹ 0.48 per kg. Calculate the variance?

Solution:

Standard quantity of materials = Actual output × Standard quantity of material per unit

= 2900 × 10 kg = 29000 kg

Standard price per kg of material = ₹ 0.50.

Standard cost = Standard quantity of actual output × Standard price per kg

= 29000 kg × 0.50 = ₹ 14500.

Actual cost = Actual quantity consumed × Actual price per kg of material

= 30000 kg × 0.48 = ₹ 14400

Material cost variance = (Standard quantity of actual output × Standard price per kg) – (Actual quantity consumed × Actual price per kg)

= ₹ 14500 – ₹ 14400 = ₹ 100 (fav).

Material price variance = (Standard price per kg of material – Actual price per kg of material) × Actual quantity used

= (0.50 – 0.48) × 30000 = ₹ 600 (fav).

Material usage variance = (Standard quantity for actual production – Actual quantity used) × Standard price per unit

= (29000 kg – 30000 kg) × 0.50 = ₹ 500 (adv).

Check:

Raw material cost variance = Material price variance + Material usage variance.

₹ 100 (fav) = ₹ 600 (fav) + ₹ 500 (adv)

Example 2

The following data are available from the records of a company for production of BX:

Standard quantity: 1000 kg of material M

Standard price per kg: ₹ 2.40.

During a certain month 1150 kg of M was actually used and the actual price paid for material M was ₹ 2.60 per kg.

You are required to:

1. Compute the total direct material cost variance

2. Analyze the total variance by computing
   (i) the material price variance
   (ii) the material usage variance

Solution:

1. Direct material cost variance = Standard cost – Actual cost
   = (1000 × ₹ 2.40) – (1150 × ₹ 2.60) = ₹ 590 (adv)
2. (i) Material price variance = Price difference × Actual quantity
   = (₹ 2.40 – ₹ 2.60) × 1150 = ₹ 230 (adv)
   (ii) Material usage variance = Usage difference × Standard price
   = (1000 – 1150) × ₹ 2.40 = ₹ 360 (adv)

Check:

Material cost variance = Material price variance + Material usage variance

₹ 590 (adv) = ₹ 230 (adv) + ₹ 360 (adv).

Example 3 Material mix and yield variances

From the following information calculate material mix variance and yield variance:

Standard mix

Material A =	120 kg @	₹ 5 =	₹ 600
Material B =	80 kg @	₹ 10 =	₹ 800
	200 kg		₹ 1400
(30% loss)	60 kg		
	140 kg		₹ 1400

Actual mix

Material A =	112 kg @	₹ 5 =	₹ 560
Material B =	88 kg @	₹ 10 =	₹ 880
	200 kg		₹ 1440
(25% loss)	50 kg		
	150 kg		₹ 1440

Solution:

Material mix variance = (Quantity in standard mix proportion – Quantity in actual mix proportion) × Standard price

Mix variance for material A = (120 – 112) × ₹ 5 = ₹ 40 (fav).

Mix variance for material B = (80 – 88) × ₹ 10 = ₹ 80 (adv).

Material mix variance = ₹ 40 (adv).

Material yield variance = (Standard yield of actual input – Actual yield of input) × Standard material cost

Standard material cost per unit = ₹ 1400/140 = ₹ 10.

Material yield variance = (140 – 150) × ₹ 10 = ₹ 100 (fav).

Example 4

The standard material inputs required for 1000 kg of a finished product are given below:

Material	Quantity (in kg)	Standard rate per kg (in ₹)
A	450	20
B	400	40
C	250	60
	1100	
Standard loss	100	
Standard output	1000	

Actual production in a period was 20000 kg of the finished product for which the actual quantities of material used and the prices paid there for are as under:

Material	Quantity used (kg)	Purchase price per kg (₹)
A	10000	19
B	8500	42
C	4500	65

Calculate:

(i) Material cost variance
(ii) Material price variance
(iii) Material usage variance
(iv) Material mix variance
(v) Material yield variance

Show reconciliation among the variances?

Solution:

Standard input of materials for actual output of 20000 kg = 1100/1000 × 20000
= 22000 kg

A = 450/1100 × 22000 = 9000 kg
B = 400/1100 × 22000 = 8000 kg
C = 250/1100 × 22000 = 5000 kg
22000 kg

Standard material cost for actual output:

	₹
A = 9000 kg @ ₹ 20	= 180000
B = 8000 kg @ ₹ 40	= 320000
C = 5000 kg @ ₹ 60	= 300000
22000 kg input	800000
(–) 2000 kg loss	–
20000 kg output	800000

Standard cost per kg of standard mix = ₹ 800000/22000 = ₹ 364/11
Standard cost per kg of output = ₹ 800000/20000 = ₹ 40

Actual cost:	₹
A = 10000 kg @ ₹ 19	190000
B = 8500 kg @ ₹ 42	357000
C = 4500 kg @ ₹ 65	292500
23000 kg input	839500
(–) 3000 kg loss	–
20000 kg output	839500

Revised standard quantity = Standard quantity/Standard mix × Actual mix

	kg
A = 450/1100 × 23000	= 9409
B = 400/1100 × 23000	= 8364
C = 250/1100 × 23000	= 5227
	23000

₹

(i) Material cost variance = Standard cost of actual output – Actual cost

= ₹ 800000 – ₹ 839500 = 39500 (adv)

(ii) Material price variance = (Standard price – Actual price) × Actual quantity

A = (₹ 20 – ₹ 19) × 10000 = 10000 (fav)
B = (₹ 40 – ₹ 42) × 8500 = 17000 (adv)
C = (₹ 60 – ₹ 65) × 4500 = 22500 (adv)
29500 (adv) = 29500 (adv)

(iii) Material usage variance = (Standard quantity for actual output – Actual quantity) × Standard price

A = (9000 – 10000) × ₹ 20 = 20000 (adv)
B = (8000 – 8500) × ₹ 40 = 20000 (adv)
C = (5000 – 4500) × ₹ 60 = 30000 (fav)
10000 (adv) = 10000 (adv)
39500 (adv)

(iv) Material mix variance = (Revised standard quantity – Actual quantity) × Standard price

A = (9409 – 10000) × ₹ 20 = 11820 (adv)
B = (8364 – 8500) × ₹ 40 = 5440 (adv)
C = (5227 – 4500) × ₹ 60 = 43620 (fav)
26360 (fav) = 26360 (fav)

(v) Material yield variance = (Standard yield for actual mix – Actual yield) × Standard cost per unit

= (Standard output for actual mix – Actual yield) × Standard cost per unit

= [(1000/1100 × 23000) – 20000] × ₹ 40

= (20909 – 20000) × ₹ 40

= 36360 (adv)

10000 (adv)

Check:

Material cost variance = Material price variance + Material usage variance

= Material price variance + Material mix variance + Material yield variance

₹ 39500 (adv) = ₹ 29500 (adv) + ₹ 26360 (fav) + ₹ 36360 (adv)

Alternative calculations

	₹
Actual cost (as per calculation shown above)	839500
Actual input at standard price:	
A = 10000 kg @ ₹ 20	200000
B = 8500 kg @ ₹ 40	340000
C = 4500 kg @ ₹ 60	270000
23000 kg	810000

1. Material cost variance:

Standard cost of actual output (20000 kg @ ₹ 40)	= 800000	
Actual cost	= 839500	
Variance	= 39500	39500 (adv)

2. Material price variance:

Actual input at standard price	= 810000	
Actual input at actual price	= 839500	
Variance	= 29500	29500 (adv)

3. Material usage variance:

Standard cost of output	= 800000	
Actual input at standard price	= 810000	
Variance	= 10000	10000 (adv)
		39500 (adv)

4. Material mix variance:

Actual mix at standard price	= 810000	
Standard mix of 23000 kg at standard cost (23000 kg × ₹ 364/11)	= 836360	
Variance	= 26360	26360 (fav)

5. Material yield variance:

Standard yield from 23000 kg input

(23000 kg × 1000/1100)		= 20909 kg	
Actual yield		= 20000 kg	
	Difference	= 909 kg	
	Variance	= 909 kg @ ₹ 40	36360 (adv)

Reconciliation Statement

		₹
Standard material cost of actual output		800000
Variances:		
	Price = 29500 (adv)	
	Mix = 26360 (fav)	
	Yield = 36360 (adv)	
	39500	39500 (adv)
Actual material cost		839500

Example 5 Direct labour cost variance

Product A is estimated to require 20 hours per unit. The standard rate of labour per hour is ₹ 1. During the month of July, 2000 units were produced. For this, 38000 hours were taken at ₹ 1.05 per hour. Out of 38000 hours, 100 hours were lost due to abnormal loss for machine breakdown. Calculate the variance?

Solution:

Standard time for actual production = 2000 × 20 hours = 40000 hours

Standard labour cost = 40000 hr × ₹ 1 = ₹ 40000

Actual labour cost = 38000 hr × ₹ 1.05 = ₹ 39900

Total direct labour cost variance = Standard cost – Actual cost = ₹ 100 (fav)

Direct labour rate variance = (Standard rate – Actual rate) × Actual hours of production

= (₹ 1.00 – ₹ 1.05) × 38000 hr

= ₹ 1900 (adv).

Direct labour efficiency variance = (Standard hours for actual production – Actual hours worked) × Standard rate per hour

= (40000 hr – 37900 hr) × ₹ 1

= ₹ 2100 (fav).

or Direct labour efficiency variance = Production difference × Standard rate per unit.

$$= \left(\frac{37900}{20} - 2000\right) \times (20 \times ₹\, 1)$$

= (1895 – 2000) × ₹ 20

= ₹ 2100 (fav).

Direct labour idle time variance = Abnormal idle hours × Standard rate per hour

= 100 hr × ₹ 1 = ₹ 100 (adv).

Check:

Direct labour cost variance = Labour rate variance + Labour efficiency variance + Labour idle time variance

₹ 100 (fav) = ₹ 1900 (adv) + ₹ 2100 (fav) + ₹ 100 (adv)

Example 6

From the following information relating to ADB Ltd. you are required to calculate and present:

(i) Direct wages cost variance
(ii) Direct wages rate variance
(iii) Direct labour efficiency variance
(iv) Direct labour idle time variance

The standard wage rate for the 500 employees in department X is ₹ 0.80 per hour. The company operates a 40-hour week, without any overtime, and the standard performance for the department for one hour is 1000 units.

During a given period of four weeks, the actual output for the department was 158000 units, all of which was transferred to finished stock. Due to a power failure, four hours of idle time were incurred. Around 15 employees were actually paid @ ₹ 0.85 per hour, 5 employees were paid @ ₹ 0.75 per hour and the balance employees were paid at the standard rate.

Solution:

Actual hours attended	= 500 × 4 × 40 =	80000 labour hours
Idle hours	= 500 × 4 =	2000 labour hours
Actual hours worked		78000 labour hours

Standard hours required to produce 158000 units = 158000 × 500/1000

= 79000 labour hours

Standard labour cost = 79000 hours @ ₹ 0.80 = ₹ 63200

Actual labour cost:	₹
15 × 4 × 40 × ₹ 0.85	2040
5 × 4 × 40 × ₹ 0.75	600
180 × 4 × 40 × ₹ 0.80	61440
	64080

Direct wages cost variance = Standard cost – Actual cost

= ₹ 63200 – ₹ 64080 ₹ 880 (adv)

Direct wages rate variance = (Actual hours attended × Standard rate) – Actual cost

= (80000 × ₹ 0.80) – ₹ 64080 ₹ 80 (adv)

Direct labour efficiency variance = Standard cost – (Actual hours worked × Standard rate)

= ₹ 63200 – (78000 × ₹ 0.80) ₹ 800 (fav)

Direct labour idle time variance = Abnormal idle time × Standard rate

= 2000 × ₹ 0.80 ₹ 1600 (adv)

Check:

Direct wages cost variance = Direct wages rate variance + Direct labour efficiency variance + Direct labour idle time variance

₹ 880 (adv) = ₹ 80 (adv) + ₹ 800 (fav) + ₹ 1600 (adv)

Example 7 Direct labour mix variance

The budgeted labour force for production of product A is:

10 skilled workers @ ₹ 1.00 per hour for 40 hours = ₹ 400

15 unskilled workers @ ₹ 0.60 per hour for 40 hours = ₹ 360

Actual labour force employed during the week was:

8 skilled workers @ ₹ 1.10 per hour for 40 hours = ₹ 352

17 unskilled workers @ ₹ 0.55 per hour for 40 hours = ₹ 374

Assuming that the labour efficiency is unaffected, find out the variance?

Solution:

Direct labour rate variance = (Standard rate – Actual rate) × Actual hours of production

For skilled workers = (1.00 – 1.10) × (8 × 40 hr) = ₹ 32 (adv)

For unskilled workers = (0.60 – 0.55) × (17 × 40 hrs) = ₹ 34 (fav)

₹ 2 (fav)

Direct labour mix variance = Standard cost of standard mix – Standard cost of actual mix

Standard cost of standard mix = Standard labour × Standard rate

For skilled = 10 × ₹ 1.00 × 40 hr = ₹400

For unskilled = 15 × ₹ 0.60 × 40 hr = ₹360

₹760

Standard cost of actual mix = Actual labour × Standard rate

For skilled = 8 × ₹ 1.00 × 40 hr = ₹ 320

For unskilled = 17 × ₹ 0.60 × 40 hr = ₹ 408

₹ 728

So, direct labour mix variance = (₹ 760 – ₹ 728) = ₹ 32 (fav)

Example 8

Calculate the variances from the following information as per the originating causes:
Standard direct cost per unit:

Material cost: 5 kg = ₹ 50.00

Labour cost: 20 hr = ₹ 10.00

₹ 60.00

For production of 500 units, materials consumption amounted to ₹ 25650 against 2700 kg. Wage payment was ₹ 6050 for 11000 hours including 20 hours idle time due to machine break-down.

Solution:

Workings

Standard material cost per kg = ₹ 50/5 kg = ₹ 10

Standard labour cost per hour = ₹ 10/20 hr = ₹ 0.50

Actual labour hour per unit = 11000 hr/500 units = 22 hr

Actual labour cost per hour = ₹ 6050/11000 hr = ₹ 0.55

Material cost variance = Standard cost – Actual cost

= (500 × 5 kg × ₹ 10) – (2700 kg × ₹ 9.50)

= ₹ 25000 – ₹ 25650 = ₹ 650 (adv)

Material price variance = (Standard price – Actual price) × Actual quantity

= (₹ 10 – ₹ 9.50) × 2700 kg = ₹ 1350 (fav)

Material usage variance = (Standard quantity – Actual quantity) × Standad price

= [(500 unit × 5 kg) – 2700 kg] × ₹ 10

= (2500 kg – 2700 kg) × 10

= 200 × 10 = ₹ 2000 (adv)

Check:

Material cost variance = Material price variance + Material quantity (usage) variance

₹ 650 (adv) = ₹ 1350 (fav) + ₹ 2000 (adv)

Labour cost variance = Standard cost – Actual cost
= (500 × 20 hrs. × 0.50) – (11000 hrs. × 0.55)
= ₹ 5000 – ₹ 6050 = ₹ 1050 (adv)

Labour rate variance = (Standard rate/hr – Actual rate/hr) × Actual hours
= (0.50 – 0.55) × 11000 hr = ₹ 550 (adv)

Labour efficiency variance = (Standard hours – Actual hours worked) × Standard rate per hour
= [(500 × 20 hr) – (11000 hr – 20 hr)] × 0.50
= (10000 – 10980) × 0.50 = ₹ 490 (adv)

Labour idle time variance = Idle hours × Standard rate/hour
= 20 hr × 0.50 = ₹ 10 (adv)

Check:

Labour cost variance = Labour rate variance + Labour efficiency variance + Labour idle time variance

₹ 1050 (adv) = ₹ 550 (adv) + ₹ 490 (adv) + 10 (adv)

Example 9

The following details relating to the product X during the month of March, 2009 are available. Compute the material and labour cost variances and also reconcile the standard and the actual cost from the variances.

Standard cost per unit:
Materials 50 kg @ ₹ 42 per kg
Labour 400 hr @ ₹ 1 per hr
Actual cost for the month:
Materials 4900 kg @ ₹ 42 per kg
Labour 39600 hr @ ₹ 1.10 per hr
Actual production 100 units.

Solution:

Standard requirements for actual production:
Materials 100 × 50 kg = 5000 kg
Labour 100 × 400 hr = 40000 hr

		₹
Material cost variance	= Standard cost – Actual cost	
	= (5000 × ₹ 40) – (4900 × ₹ 42)	5800 (adv)
Material price variance	= (Standard price – Actual price) × Actual quantity	
	= (₹ 40 – ₹ 42) × 4900	9800 (adv)
Material usage variance	= (Standard usage – Actual usage) × Standard price	
	= (5000 – 4900) × ₹ 40	4000 (fav)

Check:

Material cost variance = Material price variance + Material usage variance

₹ 5800 (adv) = ₹ 9800 (adv) + ₹ 4000 (fav)

Labour cost variance = Standard cost – Actual cost

= (40000 × ₹ 1) – (39600 × ₹ 1.10) 3560 (adv)

Labour rate variance = (Standard rate – Actual rate) × Actual hours

= (₹ 1.00 – ₹ 1.10) × 39600 3960 (adv)

Labour efficiency variance = (Standard hours – Actual hours) × Standard rate

= (40000 – 39600) × ₹ 1.00 400 (fav)

Check:

Labour cost variance = Labour rate variance + Labour efficiency variance

₹ 3560 (adv) = ₹ 3960 (adv) + ₹ 400 (fav)

Reconciliation Statement
For the period: March 2009

Actual output: 100 units

		₹
Standard costs:		
Materials 5000 kg @ ₹ 40 per kg	= 200000	
Labour 40000 hr @ ₹ 1.00 per hr	= 40000	240000
Variances:		
Material consumption	= 4000 (fav)	
Labour efficiency	= 400 (fav)	
Controllable by production manager	4400 (fav)	
Material price	9800 (adv)	
Labour rate	3960 (adv)	
Uncontrollable	13760 (adv)	9360 (adv)
Actual costs:		
Materials 4900 kg @ ₹ 42 per kg	= 205800	
Labour 39600 hr @ ₹ 1.10 per hr	= 43560	249360

Example 10 Overhead cost variance

The standard overhead rate of product X is as follows:

Variable overhead = ₹ 2.00 per unit

Standard fixed overhead = ₹ 30000

Standard units = 3000 units

Standard fixed overhead per unit = (₹ 30000/3000 units) = ₹ 10

Standard time for production of each unit of X = 10 hours

During the month of January, the following actual data are available:

Hours worked = 27000 hr

Actual output = 2600 unit

Overhead incurred:

Variable o/h = ₹ 5000

Fixed o/h = ₹ 28000

Calculate the overhead cost variance?

Solution:

Variable o/h expenditure variance = Standard variable o/h – Actual variable o/h

= (Actual production × Standard rate) – Actual variable o/h

= (2600 × ₹ 2) – ₹ 5000 = ₹ 200 (fav)

Fixed o/h (total) variance = Standard o/h of actual production – Actual o/h

= (Standard o/h rate × Actual production) – Actual o/h

= (₹ 10 × 2600) – ₹ 28000 = ₹ 2000 (adv)

Fixed o/h expenditure variance = (Standard o/h rate × Budgeted production) – Actual o/h

= (₹ 10 × 3000) – ₹ 28000 = ₹ 2000 (fav)

Fixed o/h volume variance = Standard fixed o/h – Budgeted fixed o/h

= (Standard rate × Actual production) – Budgeted o/h

= (₹ 10 × 2600) – ₹ 30000 = ₹ 4000 (adv)

Fixed o/h efficiency variance = (Standard production of actual hours – Actual production) × Standard rate per unit

= (27000 hr – 2600) × ₹ 10 = ₹ 1000 (adv)

10 hours

Fixed o/h capacity variance = (Standard production of actual hours – Budgeted production) × Standard rate per unit

= (2700 – 3000) × ₹ 10 = ₹ 3000 (adv)

Check:

Fixed o/h (total) variance = Fixed o/h expenditure variance + Fixed o/h volume variance

= Fixed o/h expenditure variance + Fixed o/h efficiency variance + Fixed o/h capacity variance

₹ 2000 (adv) = ₹ 2000 (fav) + ₹ 1000 (adv) + ₹ 3000 (adv)

Note: It is assumed that there is no calendar variance.

Example 11

The budgeted fixed overhead for the year 2008 amounted to ₹ 14400. It was estimated that 288 days would be working during the year. In February, days were worked only 20. Find out the calendar variance?

Solution:

$$\text{Fixed o/h calendar variance} = (\text{Standard working days} - \text{Actual working days}) \times \frac{\text{Budgeted fixed o/h}}{\text{Standard days in budget period}}$$

$$\text{Standard working days in a month} = \frac{288}{12} = 24 \text{ days}$$

Budgeted fixed o/h = ₹ 14400

Standard days in budget period = 288 days

$$\text{Fixed o/h calendar variance} = (24 - 20) \times \frac{₹\,14400}{288} = 4 \times ₹\,50 = ₹\,200 \text{ (adv)}$$

Example 12

The standard variable overhead for a particular production department has been budgeted as follows:

Budgeted variable overhead for the period: ₹ 20000

Budgeted volume of production for the period: 40000 units

During the period under review the actual variable overheads incurred amounted to ₹ 28000.

The actual production was 48000 units.

Compute the variable overhead variance?

Solution:

Standard variable overhead rate per unit = Budgeted overhead/Budgeted production
= ₹ 20000/40000 = ₹ 0.50 per unit

Variable overhead recovered (i.e. charged to production)
= Actual production × Standard rate per unit
= 48000 × ₹ 0.50 = ₹ 24000

Actual variable overhead = ₹ 28000

Variable overhead variance = Overhead recovered – Actual overhead
= ₹ 24000 – ₹ 28000
= ₹ 4000 (adv)

Example 13

At a certain factory the budgeted quantity of units to be produced was 10000 units for a 20 working day month. The budgeted fixed overhead for the period was ₹ 20000.

During the month the actual quantity produced was 7500 units. Actual fixed overhead incurred amounted to ₹ 24000. The standard rate of production has been set at 500 units per working day. Only 18 days could be worked actually during the month.

Compute the following variances:

(i) Fixed overhead variance

(ii) Fixed overhead volume variance

(iii) Fixed overhead expenditure variance
(iv) Fixed overhead capacity variance
(v) Fixed overhead efficiency variance

Solution:

Standard fixed overhead per unit = Budgeted overhead/Budgeted production
= ₹ 20000/10000 = ₹ 2 per unit

Fixed overhead recovered by actual production = Actual production × Standard rate
= 7500 × ₹ 2 = ₹ 15000

Standard production in actual days = Actual days worked × Standard rate of production
= 18 × 500 = 9000 units

	₹
(i) Fixed overhead cost variance = Fixed overhead recovered – Actual overhead	
= ₹ 15000 – ₹ 24000	9000 (adv)
(ii) Fixed overhead expenditure variance = Budgeted overhead – Actual overhead	
= ₹ 20000 – ₹ 24000	4000 (adv)
(iii) Fixed overhead volume variance	
= (Budgeted production – Actual production) × Standard rate per unit	
= (10000 – 7500) × ₹ 2	5000 (adv)
(iv) Fixed overhead capacity variance	
= (Budgeted production – Standard production) × Standard rate per unit	
= (10000 – 9000) × ₹ 2	2000 (adv)
(v) Fixed overhead efficiency variance	
= (Standard production – Actual production) × Standard rate per unit	
= (9000 – 7500) × ₹ 2	3000 (adv)

Check:

Fixed overhead cost variance
= Expenditure variance + Volume variance
= Expenditure variance + Capacity variance + Efficiency variance
₹ 9000 (adv) = ₹ 4000 (adv) + ₹ 2000 (adv) + ₹ 3000 (adv)

Example 14 Sales value variance

The budgeted and actual sales for a period in respect of two products are given below:

Product	Budget			Actual		
	Quantity	Price (₹)	Value (₹)	Quantity	Price (₹)	Value
A	1000	5	5000	1200	6	7200
B	1200	10	12000	1000	9	9000
Total	2200		17000	2200		16200

Calculate the necessary sales variance?

Solution:

In order to calculate all the sales variances, it is necessary to ascertain:

(a) Standard sales, i.e. Actual quantity sold × Standard selling price, and

(b) Revised standard sales, i.e. standard sales adjusted to budgeted sales ratios.

	Standard sales				Revised standard sales	
Product	Quantity	Price (₹)	Value (₹)		Budgeted ratio	Value (₹)
A	1200	5	6000		(5/17) × 16000 =	4706
B	1000	10	10000		(12/17) × 16000 =	11294
Total	2200		16000			16000

Sales value variance = Actual sales – Budgeted sales

A = ₹	7200 –	5000 = ₹	2200	(fav)
B = ₹	9000 –	12000 = ₹	3000	(adv)
₹	16200	17000 = ₹	800	(adv)

Sales price variance = Actual sales – Standard sales

A = ₹	7200 –	6000 = ₹	1200	(fav)
B = ₹	9000 –	10000 = ₹	1000	(adv)
₹	16200	16000 = ₹	200	(fav)

Sales volume variance = Standard sales – Budgeted sales

A = ₹	6000 –	5000 = ₹	1000	(fav)
B = ₹	10000 –	12000 = ₹	2000	(adv)
₹	16000	17000 = ₹	1000	(adv)

Sales quantity variance = Revised standard sales – Budgeted sales

A = ₹	4706 –	5000 = ₹	294	(adv)
B = ₹	11294 –	12000 = ₹	706	(adv)
₹	16000	17000 = ₹	1000	(adv)

Sales mix variance = Standard sales – Revised standard sales

A = ₹	6000 –	4706 = ₹	1294	(fav)
B = ₹	10000 –	11294 = ₹	1294	(adv)
₹	16000 –	16000 = ₹	nil	

Check:

Sales value variance = Sales price variance + Sales volume variance

= Sales price variance + Sales quantity variance + Sales mix variance

₹ 800 (adv) = ₹ 200 (fav) + 1000 (adv) + Nil

= ₹ 800 (adv).

Example 15

The budgeted and actual sales for a period in respect of two products are as under:

Product	Budgeted sales		Actual sales	
	Quantity (units)	Price (₹/unit)	Quantity (units)	Price (₹/unit)
A	8000	10	9000	11
B	12000	8	6000	7

Calculate the necessary variances explaining the difference between the budgeted and the actual sales and prepare a reconciliation statement?

Solution:

Budgeted sales:	₹	Actual sales:	₹
A 8000 units @ ₹ 10	80000	A 9000 units @ ₹ 11	99000
B 12000 units @ ₹ 8	96000	B 6000 units @ ₹ 7	42000
20000 units	176000	15000 units	141000

Revised standard mix (i.e. actual total quantity in budgeted ratio):

A = 8/20 × 15000 = 6000 units
B = 12/20 × 15000 = 9000 units
15000 units

Total sales variance = Budgeted sales – Actual sales

= ₹ 176000 – ₹ 141000 ₹ = 35000 (adv)

Sales price variance = Price difference × Actual quantity
A = (₹ 10 – ₹ 11) × 9000 = 9000 (fav)
B = (₹ 8 – ₹ 7) × 6000 = 6000 (adv)
3000 3000 (fav)

Sales volume variance = Volume difference × Standard price
A = (8000 – 9000) × ₹ 10 = 10000 (fav)
B = (12000 – 6000) × ₹ 8 = 48000 (adv)
38000 38000 (adv)

Sales mix variance = (Revised standard mix – Actual mix) × Standard price
A = (6000 – 9000) × ₹ 10 = 30000 (fav)
B = (9000 – 6000) × ₹ 8 = 24000 (adv)
6000 6000 (fav)

Sales quantity variance = (Budgeted quantity – Revised standard quantity) × Standard price

A = (8000 – 6000) × ₹ 10 = 20000 (adv)

B = (12000 – 9000) × ₹ 8 = 24000 (adv)

44000   44000 (adv)

Check:

Total sales variance = Sales price variance + Sales volume variance
= Sales price variance + Sales mix variance + Sale quantity variance

₹ 35000 (adv) = ₹ 3000 (fav) + ₹ 6000 (fav) + ₹ 44000 (adv)

Reconciliation Statement

	₹
Budgeted sales	176000
Variances:	
Price = ₹ 3000 (fav)	
Mix = ₹ 6000 (fav)	
Quantity = ₹ 44000 (adv)	35000 (adv)
Actual sales	141000

Alternative calculations:

	₹
Budgeted sales (as per calculation made above)	176000
Average standard price = ₹ 176000/20000 units = ₹ 8.80 per unit	
Actual sales (as per calculation made above)	141000

Actual sales at standard price:

A = 9000 units @ ₹ 10 = ₹ 90000

B = 6000 units @ ₹ 8 = ₹ 48000

15000 units = ₹ 138000

Total sales variance = Budgeted sales – Actual sales = 35000 (adv)

Sales price variance = Actual sales at standard price – Actual sales at actual price
= ₹ 138000 – ₹ 141000 = ₹ 3000 (fav)

Sales volume variance = Budgeted sales – Actual sales at standard price
= ₹ 176000 – ₹ 138000 = ₹ 38000 (adv)

Sales mix variance = Actual mix at standard price – Standard mix of 15000 units at standard price
= ₹ 138000 – (15000 × ₹ 8.80) = ₹ 6000 (fav)

Sales quantity variance = Budgeted sales – Standard mix of 15000 units at standard price
= ₹ 176000 – (15000 × ₹ 8.80) = ₹ 44000 (adv)

9.10 CONCLUSION

Standard costing is a technique which uses standards for costs and revenues for the purpose of management control through variance analysis. It involves:

(i) Ascertainment and use of standard costs
(ii) Measurement of actual costs
(iii) Comparison of standard costs and actual costs
(iv) Analysis of variances and taking appropriate actions.

This control tool is adopted by the management to find out especially the causes of adverse variation in cost of production and services so that corrective action can be taken immediately to avoid loss or wastage. Sales value variance is calculated to the management for setting up appropriate sales strategy for improving revenues. This chapter has adequately dealt with the various aspects of standard costing and explained with examples, how to analyze the causes of variation for prompt management actions.

REVIEW QUESTIONS

9.1 Define standard costing? How does it differ from budgetary control?

9.2 What are the preliminaries to be taken into account before setting up the standard costs?

9.3 Write short notes on:
(a) Current standard
(b) Basic standard
(c) Normal standard.

9.4 What is variance analysis? State the reasons for variance with examples?

9.5 Explain the components of direct material cost variance and state the reasons for such variances?

9.6 Explain the components of direct labour cost variance and state the reasons for such variances?

9.7 Explain the components of fixed overhead cost variance and state the reasons for such variances?

9.8 What is sales variance? Why do the sales variances occur?

9.9 From the following particulars calculate:
(i) Material cost variance
(ii) Material usage variance
(iii) Material price variance

Quantity of material purchased:	3000 units
Value of material purchased:	₹ 9000
Standard quantity of material required per ton of finished product:	25 units
Standard rate of material:	₹ 2 per unit
Opening stock of material:	nil

Closing stock of material: 500 units

Finished production during the period: 80 ton

9.10 Data relating to a work order are given below:

Standard rate of wages per hour = ₹ 10

Standard hours = 300

Actual rate of wages per hour = ₹ 12

Actual hours = 200

Calculate:

(i) Labour cost variance

(ii) Labour rate variance

(iii) Labour efficiency variance

9.11 From the following information of XYZ Ltd. determine:

(i) Labour cost variance

(ii) Labour efficiency variance

(iii) Labour rate variance

(a) Standard labour cost per unit of production is ₹ 15.

(b) Time allowed per unit is 30 hours.

(c) During the month of March, 2010, 3000 units are produced in 75000 hours.

(d) Actual payment of wages for the month is ₹ 45000.

9.12 A company produces a single product which passes through two operating departments. The standard cost for the product shows the following data:

	Standard time (hours)	Standard rate (₹)	Total (₹)
Department P	2.2	5.40	11.88
Department Q	1.6	6.00	9.60

The production for the month of March is 1000 units. The actual labour costs in the two departments are:

	Hours	Cost (₹)
Department P	2000	12908
Department Q	1800	10200

Calculate:

(i) Labour cost variance

(ii) Labour rate variance

(iii) Labour efficiency variance

9.13 A company has planned to manufacture 1000 units of a particular product. It has calculated its unit standard cost as follows:

Materials 10 kg @ ₹ 5 per kg

Labour 3 hr @ ₹ 8 per hr

The target of 1000 units was achieved. The following costs were incurred per unit:

Materials 11 kg @ ₹ 4.50 per kg

Labour 2.5 hr @ ₹ 10 per hr

Calculate:

(a) The total cost variance
(b) The material cost variance
(c) The material price variance
(d) The material usage variance
(e) The labour cost variance
(f) The labour rate variance
(g) The labour efficiency variance

10

Transfer Pricing

10.1 INTRODUCTION

A transfer price is defined as the price that is assumed to have been charged by one department of a company for products and services it provides to another department of the same company, in order to calculate each department's profit and loss separately. This chapter deals with transfer pricing and its various aspects as any dynamic management of an organization would like to assess the contribution of each of the profit centres.

10.2 CONCEPT OF TRANSFER PRICING

The concept of transfer price is fundamentally aimed at stimulating the external market conditions within the company so that the managers get motivated and try to perform well. However, the transfer price does not have any direct impact on the organization's profits as a whole because its effect on one department's revenue is exactly offset by the other department's costs.

The use of 'market price' as transfer price establishes the discipline of the market on the divisional managers and allows them to operate their divisions with greater autonomy. However, at times, it is difficult to get the correct market price as it may not be available or it may not be possible to estimate. In such situation, cost based transfer price comes into play. Normally, standard costs are taken into consideration. By using the standard costs, the inefficiencies of the selling department are not passed onto the buying department.

10.3 OBJECTIVES OF TRANSFER PRICING

There are many objectives of transfer pricing for the benefits of the organization. They are as follows:

(i) To distribute properly, the revenue between profit centres when they are responsible jointly for product development and marketing
(ii) To provide relevant information to the profit centres regarding the trade-off between costs and revenues of the company
(iii) To induce goal-congruent decisions to improve the profits of the department and also of the whole company
(iv) To measure the economic performance of profit centres

10.4 IDEAL SITUATION FOR OPERATION OF TRANSFER PRICING MECHANISM

The ideal situation for operation of transfer pricing is that the transfer price should be similar to the price which would be charged if the products were sold to outside customers or purchased from outside venders.

10.4.1 Goal Congruence

There should be goal congruence between profit centres and the parent organization. The pre-requisites for achieving goal congruence are as follows:

(i) Competent people
(ii) Good organizational atmosphere
(iii) Details of market price
(iv) Freedom to source
(v) Availability of information
(vi) Scope for negotiation

The company should have competent executives who are skilled at negotiation and arbitration. They should be able to determine the appropriate transfer prices. Good organizational atmosphere creates an atmosphere of trust and confidence between the selling department and the buying department of the company. The market price should reflect the same conditions in terms of quantity, quality, and time for delivery of the product to which the transfer price is applicable. Managers of the selling department should be given freedom to sell their goods in the outside market. Similarly, the managers of the buying department should be allowed to buy their goods from the outside market. They should be fully aware of market conditions and should have all the necessary information available to them before taking any decision. There must be a system of negotiation of contracts, for which the managers should be adequately trained on transfer price decisions.

10.5 CONSTRAINTS ON SOURCING IN TRANSFER PRICING

Sometimes, it becomes difficult to find an ideal situation for the operation of a transfer pricing mechanism. Due to the corporate policy being exercised in the company, the profit centre managers may not have enough freedom to make a sourcing decision. Generally, such constraints are as follows:

(i) Limited markets
(ii) Excess or shortage of industry capacity
(iiii) Sourcing constraints

10.5.1 Limited Markets

The reasons for the limited markets are as follows:

(i) In many companies the existence of excess internal capacity forces the buying department not to go for outside purchase.
(ii) In highly integrated companies, there tends to be a little independent production capacity for the intermediate products.
(iii) If the company is a sole producer of a product, then outside capacity does not exist.
(iv) If a company makes a significant investment in facilities, then it cannot buy the goods from outside sources though the outside capacity exists.

10.5.2 Excess or Shortage of Industry Capacity

In situation of excess capacity in the industry, the selling department does not sell in the outside market, whereas the buying department may buy from outside vendors, though the inside capacity is available in the company. The situation is reversed in time of shortage of industry capacity. However, in either situation, the company as a whole may not optimize its profits.

10.5.3 Sourcing Constraints

A company may allow its buying department to buy goods from market if the department gets a better deal in terms of quality, price and service. Similarly, a selling department may be allowed to sell its products in the open market if it gets a better profit there. Therefore, the management should take appropriate decisions to optimize the company's profit.

10.6 METHODS OF CALCULATING TRANSFER PRICES

The methods used, differ from company to company. The five methods used commonly are as follows:

(i) Market based pricing method
(ii) Cost based pricing method:
  (a) Actual cost approach

(b) Standard cost approach
(c) Variable cost approach/Marginal cost approach

(iii) Cost plus based pricing method
(iv) Negotiated pricing method
(v) Dual pricing method

10.6.1 Market Based Pricing Method

If a perfectly competitive market for the intermediate product exists, the best method is to follow the market price as the transfer price. However, the supplying department may offer some price concession to the extent of selling and distribution expenses which would have been incurred in case of outside sale, but not required for internal transfer.

The main difficulties in following market based pricing are the following:

(i) A perfectly competitive market is very rare.
(ii) A market for intermediate products may not be available.
(iii) Even if the market is available, market price may vary from market to market.
(iv) Quality and supply of the products that the purchase department may have to buy from the market may be uncertain.

10.6.2 Cost-based Pricing Method

The supplying/selling department may follow a transfer price based on either full (actual) cost or marginal cost. The main problem here is that there may not have any motivation on the part of the selling department to achieve optimum level. At times, the standard costs are also considered as the basis for transfer price. Here the performance may be evaluated in terms of efficiency or inefficiency of the supplying department when the standard cost (i.e., transfer price) is compared with the actual cost of the supplying department.

10.6.3 Cost Plus Based Pricing Method

In order to overcome some of the limitations of cost-based pricing method, cost plus approach (say, cost plus 10% or 20%) may be followed. This method allows the supplying department to have some margin. However, it may create the problem of stock valuation of the company because of inclusion of 'margin' to the cost by the supplying department and this additional amount gets included in the closing stock of the buying department.

10.6.4 Negotiated Pricing Method

Under this method, the transfer price may be fixed on the basis of negotiation or bargain between the managers of supplying department and the buying department.

10.6.5 Dual Pricing Method

In this method, the supplying department charges a higher transfer price, whereas the buying department gets the goods at a lower price/cost price.

General Principle

Minimum transfer price = Incremental cost per unit (+) Opportunity cost per unit.

In absence of a market for intermediate products or in case of availability of idle capacity of the supplying department, opportunity cost may be taken as 'zero'. In such situation, minimum transfer price may be taken as incremental or marginal cost only.

Example 1

A manufacturing company has two divisions—X and Y. The output of X, which may be sold in the market at ₹ 300 per unit, is also used as a component by Y for manufacturing a product. Y requires one unit of the component from X for producing every one unit of the final products which is sold in the market at ₹ 500 per unit.

The budgeted production for X and Y are 3000 and 1000 units respectively. The cost data for the budgeted level of production in respect of the two divisions are as follows:

	Division X (₹)	Division Y (₹)
Materials per unit	100	?
Wages per unit	60	50
Variable overhead per unit	40	30
Fixed overhead per unit	50	40

Show the divisional profits and the profits of the company in case of the following transfer pricing policies:

(i) Market price method
(ii) 110% of full cost method, and
(iii) Negotiated price of ₹ 290 per unit.

Solution:

(i) Market price based transfer price method

Statement showing the divisional profits and the profits of the company

Division X (₹)		Division Y (₹)		Company (₹)
Sales (3000 × ₹ 300)	= 900000	(1000 × ₹ 500)	= 500000	1400000
Less: Costs				
Variable costs (3000 × ₹ 200)		Transfer-in-costs (1000 × ₹ 300)		
	= 600000		= 300000 plus	
		Other variable costs (1000 × ₹ 80)		
			= 80000	
			= 380000	980000
Fixed costs (3000 × ₹ 50)		(1000 × ₹ 40)		
	= 150000		= 40000	190000
	750000		420000	1170000
Profit	= 150000		80000	230000

(ii) 110% of full cost based transfer price method

Division X (₹)		Division Y (₹)		Company (₹)
Sales (2000 × ₹ 300)	= 600000	(1000 × ₹ 500)		
(1000 × ₹ 275*)	= 275000			
	875000		= 500000	1375000
Less: Costs				
Variable cost (3000 × ₹ 200)		Transfer-in-costs (1000 × ₹ 275)		
	= 600000		= 275000 plus	
		Other variable costs (1000 × ₹ 80)		
			= 80000	
			= 355000	955000
Fixed costs				
= (3000 × ₹ 50)	= 150000	(1000 × ₹ 40)	= 40000	190000
	750000		395000	1145000
Profit	= 125000		105000	230000

Note: Full cost per unit of the component in Division X = (₹ 100 + 60 + 40 + 50) = ₹ 250. So, 110% of full cost = 110% × ₹ 250 = ₹ 275.

(iii) Negotiated price based transfer price method

Division X (₹)		Division Y (₹)		Company (₹)
Sales (2000 × ₹ 300)	= 600000	(1000 × ₹ 500)		
(1000 × ₹ 290*)	= 290000			
	890000		= 500000	1390000
Less: Costs				
Variable costs (3000 × ₹ 200)		Transfer-in-costs = (1000 × ₹ 290)		
	= 600000		= 290000 plus	
		Other variable costs = (1000 × ₹ 80)		
			= 80000	
			370000	970000
Fixed costs (3000 × ₹ 50)	= 150000	(1000 × ₹ 40)	= 40000	190000
	750000		410000	1160000
Profit	140000		90000	230000

Note: Negotiated price of the component is ₹ 290 as given in the example.

It may be noted that the profit of the company as a whole is the same irrespective of the transfer pricing policy followed. Only divisional profits differ on the basis of the transfer prices being charged. Profit of the supplying division, i.e. Division X is more when transfer price is higher as in (i) above, and the profit of the buying division, i.e. Division Y is more when transfer price is lower as in (ii) above.

10.7 TRANSFER PRICING AND OPTIMUM LEVEL OF PRODUCTION

In absence of any market for intermediate products, and if there is no capacity constraints in the supplying units, then the transfer price for achieving the organizational optimality will be the marginal cost of production of the intermediate product at the optimal level of output for the company as a whole. Therefore, the optimum output level is the level where marginal cost of the supplying department equals to the net marginal revenue of the receiving/buying department.

Total net revenue = Total revenue – Conversion cost

Company's profit = Total revenue of the buying department – Total cost of the selling department

Example 2

From the following data, find out:

(i) The optimum output level
(ii) The transfer price
(iii) Company's profit
(iv) The profit of the supplying division
(v) The profit of the buying/receiving division

Supply Division		Receiving Division	
Units produced	Total costs (₹)	Units produced	Total net revenue (₹)
1000	8000	1000	20000
2000	14000	2000	38000
3000	20000	3000	54000
4000	22000	4000	68000
5000	26000	5000	80000
6000	30000	6000	90000
7000	38000	7000	98000
8000	48000	8000	104000
9000	62000	9000	108000

Solution:

Supply Division			Receiving Division			
Units production	Total cost (₹)	Marginal cost (₹)	Units production	Total net revenue (₹)	Marginal net revenue (₹)	Company profit (₹)
1000	8000	8000	1000	20000	20000	12000
2000	14000	6000	2000	38000	18000	24000
3000	20000	6000	3000	54000	16000	34000
4000	22000	2000	4000	68000	14000	46000
5000	26000	4000	5000	80000	12000	54000
6000	30000	4000	6000	90000	10000	60000
7000	38000	8000	7000	98000	8000	60000
8000	48000	10000	8000	104000	6000	56000
9000	62000	14000	9000	108000	4000	46000

It is seen from the example that at the output level of 7000 units, the marginal cost of the supplying division and the marginal net revenue of the receiving division is equal and the total profit of the company as a whole is the maximum. Therefore, 7000 units may be considered as the optimum output level, and the transfer price is the marginal cost of the supplying division at the optimum level, i.e. ₹ 8000 for 1000 units or ₹ 8 per unit. Now taking transfer price as ₹ 8 per unit, the profitability of both the divisions and the company as a whole may be shown below:

Supply Division				Receiving Division			
Units production	Total cost (₹)	Revenue (Transfer price) (₹)	Profit (₹)	Total net revenue (₹)	Transfer-in cost (₹)	Profit (₹)	Company profit (₹)
1000	8000	8000	—	20000	8000	12000	12000
2000	14000	16000	2000	38000	16000	22000	24000
3000	20000	24000	4000	54000	24000	30000	34000
4000	22000	32000	10000	68000	32000	36000	46000
5000	26000	40000	14000	80000	40000	40000	54000
6000	30000	48000	18000	90000	48000	42000	60000
7000*	38000	56000	18000*	98000	56000	42000*	60000*
8000	48000	64000	16000	104000	64000	40000	56000
9000	62000	72000	10000	108000	72000	36000	46000

It may be observed from the above that both the divisions' profit is increasing upto the output level of 7000 units. Thereafter, the profits are decreasing. Therefore, the output level of 7000 units is considered as optimum level.

10.8 INTERNATIONAL TRANSFER PRICING

International transfer price is the price charged on transfer of intermediate products across national boundaries. Additional factors, such as, difference in the tax rates, freights, duties, government policies in respect of exports, imports, dividend repatriation, etc., in different countries are to be considered for fixing the transfer prices in such cases. The transfer prices are set up in such a way as to reduce the total burden of taxes, freight and duties etc., in order to increase the profit of the organization as a whole.

Example 3

Two divisions of a company, P and Q are located in two different countries having different income tax rate—30% in P and 20% in Q. Operating income of the divisions under different transfer price methods are given as follows:

Transfer price methods	Operating income (₹)	
	Division P	Division Q
Market price	40000	20000
110% of full cost	25000	35000
Negotiated price	32000	28000

Suggest the most appropriate transfer price method that will maximize the operating income of the company as a whole.

Solution:

Transfer price Methods	Operating income (₹)			Tax payable (₹)		Total
	Division P	Division Q	Company	Division P @ 30 %	Division Q @ 20 %	
Market price	40000	20000	60000	12000	4000	16000
110% of full cost	25000	35000	60000	7500	7000	14500
Negotiated price	32000	28000	60000	9600	5600	15200

From the example it is evident that the total tax payable is the lowest in case of transfer price based on 110% of full cost. So the post-tax income of the company will be maximum if a transfer price based on 110% of full cost method is followed.

MNCs can manipulate their income by use of transfer pricing in the following ways:

(i) MNCs set high transfer prices for subsidiaries in countries with a relatively high rate of taxation.

(ii) MNCs set low transfer prices when goods are subjected to high import duties in a particular country.

(iii) MNCs set relatively high transfer prices for their subsidiaries in countries experiencing hyper inflation and currency devaluation.

(iv) MNCs set high transfer prices for goods and services that are purchased by the subsidiaries situated in countries, which restrict repatriation of income.

10.9 UPSTREAM FIXED COSTS AND PROFITS

At times, a typical transfer pricing problem is faced by the process industry, and the integrated process companies in which the marketing department sells the final product to the outside customers without considering the fixed costs involved in the internal purchase price. This may happen due to absence of proper transfer pricing mechanism. The companies should adopt the following methods to sort out this problem:

(i) Two step pricing

(ii) Profit sharing

(iii) Two sets of prices

10.9.1 Two Step Pricing

It involves charging for the (transferred) product twice. In the first stage, the product is priced based on variable cost incurred. In the second stage of pricing, the fixed costs incurred are included. The sum of these two charges constitutes the transfer price for the product.

10.9.2 Profit Sharing

Under this method, the product is transferred to the marketing department at the standard variable cost. After the product is finally sold, the departments share the profits earned.

10.9.3 Two Sets of Prices

Under this method, revenue is credited to the manufacturing department at the market price and the buying department is charged for the total standard costs. The difference between the outside sales price and the standard costs is charged to the parent company's account. These charges are later eliminated while preparing consolidated financial statements.

10.10 ADMINISTRATION OF TRANSFER PRICING

Implementation of transfer pricing can be successful in an organization which has strong administrative machinery. It involves the following actions:

(i) Negotiation of transfer price
(ii) Arbitration and conflict resolution
(iii) Product classification
(iv) The departments negotiate between them while fixing up the transfer price

Generally, the corporate office does not interfere in the formulation of transfer price. In case there is a dispute in fixing the transfer price, the responsibility for arbitration and conflict resolution rests with the corporate office. Generally, a committee is formed with the responsibility to settle the conflicts regarding fixation of transfer price. In some organizations, products are classified into various categories in order to exercise control over the fixation of transfer price.

10.11 CONCLUSION

A transfer price is the price that is assumed to have been charged by one department of an organization for products and services it provides to another department, in order to calculate each department's profits or losses separately. However, the transfer price does not have any direct impact on the organization's profits as a whole because its effect on one department's revenue is exactly offset by the other department's costs. This chapter explained the various aspects of transfer pricing with examples to understand its concepts and application.

Review Questions

10.1 (a) Define transfer price?

(b) What effect does the transfer pricing have on the profitability of individual departments and the profitability of the company as a whole?

(c) What are the objectives of transfer pricing?

10.2 Discuss the pre-requisites for achieving goal congruence for operation of transfer pricing mechanism?

10.3 Explain various constraints on sourcing in transfer pricing?

10.4 "There are five methods commonly used for calculating transfer prices". Explain each of these methods fully?

10.5 What is meant by international transfer pricing? Explain how MNCs can manipulate their income by use of transfer pricing?

10.6 Write short notes on:

(a) Two step pricing

(b) Negotiation of transfer price

(c) Arbitration and conflict resolution.

11

Reward System

11.1 INTRODUCTION

The reward system is an important mechanism that encourages and motivates managers to achieve objectives. It is meant to induce a high level of individual, group or organizational performance to achieve the overall goals and objectives of the company. Employee output, profitability, cost reduction, level of customer service, etc., form the criteria of reward systems. Rewards provide the right amount of motivation for desired increase in performance. This chapter deals with the needs for and components of reward systems and incentive plans as a major motivational tool for management control. It also discusses the framework or guidelines for resolving the conflicts among employees in an organization.

11.2 NEED FOR REWARD SYSTEMS

Various needs for implementation of reward systems in a company can be enumerated as follows:

(i) To secure participation of individual employees for achieving corporate goal and objectives

(ii) To pay for the contributions of the stakeholders—the customers, shareholders, creditors and the public

(iii) To be a source of communication and feedback

(iv) To create a sense of belonging and to make the employees more committed to the tasks

(v) To boost the morale of workers of the organization

(vi) To ensure payment of suitable reward to those workers in jobs requiring high level of skill and responsibility

The control systems designed for rewards should be based on factors, viz., responsibility, education, skill and physical requirements.

11.3 COMPONENTS OF COMPENSATION PLANS

A manager of an organization has a remuneration package consisting of the following components:

(i) Salary
(ii) Benefits/perks
(iii) Incentives

11.3.1 Salary

Salaries are generally paid each month. These are paid based on factors, e.g., age, qualifications, experience and performance. There are various factors affecting administration of salary:

(i) Remuneration in peer industries
(ii) Company's ability to pay
(iii) Cost of living
(iv) Productivity
(v) Union strategy and pressure
(vi) Government legislation

Salary administration must follow a systematic approach to ensure payment of salary in a logical, equitable and fair manner. In this regard, the objectives of salary administration deserve mention. They are as follows:

- To acquire and retain qualified and competent personnel
- To reinforce desired behaviour and good performance, loyalty, willingness to shoulder additional responsibilities
- To pay employees as per their efforts and merit

11.3.2 Benefits/Perks

The benefits satisfy an employee's economic, social and psychological needs. These include: safety measures, health benefits, pension, perks, etc. The objectives of providing benefits/perks to the employees are as follows:

(i) To boost employee morale
(ii) To improve quality of work environment and work life
(iii) To identify and satisfy the unsatisfied needs
(iv) To create a sense of belonging among employees
(v) To protect health of staffs and employees and ensure their safety

11.3.3 Incentives

The incentive plans are approved by the board of directors of the company and finally get approval of the shareholders in the general meeting before implementation. The incentives are classified into two plans:

(i) Short-term incentive plans
(ii) Long-term incentive plans

Short-term incentive plans

These plans are usually based on the performance of employees in the current year. Here, the bonus is paid in cash. The different methods of short-term incentive plans are:

(i) The total bonus pool
(ii) Carryovers
(iii) Deferred payments

The total bonus pool

It refers to a system wherein shareholders approve on the formula to be used for deciding the total bonus to be paid in a given year. In this connection, several methods under the total bonus pool calculation are mentioned as follows:

(i) Percentage of profits earned
(ii) Percentage of return on capital employed
(iii) Percentage of PBIT–A capital charge on shareholders' equity and long-term debt
(iv) Increase in profitability in the current year as compared to the previous year
(v) Increase in profitability of the company as compared to the industry profitability

It should however, be noted that while calculating bonuses, adjustments are needed to be made in the net income and shareholders' equity.

Carryovers

It refers to an annual carryover of a part of the amount determined by the bonus formula to the bonus pool. The board of directors decides the percentage to be carried every year. This method is flexible as the payment of bonus is not determined by any formula. In good year the management might pay only a portion of the bonus to its employees, but in a poor year it may pay more than the amount eligible by the year's performance by way of drawing from the carryover bonus.

Deferred payments

Under this system, the bonus is calculated annually, but the employees receive the payments over a period of say 3 years. Employees receive only one-third of the bonus in the year in which it is earned. The balance two-thirds is paid equally over the next two years and so on.

Under this system, the employees can estimate their cash income for the coming year. Also it guarantees payment of bonus to the retired employees as the bonus payment is spread out. However, the employees lose the deferred payment, if they leave the company.

Long-term incentive plans

These plans are designed to reward the performance of an employee over a long period. Different types of long-term incentive plans are discussed below:

(i) Stock options
(ii) Stock appreciation rights
(iii) Phantom stock plans
(iv) Performance shares

Stock options

A stock option gives an executive the right to buy a certain number of shares in the company at a fixed price for a certain number of years. The managers, who obtain stock, gain when they sell the stock at a price higher than the price paid for. They can, of course, retain stock even if they leave the company. But they are not allowed to dispose of the stock for a specified period after they acquire it.

Stock appreciation rights

This incentive plan gives the executives the right to receive cash payments based on the increase in value of stock from the time of the award until a specified future date depending on market price.

Phantom stock plans

This plan provides incentives to the executives either in the form of cash or shares. After a specified date, the manager is entitled to receive the amount of fair market value of phantom shares credited to his account. It has two plans like,

(i) Growth plan—In this, an executive receives equal amount of appreciation in the market value of shares;
(ii) Basic plan—In this, an executive receives the original value of the shares as well as the amount appreciated.

Performance shares

Under this incentive plan, employees are awarded a specified number of shares when they meet specific long-term goals. They are given the shares based on performance and are not affected by increase or decrease in stock price. However, this entire plan is measured as per accounting calculation of performance which may not have a bearing on the economic worth of the firm. It should be noted that while calculating bonuses, adjustments are to be made in the net income and the shareholders' equity.

11.4 COMPENSATION TO CEOs

The compensation of CEO of a company is decided after a discussion by the board of directors. The percentage of incentive payment decided by the CEO for his subordinates can be taken as the basis for determining his compensation.

In most cases, CEOs are paid extraordinary bonuses, lavish perks that are not related to the profits of the company. Of late, the exorbitant salaries paid to them have come under scrutiny. The recent scandals in Global Crossing, Xerox, etc., have highlighted this issue. The problem lies not only with the pay packages the CEOs receive, but also with the methods they adopt to raise the stock price up in time to cash in their options.

The family-run organizations in India also pay exceptionally high salaries to their CEOs especially in the manufacturing sector where profits and stock prices have increased continuously.

11.5 INCENTIVES FOR STRATEGIC BUSINESS UNIT (SBU) MANAGERS

Incentives for SBU managers include financial incentives, psychological incentives, and social incentives. Financial incentives are provided in the form of salary, bonus, perks, etc. Psychological and social incentives are provided in terms of promotions, increased power and responsibility, better placement, etc.

11.5.1 Criterion for Providing Incentives

Following are the criterion for incentives to the SBU managers:

(i) Size of bonus
(ii) Cut-off level of bonus payment
(iii) Basis of bonus/incentive payment

Size of bonus

There are two schools of thought on designing the mix between fixed salary and incentive bonus payment to the managers. One school believes that it is important to appoint good managers, pay them well and expect good performance from them. In this type of compensation performance is not related to pay. The other school believes that compensation should be based on performance. So, the emphasis is on incentive bonus payment and not salary. While the first philosophy assures managers' monthly salary, the second philosophy encourages managers to put greater effort and perform to the best of their ability.

Cut-off level of bonus payment

The upper cut-off indicates the level of performance at which maximum bonus can be earned. The lower cut-off indicates the level below which no bonus can be paid.

Basis of bonus/incentive payment

It is important to base bonus/incentive payment upon the performance of each SBU as the decisions and actions of the manager have a direct impact on the performance of that SBU. However, the managers' ability to foster co-operation should also be given due consideration.

11.6 PERFORMANCE VARIABLES

These variables ensure that the reward system is able to match the pay to individual performance, taking into consideration individual competencies, skills and team outputs.

11.6.1 Types of Performance Variables

There are various types of performance variables as follows:

(i) Controllable variables
(ii) Non-controllable variables
(iii) Financial variables
(iv) Non-financial variables
(v) The Balanced Score Card (BSC)
(vi) Feedback

Controllable variables

Managers should be rewarded based on the variables whose values are under their own control and influence.

Non-controllable variables

Some amount of unfairness creeps into the reward system when the managers hold their subordinates accountable for variables that are out of their control.

Financial variables

These variables are usually derived from the accounting system of the organizations. For example, Profit Before Taxes (PBT), Earning Per Share (EPS), Return On Equity (ROE), cash flow, sales, operating profit, etc.

Non-financial variables

These key success factors are cycle time, quality measures, complaints from customers, on-time delivery, etc.

The Balanced Score Card (BSC)

In this rapidly changing world of business, the traditional measures of performance appraisal are insufficient for making decisions. The financial measures alone are inadequate for guiding and evaluating how information age companies create future value through investment in customers, suppliers, employees, technology, process, and innovation. It is now important to take into consideration both financial and non-financial measures of performance. The BSC translates mission and strategy into objectives and measures.

The BSC takes into account financial and non-financial measures, short-term and long-term goals, external goals, internal improvements, past outputs, and on-going requirements, as the indicators of future performance.

Advantages of BSC are enumerated as follows:

(i) BSC acts as a strategic planning and communication device
(ii) It directs managers' attention towards the strategic goals of the organization
(iii) It identifies the links between the lagging and leading indicators of performance
(iv) It helps business managers to measure the value created by the firm for existing and future customers.
(v) It enhances the internal capabilities of managers and the investment in people, systems and procedures in order to improve future performance.

(vi) It reveals the value drivers for superior long term financial and competitive performance.

(vii) It translates a firm's mission and strategy into tangible objectives and measures.

According to Robert Kaplan and David Norton, there are four groups of performance measures, viz. financial, customer, internal, and innovation and learning. The roles and functions of BSC are that it measures performance from the four important perspectives as follows:

(i) Financial perspective that involves the strategy for growth, profitability, and risks viewed from the shareholders' perspective

(ii) Customer perspective that concentrates on creating value and differentiation from that of the competitors

(iii) Internal business perspective that focuses on various strategic priorities for business processes, resulting in customers' and shareholders' satisfaction

(iv) Learning and growth perspective that determines priorities to create a climate that supports organizational change, innovation and growth (see Figure 11.1).

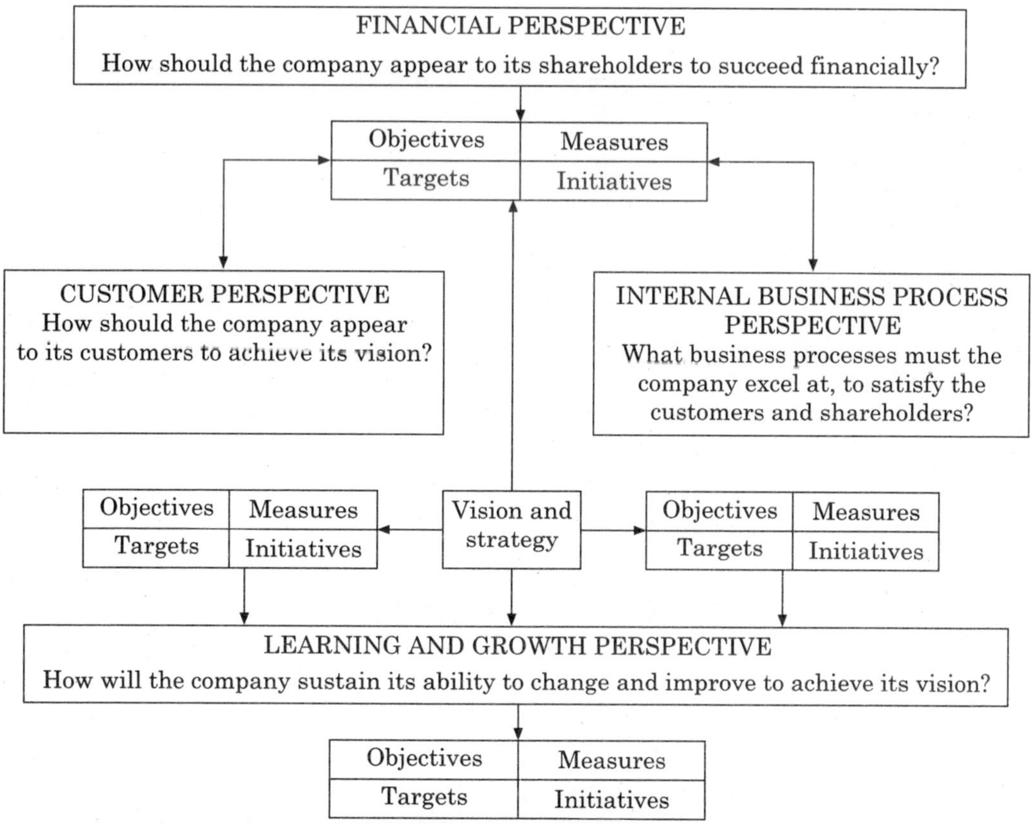

Figure 11.1 Translating Vision and Strategy into Objectives and Measures: Four Perspectives.

Let us discuss these perspectives in some details.

Financial perspective

The BSC recognises the financial perspective, because financial measures are valuable in readily disclosing the economic results of actions already taken by the management. These measures indicate whether a company's strategy and its execution have contributed towards improvement in the bottom-line. Financial objectives are directly related to the profitability of the company, measured in terms of ROCE, ROI, EVA, etc.

Customer perspective

In this perspective, the managers identify the customer and market segments in which the company should compete and the measures of its performance in these targeted segments. The core outcome measures from customer perspective are interpreted in terms of customer satisfaction, customer retention, customer acquisition, customer profitability and market share in targeted segments (Figure 11.2).

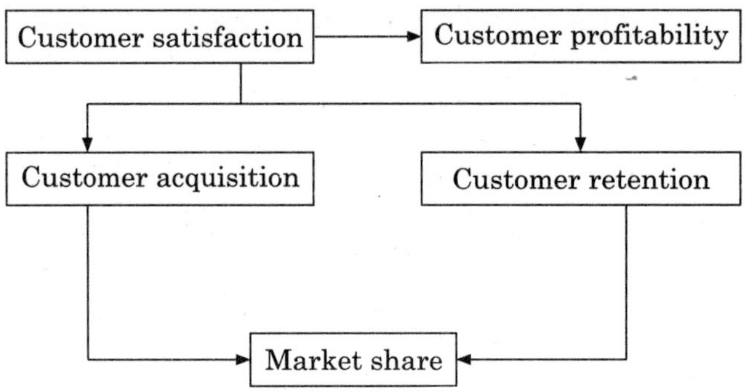

Figure 11.2 Customer Perspective: Core Outcome Measures.

The real strategy of the business is value proposition decided by the management to attract, deliver, and retain customers in the targeted segments. However, a common set of the following attributes that organizes the value proposition in many industries, is observed:

(i) Product and service attributes
(ii) Customer relationship
(iii) Image and reputation of the company

Product and service attributes encompass the functionality of the product/service, its price and quality. Customer relationship attributes include prompt response and delivery of the product/service, customers' opinion of purchasing from the company, etc. Image and reputation attributes enable a company to proactively define itself for its customers.

Internal business process perspective

In this perspective, the managers identify the critical internal processes in which the company should work. Each company has its own generic value chain model to create value for customers and produce financial results. This model takes into account the following core business processes:

(i) Innovation
(ii) Operation
(iii) After-sales service (Figure 11.3).

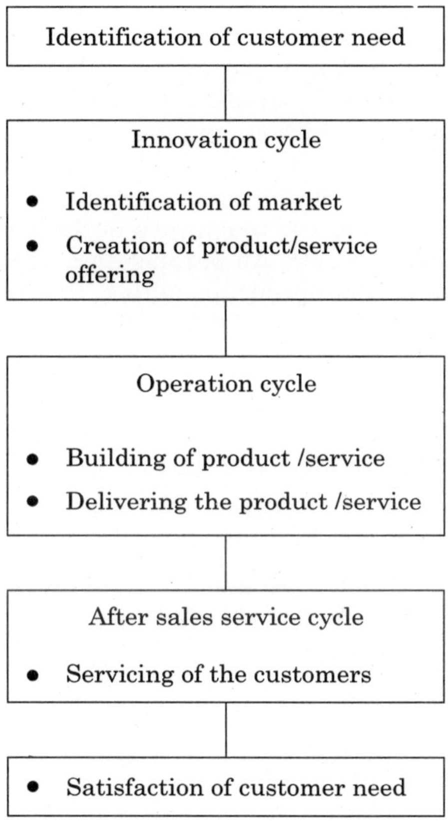

Figure 11.3 Internal Value Chain Model.

The innovation process represents the long wave of value creation in which a company initially identifies and nurtures new markets, new customers, along with the latent needs of the existing customers. The operation process represents the short wave of value creation. It commences with receipt of order from a customer and finish with efficient and timely delivery of the product/service to the customer. The third and final process in the internal value chain is the after-sales service that includes warranty and repair activities, treatment of defects, training programme for customers' employees, etc. The internal business process perspective of BSC incorporates objectives and measures for both long wave innovation cycle and the short wave operation cycle.

Learning and growth perspective

This perspective identifies the infrastructure that a company must build to create long term growth and improvement. As we are aware that organisational growth and learning originate from two sources. They are:

(i) employees

(ii) organisational systems and procedures.

In order to achieve long-term growth and all round improvement a company must invest in training the employees, improving information technology, and aligning with organisational systems and procedures. Here, several generic outcome measures include employee satisfaction, employee retention, employee training, employee skills etc.

BSC plays an important role in strategy implementation and performance measurement. The measures of performance should be accurate, objective and verifiable. It should motivate employees to improve in the key areas of competition, viz. customer satisfaction, productivity, etc. An organization's BSC will be effective, if it is linked with best rewards and appropriate penalties. Rewards and penalties help an employee to understand the expectations of the management and work towards the achievement of the goals.

An effective management control device should have the following attributes:

(i) Performance variables should be linked to the strategic goals

(ii) Goals should be accurate, objective and attainable

To promote positive motivation, management control system should have the following:

(i) Performance measures that are helpful in measuring the managers' actions

(ii) The targets that are challenging but attainable

(iii) Achieving targets should be followed by rewards

Feedback

The most powerful feedback provided by the managers to the employees is: what the organization measures and rewards.

11.7 DESIGN CONSIDERATIONS FOR REWARD SYSTEM

The control system designers assess certain aspects in order to develop efficient reward systems.

11.7.1 Rewards Integrated with Mutually Supportive Systems Model (MSSM)

The MSSM developed by Barnard states that the values of an organization are the effective rewards. They have the ability to produce incentives or disincentives depending on the design and performance variables. Employee participation in decision making and problem solving which is generally highly valued by the employees is considered to be the powerful incentive.

11.7.2 Attainability

Targets for the employees should be challenging, but attainable. Individuals who are highly motivated strive to achieve challenging but attainable targets.

11.7.3 Formal Rewards

The criteria for setting up formal rewards to the employees are as follows:

(i) Definition of goals
(ii) Definition of responsibilities
(iii) Performance measures to be congruent with the goals and objectives of the organization
(iv) Reward system to be competitive and simple

11.7.4 Informal Rewards

Informal rewards are usually meant to satisfy the psychological needs of the employees. These rewards promote self-respect, reinforce the values of the organization and encourage self-learning. Informal rewards lead to improvement in personal expertise and the powerful motivation towards achieving organizational objectives.

11.8 AGENCY THEORY

The shareholders are considered to be the principal, and the CEO is their agent in the organizational set up. At the lower level, the CEO is the principal and the managers of SBUs are agents.

The principals and agents possess divergent preference and objectives. This divergence in preference can be reduced through incentive contracts.

11.8.1 Assumptions of Agency Theory

There are certain assumptions of agency theory, which are as follows:

(i) The financial compensation cannot satisfy the agents. Perks like leisure time, attractive working conditions, flexi-working hours etc. are also needed.
(ii) The managers prefer more wealth to less, but satisfaction decreases with the accumulation of more and more wealth.
(iii) Agents (subordinates) try to avert risk when much of their wealth is dependent upon the company. Owners are 'risk neutral' as they own the shares of the company. The shareholders (owners) are more interested in the expected value of their investment.

11.8.2 Non-observability of Agent's Actions

Certain aspects of non-observability of agent's actions can be highlighted as follows:

Information asymmetry

When the principal (manager) has inadequate information about the activities of the agents (subordinates), he cannot ascertain the agent's contribution to the company's results. This situation is called 'information asymmetry'.

Private information

Sometimes, the agent may have more information than the principal about the task assigned to him. This added information is termed as private information.

Moral hazard

A situation in which the agent misinterprets private information to his principal due to divergence in preference is termed as 'moral hazard'.

11.8.3 Control Mechanisms against Information Asymmetry and Divergent Preference

Following control mechanisms are applied by the principal against information asymmetry and divergent preference of the agents.

Monitoring

The principal can design control systems to monitor the actions of his agents. Monitoring becomes easy when the tasks assigned to the agents are well-defined, and the information used is accurate. For example, auditing of financial statements.

Incentive contracting

These are established to limit divergence in preference. The principal should define the performance measure appropriately to the agents who get motivated to work in the best interest of the principal. Then such contract is said to be goal congruent. The cost of monitoring is termed as 'agency costs'.

11.9 CONFLICT RESOLUTION

Conflicts among the employees are very common in an organization. The management must know how to handle a conflict situation which, at times, may turn out to be a serious problem for the management to resolve at the earliest. In order to resolve the conflicts amicably between the employees and management, the following guidelines or framework may be considered by the management for implementation:

(i) Achieve goal congruence
(ii) Establish accounting and control departments
(iii) Encourage participative management, teamwork, and break up organizational goals into specific tasks
(iv) Involve as many people as possible in the planning process
(v) Adapt an 'information systems approach' rather than an 'overseeing approach' while reporting performance
(vi) Provide 'cross-functional training' to the employees

(vii) Review the mechanisms of control systems regularly on issues such as employee morale, tension, stress, grievances, and employee participation

(viii) Conduct attitude surveys on:

(a) Span of control

(b) Levels in hierarchy and their appropriateness

(c) Ratio of administrative to production personnel

(d) Time span for appraisals

11.10 CONCLUSION

Reward system is an important tool for management control. It is meant to induce a high level of individual, group or organizational performance to achieve the overall goals and objectives of the company. The major components of rewards and incentive plans are: salary, perks/benefits, and incentives. Short-term incentive plans are based on performance of employees in the current year. Long-term incentive plans are based on employees' performances over a long period. As one of the performance variables, the balanced score card can be used for comparing the performances of individual employees within an organization. The various aspects of agency theory and guidelines for conflict resolution have also been explained in this chapter.

REVIEW QUESTIONS

11.1 What do you mean by reward system? What are the criteria for reward system?

11.2 Explain the needs for and components of reward systems and incentive plans as a major motivational tool for management control?

11.3 Discuss fully the various components of compensation plans?

11.4 (a) What is incentive?

(b) What are the criterion for providing incentives to the managers and executives?

(c) Explain the various types of incentive plans?

11.5 Explain in brief, the various types of performance variables?

11.6 What is Balanced Score Card (BSC)? Discuss the concept of BSC?

11.7 "The control system designers assess certain aspects in order to develop efficient reward system in an organization". Explain.

11.8 What is meant by agency theory? Discuss the concept of agency theory?

11.9 What is meant by conflict resolution? Explain the guidelines to be considered by the management for conflict resolution?

11.10 Write short notes on:

(a) Stock options

(b) Phantom stock plans

(c) Deferred payments

(d) Carryovers

(e) Total bonus pool.

12

Management Control of Operations

12.1 INTRODUCTION

Operations management is one of the most important managerial functions. As management control of operations involves working through others, managers should have the right kind of information to understand the different activities which directly or indirectly influence control. This chapter deals with the different types of information and the techniques that are useful in the management control of operations.

12.2 NATURE AND TYPES OF INFORMATION IN CONTROL OF OPERATIONS

The operations managers require information in order to carry out the operations in an organization. Basically, there are two types of information. They are:

(i) Informal information
(ii) Formal information

12.2.1 Informal Information

Information that is received by the managers in the organization is mostly informal in nature. It is obtained through observation, face-to-face conversations, telephonic discussions, and meetings. By walking around, the managers try to understand problems of the workers.

12.2.2 Formal Information

In formal information, the managers rely principally on the formal reports, which include task control information, budget reports, budget signals, internal audit and non-financial information.

Task control information

It constitutes most of the formal information that flows through an organization in its day to day operations. Management control information is nothing, but a summary of task control information. The advancement and use of technology has made it possible for managers to acquire daily information.

Budget reports

A budget report serves as an important guide for the manager. The manager is expected to operate according to the budget to get a clear idea of the financial position of the responsibility centre.

Budget signals

Budget signals help the operations manager to determine the amount of money which needs to be spent on various activities. Though the expenses are stated in the budget, the manager should decide the amount that has to be spent on each activity based on the requirement of the department.

Internal audit

All good corporate houses have their own internal audit department. The internal audit reports help detect the manipulative behaviour of employees. The audit committee ensures that appropriate action is taken by the management on internal audit reports and that there are adequate and effective internal control systems to minimize the fraud and malpractices.

Non-financial information

In order to make management control systems effective in control of operations, non-financial information is also needed. It shows the means to achieve the end result of performance in an organization. It is observed that non-financial measures are provided greater importance at the lower levels of organizational hierarchy and the financial measures are given greater emphasis at the higher levels of management structure.

12.3 JUST-IN-TIME (JIT) TECHNIQUE

Just-In-Time (JIT) technique is a Japanese philosophy developed by Taichi Okno. It is used for managing all types of inventory, purchase, and production functions in an organization. The main purpose of this philosophy is to reduce inefficiency and unproductive time and cost in the production process.

Evaluation

(i) It reduces buffer inventory
(ii) It decreases set-up costs

(iii) It decreases procurement costs
(iv) It provides good relationship with customers

12.3.1 Implications of JIT for Management Control

JIT has some implications for management control which are mentioned as follows:

(i) JIT system disregards WIP inventory in the company because inventories exist only for raw materials and finished goods. Therefore, the system reduces record keeping considerably.

(ii) It focuses management attention on time. A reduction in cycle time may result in reduction of costs.

(iii) The progress of JIT system can be effectively monitored by application of the following ratio:

$$\frac{\text{Processing time}}{\text{Cycle time}} = 1$$

The JIT system is an evolutionary system which improves the manufacturing process continuously. The management can establish targets and monitor progress against the targets.

12.4 TOTAL QUALITY MANAGEMENT (TQM)

TQM is a management concept that directs the collective efforts of all employees and officers towards satisfying customer expectations by continuously improving the operations management processes and products.

TQM emphasizes three important aspects. They are as follows:

(i) Customer satisfaction
(ii) Employee involvement
(iii) Quality improvement

The TQM emphasizes manufacturing products with zero defects. Emphasis is also given on detecting the problems at the initial stage as the earlier a defect is detected, the lower will be the cost penalty.

12.4.1 Total Quality Management Approach (TQM approach)

There are three approaches to TQM. They are as follows:

(i) Quality responsibility
(ii) Product design
(iii) Relationship with suppliers

Quality responsibility

The responsibility for quality should be shared by all departments, as quality assurance is the responsibility of every single department, and of the management as well. Therefore, management must foster an environment for detecting and solving quality problems. This can be avoided by identifying the errors at an early stage. Employees in every department should ensure that they do not pass on a defective product to the next stage of production. The TQM approach, thus, emphasizes ensuring quality when the product is being manufactured rather than inspecting it for quality after it has been produced.

Product design

Under TQM approach there is an effort to coordinate the activities of designers and the production engineers/managers. While designing a product, the customer preference should be given due importance.

Relationship with suppliers

In TQM approach, the supplier is selected not just based on the lowest price but also on quality, and timely delivery of the product. So, one or two suppliers are selected and a long-term relationship is set up with them.

12.4.2 TQM Implications for Management Control

For management control system to be effective in an organization, two implications of TQM deserve mention. They are as follows:

- (i) Financial measures
- (ii) Non-financial measures

Financial measures

The total cost of quality for a firm is the sum total of four costs. They are as follows:

- (i) Preventive costs, e.g., inspection, preventive maintenance, etc.
- (ii) Appraisal costs, e.g., design analysis costs, etc.
- (iii) External failure costs, e.g., cost of returns, repair costs, etc.
- (iv) Internal failure costs, e.g., yield loss, rework costs, etc.

Non-financial measures

These measures relate to collection of non-financial information about:

- (i) Number of defective units delivered by each supplier
- (ii) Number and frequency of late deliveries
- (iii) Number of customer complaints received
- (iv) Machine breakdowns occurred
- (v) Number and frequency of product returns

The non-financial measures are important to provide continuous feedback to the managers and workers for improved quality.

12.5 COMPUTER AIDED MANUFACTURING PROCESS

It is a complete process whereby the product design and engineering, planning, and manufacturing are all integrated by the help of advanced computer systems.

Costly and technologically advanced computers are used to integrate different stages of production, whereby manufacturing operations are scheduled automatically, and availability of manpower is monitored by the systems. The systems send instructions to various workstations through computer screens.

12.5.1 Implications of Computer Aided Manufacturing for Management Control

(i) Operations managers are relieved from day-to-day supervision of the performance of their workers.

(ii) The information provided by the computers is authentic and accurate to the management for actions.

(iii) Employees are rewarded based on their work performance in terms of quantity and quality.

12.6 DECISION SUPPORT SYSTEMS

These systems aid decision making by providing the answers to a series of questions. These are so called because they help the decision-maker to arrive at a decision.

12.6.1 Implications of Decision Support System for Management Control

(i) They can increase the quality decisions and reduce the time required to take decisions.

(ii) They permit many decisions to be made by computer or by lower level personnel.

12.7 CONCLUSION

Operations management is one of the most important managerial functions. Management control of operations involves working through others. Two types of information, informal and formal, are required by the managers to understand the different activities which influence control. Formal information includes task control information, budget reports, budget signals, internal audit, and non-financial information. This chapter also examined the various techniques viz. JIT, TQM, computer aided manufacturing, and decision support systems and their implications which are useful in the management control of operations.

REVIEW QUESTIONS

12.1 What is operations management? Explain the nature and types of information required by the management to carry out operations in an organization?

12.2 What is Just-In-Time (JIT) technique? State how JIT can assist management as an aid to management control?

12.3 Explain the various concepts of TQM and their implications for management control?

12.4 What is computer aided manufacturing process? Discuss the implications of computer aided manufacturing for management control?

12.5 State the implications of decision support system for management control?

Part IV

Strategic Cost Management

13

Strategic Cost Management and Continuous Process Improvement

13.1 INTRODUCTION

In the present era of competition, an organization has to offer quality products and services at a reasonable or lower cost to the customers in order to survive in the market place. Therefore, the companies have started using cost management as a strategic tool of management control process. The focus of cost management has now shifted from product costing and financial reporting to the development of cost information to help management achieve strategic goals and objectives.

This chapter deals with two broad aspects of management strategy and control separately. The first part discusses the strategic cost management and the second part explains various methods in vogue for continuous process improvement in an organization.

13.2 STRATEGIC COST MANAGEMENT (SCM)

Strategic Cost Management (SCM) is defined as the application of costing information to the development and implementation of a company's strategy. Rapid changes in the business environment and corresponding changes in product and manufacturing processes have forced the organizations to adopt a more proactive and strategic approach towards costing. They realized that costing system should be flexible enough to support changes in the business environment and help management take better strategic decisions and control.

13.2.1 Processes of Strategic Cost Management (SCM)

There are three processes of strategic cost management. They are:

(i) Value chain analysis
(ii) Cost driver analysis
(iii) Strategic positioning analysis

Value chain analysis

Value chain is the linked set of value-creating activities from the basic raw material sources from suppliers to the ultimate end-use product delivered into the final customers' hands. Each company should be understood in the context of the overall value chain of value-creating activities. Value chain requires an external focus. Value chain analysis is a tool of strategic analysis that can be used to identify areas in which value can be enhanced for customers or costs can be reduced. It helps an organization to gain competitive advantage. It is centered around a product or service and discharges all the activities necessary to achieve competitive advantage.

Value chain analysis is essential to determine exactly where, in the chain, customer value can be enhanced or costs can be lowered. The value chain concept highlights four profit improvement areas as follows:

(i) Linkage with suppliers
(ii) Linkage with customers
(iii) Process linkage within the value chain of a company
(iv) Linkage across business unit value chain within the company

Value chain analysis involves following three distinct activities:

(i) Identify value chain activities
(ii) Identify the cost driver(s) at each value activity
(iii) Develop a competitive advantage by reducing cost or adding value

In the initial stage, all the activities should be identified and differentiated from other activities so that they can be regarded as separate business activities. In the second stage, those activities that have potential for cost reduction are identified. In the final stage, the companies conduct a detailed study of the value activities and cost drivers to determine the nature of current and potential competitive advantage. The analysis of value activities enables the company to identify areas in which the company can provide greater value.

Cost driver analysis

It is a useful technique which integrates the problem-solving and analytical tools for quality and process improvement. It generates information needed to reduce costs and improve the overall financial performance of the organization.

Cost drivers are of two types—structural cost drivers and executional cost drivers.

Structural cost drivers: There are five structural cost drivers. They are scale, scope, experience, complexity, and technology.

Executional cost drivers: Executional cost drivers are those drivers that determine a company's ability to execute value activities. The basic executional cost drivers are commitment of workforce to continuous improvement; management's attitudes towards quality; cycle time for getting new products into the market; utilization of existing capacity; proper design of internal business processes; and management's ability to work efficiently with the suppliers and customers to reduce costs.

Strategic positioning analysis

It refers to the way in which an organization positions itself against the competitors in the market. A company can choose to compete in the market either on the basis of cost leadership or differentiation. It means that in order to remain competitive, a company has to offer its products either at a lower cost or with a greater number of features.

Cost leadership strategy

If a company produces its products or services at a cost lower than its competitors, then the company is said to be following a cost leadership strategy for gaining competitive advantage.

An organization can adopt a cost leadership strategy only when its productivity is high and its manufacturing processes run smoothly. Its administrative expenses and selling and distribution costs must be low and minimum.

The primary focus of the low-cost strategy is to achieve low cost relative to competitors, viz. tight control of cost, cost reduction, etc. Examples of companies following low-cost strategy are: Nirma in detergents, Times in wrist watches, etc.

Differentiation strategy

The differentiation strategy consists in differentiating the product by creating something unique. Product differentiation can be achieved through the following:

(i) Brand loyalty
(ii) Superior customer service
(iii) Dealer network
(iv) Product design and features

Examples of companies following differentiation strategy are: HUL in detergents, Wipro in computers, Titan for wrist watches.

The companies which adopt a differentiation strategy try to make their customers feel that their products are different, qualitatively superior and have a greater number of features than their competitors' products. Most companies in the automobile, telecom, consumer electronic sectors use a differentiation strategy for their customers.

13.2.2 Methods of Strategic Cost Management

There are various methods or techniques used by the management along with the strategic management tools. They are as follows:

(i) Target costing
(ii) Activity based costing
(iii) Quality costing
(iv) Life cycle costing

Target costing

Target cost is the maximum manufacturing cost of a product. Target costing is done to encourage various design and production departments to find less expensive ways of achieving similar or better features and quality of product. It is decided after analyzing market, assessing customer requirements, determining elasticity of demand and analyzing cost-volume-profit relationships.

There are three phases followed in target costing. They are: planning phase, development phase, and production phase.

Planning phase: Before establishing a reasonable target cost, a market research is conducted by the organization to determine what the competitors are doing. Their products are analyzed with regard to price, service and support, promotion, work culture, and technology. Thereafter, the researcher should determine the significance of various features of the product to find out a 'niche' market.

Development phase: The company identifies the cost associated with the best possible design as per internal cost structure of the company. It tries to reduce internal costs and compares it with the competitors' cost structure. The designers, manufacturers, marketers, and engineers conduct a brainstorming session to generate ideas to substantially reduce costs or to add different features into the product without increasing target costs.

Production phase: Target costing becomes a tool for reducing costs of existing products if production is carried out with perfect planning and optimal cost-effective processes. It ensures less expensive means of production.

Benefits of target costing are as follows:

(a) It provides detailed information on costs involved in production of new product.
(b) It reduces the development cycle of a product by reducing wastage of time and resources.
(c) It provides an excellent understanding of the dynamics of production costs and simplifies the production process and costing procedure.
(d) It increases profitability of new products and reduces manufacturing costs and improves product quality.
(e) It forecasts the future costs and motivates the management to meet that goal.
(f) It inculcates a sense of continuous process improvement and promotes competitiveness in the long run.

Activity Based Costing (ABC)

Activity Based Costing (ABC) is a system that focuses on activities as the fundamental cost objects and uses the cost of these activities for compiling the costs of products and other cost objects. The product cost is built up from the cost of the specific activities undertaken to manufacture it.

In ABC, allocation of overhead cost to products is done based on activities involved rather than on a single application base such as machine hour or direct labour hour.

Allocating overhead cost to production based on a single cost driver (allocation base) can result in an unrealistic product cost because the traditional system fails to capture cause-and-effect relationship. In order to manage activities better and to make wiser economic decisions, managers need to identify the relationship of causes (activities) and effects (costs) in a more detailed and accurate manner.

ABC focuses on this aspect as activities drive costs. ABC is valuable for planning process and leads to better performance measurement in an organization.

There are three major kinds of activities in the organizations. They are as follows:

(i) Unit level activities
(ii) Batch level activities
(iii) Product sustaining activities

The above major activities drive costs or expenses which can be classified as costs at the unit level, costs at the batch or production run level, and product sustaining costs. The activities are categorised in Table 13.1.

Table 13.1 The activity related product costs

Product Line		
Unit level activities (Cost varying with units)	**Batch level activities (Cost varying with number of batches)**	**Product sustaining activities (Cost varying with product line)**
Materials	Set-ups	Production specification
Energy	Inspection	Product enhancement
Machine hours	Purchase orders	Process engineering
Labour hours	Material movements	Customer satisfaction

Profs. Robin Cooper and Robert S. Kaplan explained ABC as a resource usage model. Table 13.2 depicts resource usage model.

Table 13.2 Resource usage model

Resources–Activities–Costs Relationship Model		
Resources	Create	Activities
Activities	Drive	Costs/Expenses (Measure of consumption of resources)

ABC focuses on the important distinction between measuring the costs of resources supplied and the costs of resources used in terms of activity. Some resources are used as needed, e.g., materials, power, temporary daily labour, etc. The costs of supplying such resources are referred to as variable costs. There are other resources which are supplied in advance of usage, e.g. land and building, plant and machinery, employees, etc. The costs of such resources are independent of how much they are used.

In ABC system, short-term contribution is measured as:

Revenues – Cost of resources acquired as needed.

The remaining operating expenses represent resources that have been acquired prior to actual usage. The costs of such resources are unaffected by actual activity levels during the period.

Example 1

ABC Income Statement

Particulars			₹	₹
Sales				40000
Less: Expenses of resources supplied as used:				
Material			15200	
Energy			1200	
Short-term contract labour			1800	18200
Contribution				21800
Less: Activity expenses: committed resources:				
	Used (₹)	Unused (₹)		
Permanent direct labour	2800	400		
Machine run–time	6400			
Purchasing	1400	200		
Receiving inventory	900	100		
Production run	2000	200		
Administration	1400	400		
Engineering changes	1500			
Others	1500	300		
	17900	1600		19500
Operating profit				2300

Ascertainment of full product costs under ABC

In ABC, multiple activities in an organization are identified in the production processes that are associated with the costs. The events within these activities that cause costs are called cost-drivers. Examples: Machine set-ups, material handling, machinery, assembling, etc.

Multiple cost-drivers (a cost-driver is an allocation base) should be selected keeping in view the major activities of the firm and how each item of cost is linked up with these activities at different levels. Costs incurred at the batch level and those incurred for product sustaining level need to be allocated.

Steps for application of costs to product under ABC system are as follows:

(i) Identify activities involved in the manufacture of a product line
(ii) Identify cost of each activity
(iii) Identify cost-driver of each activity
(iv) Choose the primary cost-driver as the allocation base for each activity
(v) Apply the costs to the product

Example 2

A company furnishes the following information:

Manufacturing activities	Cost of activity (₹)
Material handling	8000
Machining	5000
Assembling	4800
Inspecting	1400

The cost-drivers chosen by the company as an application base are:

(i) Number of parts = 80000 for material handling
(ii) Machine hours = 250 for the purpose of machining
(iii) Number of parts = 8000 for assembling activities
(iv) Number of finished units = 1000 for inspection job

The cost of direct materials of a product is ₹ 100. The power cost per unit of finished product is ₹ 10. Each product uses 8 units of materials, one-fourth machine hour and 8 assembly parts.

Find out the total manufacturing cost per unit of finished product?

Also find out the full cost of the product if the unit cost of upstream activities (say, product design) and the downstream activities (say, marketing, customer service, etc.) are assumed to be ₹ 10 and ₹ 22 per unit, respectively?

Solution:

Let us first find out cost per unit of cost-driver (application base).

Manufacturing activity	Cost of activity (₹)	Cost-drivers (Application base)	Cost per unit of application base (₹)
Material handling	8000	Number of parts (80000)	0.10
Machining	5000	Machine hours (250)	20.00
Assembling	4800	Number of parts (8000)	0.60
Inspecting	1400	Number of finished units (1000)	1.40

Calculation of manufacturing cost

Particulars	₹	Amount (₹)/unit
Direct material		100.00
Cost of power		10.00
Other costs:		
Material handling (8 parts × ₹ 0.10)	0.80	
Machining (1/4 × ₹ 20)	5.00	
Assembling (8 parts × ₹ 0.60)	4.80	
Inspecting (1 finished unit × ₹ 1.40)	1.40	12.00
Total manufacturing cost per unit		122.00

Calculation of full product cost

Particulars	Amount (₹)/unit
Upstream activities (product design) cost	10.00
Manufacturing cost	122.00
Downstream activities (marketing, customer service) cost	22.00
Full product cost per unit	154.00

Quality costing

It is a system which monitors and accumulates the costs incurred by a firm in maintaining or improving product quality. The quality costs deal with the costs associated with the quality of conformance rather than the quality of design. Quality of design refers to the variations in products having same functional use. Quality of conformance refers to the degree with which the final product meets its specifications. It refers to the product's fitness for use. Thus, higher quality may mean lower total costs when quality of conformance is considered.

Classification of costs associated with quality of conformance

(i) Prevention costs
(ii) Appraisal costs
(iii) Internal failure costs
(iv) External failure costs

Prevention costs are the costs incurred to reduce the number of defective units produced or the incidence of poor quality service. For example, design and engineering cost of the product.

Appraisal costs are the costs incurred to ensure that materials, products, and services meet quality standards. Example: cost of inspection of raw material received from vendors, cost of quality audits and reliability tests, etc.

Internal failure costs are associated with materials and products that fail to meet quality standards and result in manufacturing losses. These defects are identified before they are sent to customers. For example, costs of spoiled units, cost of analyzing, investigating and reworking defects.

External failure costs are the costs incurred when inferior quality products or services are sold to customers. Example: cost of repairs, replacement, or product recall.

The desired level of product quality occurs when the costs of prevention, appraisal and failure are minimized. The magnitude of quality costs has prompted many companies to install quality costing systems to monitor and help reduce the costs of achieving high quality production.

Total Quality Control (TQC): TQC is a management process based on the premise that quality costs are minimized with zero defects. The reduction of failure costs due to improved quality outweighs additional prevention and appraisal costs.

Table 13.3 Format of quality cost report

Particulars	Current month cost (₹)	% of total
Prevention costs:		
Quality training		
Reliability engineering		
Pilot studies		
Systems development		
Total prevention costs		
Appraisal costs:		
Material inspection		
Supplies inspection		
Reliability testing		
Laboratory		
Total appraisal costs		
Internal failure costs:		
Scrap		
Repair		
Re-work		
Down time		
Total internal failure costs		
External failure costs:		
Warranty cost		
Repair and replacement		
Customer complaint		
Product liability		
Transportation losses		
Total external failure costs		
Total quality costs		

TQC begins with the design and engineering of the product. It is often associated with Just-In-Time (JIT) manufacturing. Under JIT, each worker is trained to be a quality inspector. Total quality control is referred to as Total Quality Management (TQM). Further discussion on TQM has been made in Chapters 3 and 12.

Life cycle costing

It is defined as the accumulation of costs for activities that occur over the entire life cycle of a product from inception to abandonment by the manufacturing organization and the customers. It provides a framework for managing the cost and performance of a product over duration of its life.

The life cycle begins with initial identification of a consumer need and extends through planning, research, design, development, production, evaluation, use, logistic support in operation and disposal. Life cycle is important to cost control due to the interdependencies of activities in different time periods. Life cycle costing and reporting provide management with a better picture of product profitability and help managers to understand their planning activities.

(a) **Product life cycle costing:** The cycle begins with identification of new consumer needs and the invention of a new product and is often followed by further development to make it saleable. This is followed by a rapid expansion in its sales. Then competitors enter the field with rival products and therefore, the distinctiveness of new product starts diminishing. The innovation of a new product and its degeneration into a common product is termed as the life cycle of a product.

(b) **Characteristics of product life cycle:** The characteristics of product life cycle can be enumerated as follows:

- The products have finite life and pass through the cycle of development, introduction, growth, maturity, decline and deletion or withdrawal
- Profitability first appear during the growth phase and after stabilizing during the maturity phase, decline thereafter to the point of deletion
- Per unit profit varies as the product move through their life cycle
- Each phase of the cycle possess different threats and opportunities

(c) **Activities in product life cycle:** There are various activities in product life cycle. They are as follows:

- Market research
- Specification
- Design
- Prototype manufacture
- Development of the product
- Tooling
- Manufacturing
- Selling
- Distribution
- Product support by way of after-sales service
- Replacement

(d) **Phases in product life cycle:** Phases in product life cycle can be explained as follows:

Phases	Effect
Introduction phase	Promotional cost high, sales revenue low and negative profit
Growth phase	Product penetration in the market, increased sales and profits
Maturity phase	Continued sales growth but at a diminishing rate, emergence of competitors with substitute products

Phases	Effect
Saturation phase	Pressure of new products in the market, decrease in sales and profit
Decline phase	Declining sales due to technological advancement, change of fashion and tastes of the customers, economic, technological and social change

(e) **Turning points indices in product life cycle:** The turning points of the life cycle of a product can be observed from the following indices:

- Market saturation
- Nature of competition
- Alternative products and technologies

(f) **Project life cycle costing:** It is the cost associated with acquiring, using, caring for and disposing of physical assets, including the feasibility studies, research design, development, production, maintenance, replacement and disposal, as well as support, training, operating costs generated by the acquisition, use, maintenance and replacement of permanent physical assets by an organization.

(g) **Elements of project costs over its life cycle:** There are various elements of project costs over its life cycle. They are as follows:

- Acquisition costs including cost of research, design, testing, production, construction or purchase of capital asset;
- Transportation and handling cost of capital asset;
- Maintenance cost of capital asset;
- Operation cost including engineering cost, utility cost;
- Training cost;
- Inventory cost;
- Cost of technical data collection;
- Disposal cost at the end of the life of the capital asset.

(h) **Uses of project life cycle costing:** The life cycle costing can be used in various types of projects, e.g.,

- Projects operating in capital intensive industries;
- Projects having a sizeable, on-going construction program;
- Projects dependent on expensive plants;
- Expansion projects;
- Projects incorporating expensive new technology, etc.

13.3 CONTINUOUS PROCESS IMPROVEMENT (CPI)

Continuous process improvement is the philosophy of doing business in such a way that every member of the organization is encouraged to strive and serve the customers efficiently.

The objectives of continuous process improvement can be enumerated as follows:

(i) To sustain continuous improvement within the company and align improvement activities with strategic objectives through continuous modification in all processes.
(ii) To achieve complete customer satisfaction as also to reduce costs.
(iii) To increase product quality while maintaining the schedules.

13.3.1 Methods of Process Improvement

There are three methods by which process improvement can be made in an organization. They are:

(i) Benchmarking
(ii) Bench trending
(iii) Process quality teaming

Benchmarking

Benchmarking is a continuous process of comparing products and operations against the best practices in the industry. It consists of the following four sub-processes:

(i) Planning the variables to be benchmarked
(ii) Analyzing the current and projected gap in performance
(iii) Communicating the benchmark standards to operating personnel
(iv) Developing the implementation plans

All these processes are accomplished by the management in two phases: planning phase, and analysis phase.

The process under the planning phase is to identify those companies whose performance constitutes the best practices for a product or service to be benchmarked, through internal and external sources, professionals, libraries, journals, consultants, etc. The next phase, i.e. analysis phase is to analyze the current gap in performance between the current internal operations and the best practices. This analysis provides useful information to the management about the gaps in competitiveness for an operation or process while conducting the study. A format of general benchmarking process is given in Appendix V.

Bench trending

The bench trending includes a projection of the critical market conditions and the consumer preference variables. It identifies consumer preference, new entrants, innovation threats and other market critical variables for long run success of the organization. It involves identifying important trends and evaluating their impact in order to meet future contingencies.

The following steps are followed while applying bench trending by the management:

(a) Determination of the market—its size, customer preference, competitors, etc.
(b) Assessment of industry direction, technology shifts, geopolitical changes, potential threats, from outside sources
(c) Determination of strong, current, and potential competitors by evaluating the trends in the industry
(d) Collection of information on performance of competitors and comparison of current and future performance of the organization with its competitors
(e) Setting up of a performance base line for the company
(f) Identification of a set of initiatives to maintain strengths of the organization

Process bench trending: The process bench trending is used when a company wants to improve a specific function or process.

Following steps are followed by the management in the process bench trending:

- Understanding the requirements of the process to be bench trended
- Understanding the process flow charts, procedures and quality control parameters
- Identifying and evaluating the specific objectives of the bench trending project
- Identifying the bench trending methods to be adopted by the different competitor companies
- Choosing the practices best-suited to the organization
- Determining specific process gaps

The concept of benchmarking and bench trending should be explained to all employees so that they get motivated. Informal networks should be established to share the examples of success, discuss problems, and provide assistance in attaining goals. In the implementation phase, action plans are designed by the management to attain the desired goals. Teams are formed and responsibilities are assigned, tasks are specified and sequenced, resources are allocated and results are monitored by the managers.

Process quality teaming

It is a popular concept which combines several successful total quality techniques into a cybernetic control system with features like, feedback loops, action plans, and environmental scanning. This method is effective in improving organizational yields as long as customers and suppliers are satisfied with the management.

A format of quality process teaming structure is shown in Appendix VI.

(a) **The control loop:** The control loop involves the following activities of the management:
    - Sense the environment – either the customer or the current yields
    - Detect the gap between expectations and results
    - Perform an analysis to determine appropriate action
    - Take actions
    - Return to step one, by sensing the customer needs or observing the yields

This cycle is repeated several times and each time an improvement results. This concept can be applied by the managers to almost any service, production or support process.

The steps for implementation of process quality teaming can be enumerated as follows:

(i) The management selects a unit, viz. a manufacturing department within which a quality improvement team is formed, the output to be improved is determined and the inputs are processed.

(ii) A team of personnel from all key departments is formed

(iii) The responsibility of each department is clarified and assigned to the production supervisors and workers

(b) Closed-loop corrective action system: Various activities to be performed by the management under this system are as follows:

- Make a flow chart of the process, and critical control parameters and associated measurements are to be noted at every step.
- Establish appropriate process control limits for each step in the process.
- Run the process and calculate the output after completion of major steps.
- Perform a cause and effect analysis of the major problems, and determine a specific corrective action.

The implementation of continuous process improvement methods may be complex. Therefore, management should have a good understanding of the total improvement, a support culture, and abundant personnel support.

13.4 CONCLUSION

Strategic Cost Management (SCM) is the application of costing information to the development and implementation of a company's strategy. Three processes of SCM are value chain analysis, cost driver analysis, and strategic positioning analysis. Value chain analysis is a tool of strategic analysis that can be used to identify areas in which value can be enhanced for customers or costs can be reduced. Cost driver analysis integrates the problem-solving and analytical tools for quality and process improvement. Strategic positioning analysis refers to the way in which an organization positions itself against the competitors in the market. Various methods of SCM are target costing, activity based costing, quality costing, and life cycle costing and their implications have been dealt with in this chapter.

Continuous Process Improvement (CPI) is the philosophy of doing business in such a way that every member of the organization is encouraged to strive and serve the customers efficiently. Different methods of process improvement viz., benchmarking, bench trending, and process quality teaming and their effectiveness on process improvement have been discussed in this chapter. However, as both SCM and CPI methods are intertwined, therefore SCM cannot be effective in an organization without the support of various process improvement methods in a continuous manner.

REVIEW QUESTIONS

13.1 Define Strategic Cost Management (SCM)? Discuss the processes of SCM?

13.2 What is value chain analysis? Explain the concept of value chain analysis?

13.3 What is cost driver analysis? Discuss its concepts?

13.4 What is strategic positioning analysis? Explain the various aspects of strategic positioning analysis?

13.5 (a) Define target costing?

(b) Examine the various phases in target costing followed by the management?

(c) What benefits are derived by the management from target costing?

13.6 What do you understand by Activity Based Costing (ABC)? Discuss the various aspects of activity based costing?

13.7 What is meant by quality costing? Explain the various types of costs associated with quality of performance?

13.8 "The life cycle begins with initial identification of a consumer need and extends through planning, research, design, development, production, evaluation, use, logistic support in operation and disposal". Justify the statement critically.

13.9 Explain the various phases in product life cycle?

13.10 What is project life cycle costing? Explain the elements and uses of project life cycle costing?

13.11 What is meant by Continuous Process Improvement (CPI)? Discuss the various methods of process improvement used in an organization?

13.12 Write short notes on:

(a) Benchmarking

(b) Bench trending

(c) Process quality teaming.

14

Marginal Costing

14.1 INTRODUCTION

In the present age of competition every organization has to strive hard for survival and growth. Gone are those days when the organizations use to enjoy monopoly for their products in the market place. In those days they use to dictate the selling price and the customers had no other alternative but to pay the same in the sellers' market. In the opening up of the economy and global competition the situation has now completely changed. The organizations can no longer dictate the market and the products manufactured by various companies are at present sold at competitive prices. In such buyers' market, the management of companies have realized that if they are to survive and maintain their profitability and market share, they have to analyze, and control the cost of production which is in their domain, and offer the quality products at competitive price.

In this chapter, we discuss the concept of marginal costing and cost-volume-profit analysis to form a basis or platform for better appreciation of the concept on managerial decision-making discussed in the next chapter.

14.2 MARGINAL COSTING AND ITS RELATED ISSUES

Before we discuss about marginal costing, it will be prudent for us to know about the meaning of marginal cost. Marginal cost is the cost that is incurred in producing one additional unit. Marginal cost is thus equal to variable cost. In accounting language, it is equal to the amount by which total costs change for producing one additional unit. Let us take an example.

Suppose the cost of producing 100 units of a product is ₹ 5000. If 101 units are produced the total costs increase to ₹ 5550. Therefore, marginal cost for producing 101th unit or 1 additional unit is ₹ 5550 – 5000 = ₹ 550. The same logic applies to the fact that if 99 units are produced, total costs will be ₹ 4450, i.e. ₹ 5000 – 4450 = ₹ 550. So, marginal cost or variable cost in this case is ₹ 550.

What is Marginal Costing?

It is a technique of ascertaining cost used by the management in any particular method of costing. Under this technique, all costs are classified into two groups:

(i) Fixed costs

(ii) Variable costs

Variable costs such as, direct materials, direct labour, direct expenses can be ascertained. These costs tend to be a constant amount per unit. Semi variable items of expenses should be segregated into variable and fixed elements and be included in the respective groups. Fixed costs tend to remain fixed or constant irrespective of the volume of output or activity. Fixed costs are considered as period costs and the variable costs as product costs.

Let us take another example to bring in clarity in understanding.

Suppose the material cost and labour cost for manufacture of a unit of product are ₹ 5 and ₹ 3, respectively. The cost of producing 100 units will be:

Material cost = 100 × 5 = ₹ 500 and Labour cost = 100 × 3 = ₹ 300.

If 200 units are produced, the material and labour cost will be double. It is evident that material and labour cost vary or change directly proportionate to the volume of production. Hence, these are called variable costs.

There are costs, which are not directly proportionate to the volume of output, for example, salary paid to the works manager, factory rent, or depreciation on plant and machinery, etc. The said costs remain fixed irrespective of the volume of production, i.e. 100 or 200 or more. Therefore, the costs which are not directly proportionate to the volume of production are called fixed costs.

Marginal cost is equal to the variable cost. Marginal costing is the technique that deals with marginal cost.

14.2.1 Concept of Profit

Profit is expressed by the management as gross margin or contribution and net margin or net profit. Contribution or gross margin is the difference between sales value and the variable costs.

$$\text{Contribution (C)} = \text{Sales (S)} - \text{Variable costs (V)}.$$

$$\text{Net margin} = \text{Contribution (C)} - \text{Total fixed costs (F)}$$

14.2.2 Profit/Volume Ratio (P/V Ratio)

The profit/volume ratio expresses the relation of contribution to sales $\left(\frac{C}{S}\right)$.

$$\frac{P}{V} \text{ ratio or } \frac{C}{S} \text{ ratio} = \frac{\text{Contribution (C)}}{\text{Sales (S)}} = \left(\frac{S-V}{S}\right)$$

$$= \frac{\text{Change in contribution}}{\text{Change in sales}}$$

$$= \frac{\text{Change in profit (or loss)}}{\text{Change in sales}}$$

An improvement of $\frac{P}{V}$ ratio would mean increase in the gap between sales and variable costs. This can be done by the management by way of:

(i) Increasing selling price
(ii) Reducing variable costs
(iii) Changing sales mix, i.e. substitution of a product with low $\frac{P}{V}$ ratio by a product with high $\frac{P}{V}$ ratio.

14.2.3 Break Even Chart (BEC)

It is the chart which shows the profit or loss of a firm at various levels of activity. It indicates the point at which neither profit nor loss is made [see Figures 14.1(a) and (b)]. A BEC shows the following information to the management at various levels of activity:

(i) Variable costs, fixed costs, and total costs
(ii) Sales value
(iii) Profit or loss
(iv) Break even point, i.e. the point at which total costs equals sales, or break even with sales. This is the activity point at which neither profit nor loss is incurred by the firm
(v) Margin of safety

Assumptions for making BEC

Following assumptions are made for making a Break Even Chart (BEC):

(i) Fixed costs will tend to remain constant.
(ii) Price of variable cost factors, i.e. price of raw material, labour rate etc. will remain unchanged so that variable costs are truly variable.
(iii) Semi-variable costs can be segregated into variable and fixed elements.
(iv) Product specifications and methods of manufacturing and selling will not change.
(v) Operating efficiency would not increase or decrease.
(vi) There will be no change in pricing policy.
(vii) The number of units of sales will be the same with the units produced so that there is no opening or closing stock.
(viii) Product mix will remain unchanged.

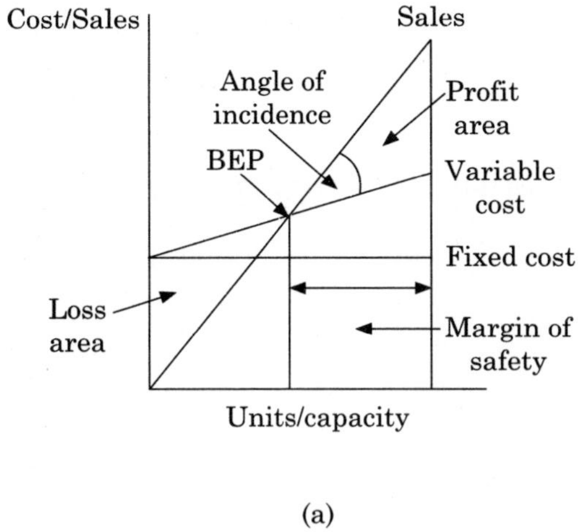

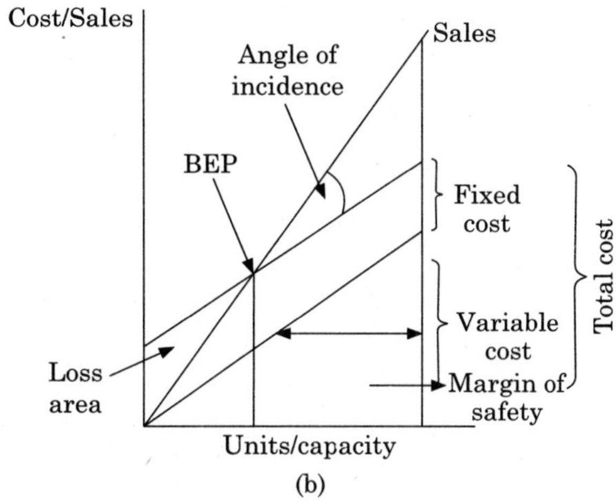

Figure 14.1 Break Even Chart.

$$\text{BEP (units)} = \text{Total fixed costs/Unit contribution}$$

$$\text{BEP (sales value)} = \text{Total fixed costs/P/V ratio}$$
$$= \text{Total fixed costs/C/S ratio}$$
$$= (\text{Total fixed costs} \times \text{Sales})/\text{Contribution}$$

14.2.4 Margin of Safety (M/S)

It is represented by excess sales over and above the break even point sales.

$$\text{Margin of Safety (M/S)} = \text{Total sales} - \text{BEP sales}$$
$$= \frac{\text{Profit}}{\text{Profit} - \text{Volume ratio}}$$

The high margin of safety indicates that profit will be made by the firm even if there is a substantial fall in sales or production. If the margin is small, a small drop in sales or production will be a serious matter. In such case the management may take various decisions as follows:

(i) Increase the level of activity
(ii) Increase the selling price
(iii) Reduce costs—fixed and/or variable
(iv) Substitute the existing products with more profitable products

For example, let us assume that the present sales volume is ₹ 500000 and the BEP sales value is ₹ 300000. Hence, the safety margin is ₹ 200000.

14.2.5 Angle of Incidence

It is the angle between sales and total cost line. This angle is an indicator of profit earning capacity of the firm over the BEP sales. So the aim of the management should be to have a large angle which would indicate earning of high margin of profit once fixed costs are covered. A small angle means that even if profits are being made, they are made at a low rate.

14.3 PROFIT-VOLUME GRAPH (P/V GRAPH) OR PROFIT CHART

This chart shows the relationship between profit and volume. A P/V graph can be constructed, if any two of the following data are known:

(i) Fixed overhead
(ii) Profit at a given level of activity
(iii) Break-Even Point

Procedure

1. The graph is divided into two areas – the vertical axis above the 0 line represents profit area, and the vertical axis below the 0 line represents the loss or fixed cost area.
2. A scale on the horizontal (0) axis is selected for sales.
3. A scale on the vertical axis is selected for profit and fixed cost.
4. Points are plotted for profits and fixed costs, and then they are connected by a straight line which intersects the sales line at the horizontal axis. The point of intersection is the Break-Even Point.

Let us take an example to understand how a P/V graph is prepared.

Example 1

The following data relate to a company for the year ended 31/12/2007:

Units produced: 20000
Variable cost per unit: ₹ 6
Fixed overhead: ₹ 50000
Selling price per unit: ₹ 10
Prepare a P/V graph?

Solution:

		₹
Sales = (20000 × ₹ 10)	=	200000
Less: variable cost = (20000 × ₹ 6)	=	120000
Contribution	=	80000
Less: fixed overhead	=	50000
Net Profit	=	30000

BEP sale = ₹ 125000.

Margin of safety = (₹ 200000 – ₹ 125000) = ₹ 75000.

Now a P/V Graph can be drawn in the following manner as shown in Figure 14.2

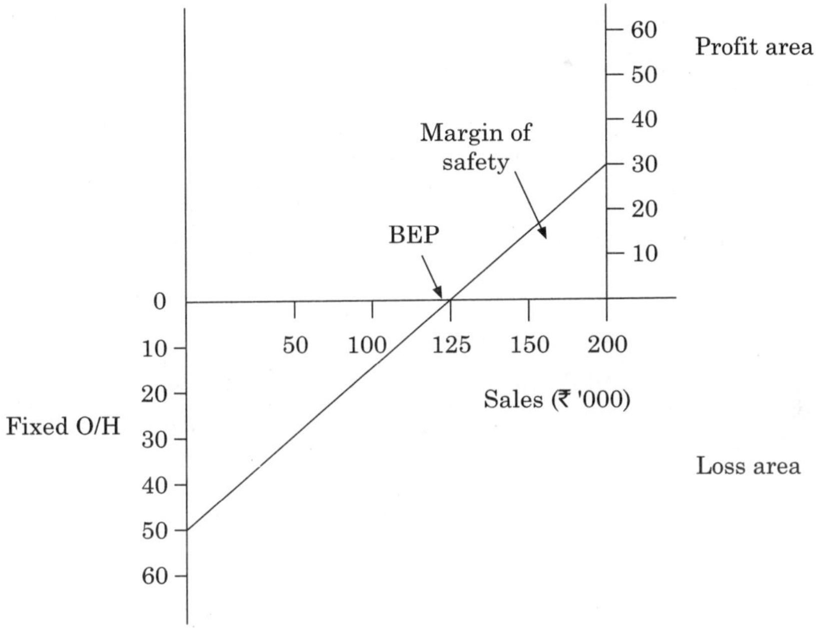

Figure 14.2 P/V Graph.

A P/V graph may be used for a variety of purposes:

(i) Determining BEP and showing the impact on profits, of selling at different prices for a product

(ii) Forecasting costs and profits resulting from changes in sales volume

(iii) Showing the deviations of actual profit from anticipated profit

(iv) Relative profitability under conditions of high or low demand for a product, etc.

Let us take one example to understand how the Break-Even Point and margin of safety, etc. is derived.

Example 2

On relative profitability under conditions of high and low demands

Two firms XY Ltd. and PQ Ltd. sell the same type of product in the same market. Their budgeted profit & loss a/cs for the year ended 2007 are as follows:

		XY Ltd. (₹)		PQ Ltd. (₹)
Sales		150000		150000
Less: Variable costs:	120000		100000	
Fixed costs:	15000		35000	
		135000		135000
Net budgeted profit		15000		15000

(i) Calculate the Break-Even Point and margin of safety of each business firm

(ii) State which firm is likely to earn greater profit in conditions of:

(a) heavy demand for the product

(b) low demand for the product

Solution: (i)

	XY Ltd. (₹)	PQ Ltd. (₹)
Sales	150000	150000
Less: Variable costs	120000	100000
Contribution	30000	50000

P/V ratio = (Cont. /Sales) × 100 = 20%   33.33%

BEP Sales = (Fixed cost/P/V ratio) = $\frac{15000}{20\%}$ = $\frac{35000}{33.33\%}$

= ₹ 75000   = ₹ 105000

Margin of safety = (Present sales – BEP sales) = ₹ 75000 = ₹ 45000

(ii) Although total costs of both the firms are the same, the fixed costs of XY Ltd. are lower than that of PQ Ltd. So the BEP in the former case is reached sooner (i.e. at lower level activity), which is evident from the following graph as shown in Figure 14.3.

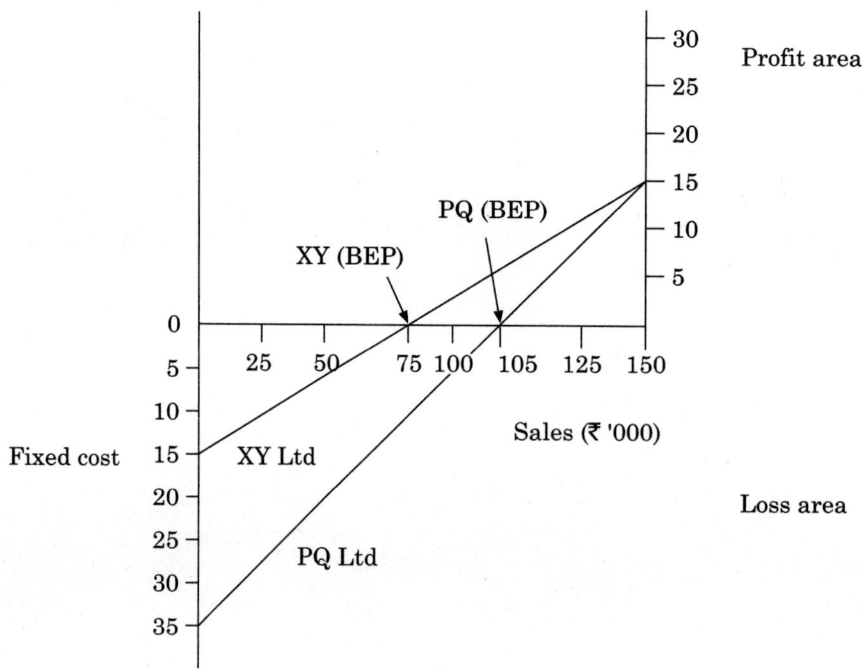

Figure 14.3 P/V Graph.

It appears from the graph that for demand below ₹ 150000 sales, XY Ltd. will earn greater profit than PQ Ltd., once a BEP has been reached. At ₹ 150000 sales, both the firms will earn same profit. But the rate of profit earning capacity of PQ Ltd. is greater than XY Ltd. due to wider angle of incidence. Therefore, in case of heavy demand, PQ Ltd. will earn greater profit, while XY Ltd. will earn greater profit in condition of low demand for the product.

14.4 MULTI–PRODUCT BREAK-EVEN CHART

In this chart it is possible to draw a break-even chart for the company as a whole, considering all products in one chart. In such case the BEP is where the average contribution line cuts the fixed cost line, assuming proportions of sales mix remaining unchanged.

Procedure

(i) Calculate P/V ratio for each product and arrange the products in descending order on the basis of P/V ratios.

(ii) X axis would represent sales value while Y axis would represent contribution and fixed costs.

(iii) Plot the total fixed costs line.

(iv) Take the product having highest P/V ratio and plot its contribution against sales. Then take the product having second highest P/V ratio, and plot cumulative contribution against cumulative sales. The process will end with plotting the product having the lowest P/V ratio.

(v) Obtain the average contribution slope by joining the origin to the end of the last line plotted. The BEP is the point of intersection of average contribution line and the fixed cost line. Let us see an example.

Example 3

ABC Ltd. produces and sells three products – X, Y, Z. From the following information relating to these products for a period, draw a break-even chart to determine the BEP of the company.

	X (₹)	Y (₹)	Z (₹)	Total (₹)
Sales	40000	25000	35000	100000
Variable costs	20000	15000	28000	63000
Fixed costs				18500

Solution:

Let us find out P/V ratio.

$$\text{P/V ratio} = \frac{(S - V)}{S} \times 100$$

$$\text{P/V ratio for product X} = \frac{20000}{40000} \times 100 = 50\%$$

$$Y = \frac{10000}{25000} \times 100 = 40\%$$

$$Z = \frac{7000}{35000} \times 100 = 20\%$$

Product	P/V ratio	Sales (₹)		Contribution (₹)	
	%	Product wise	Cumulative	Product wise	Cumulative
X	50	40000	40000	20000	20000
Y	40	25000	65000	10000	30000
Z	20	35000	100000	7000	37000

Now we can draw a multiple break-even chart as shown in Figure 14.4.

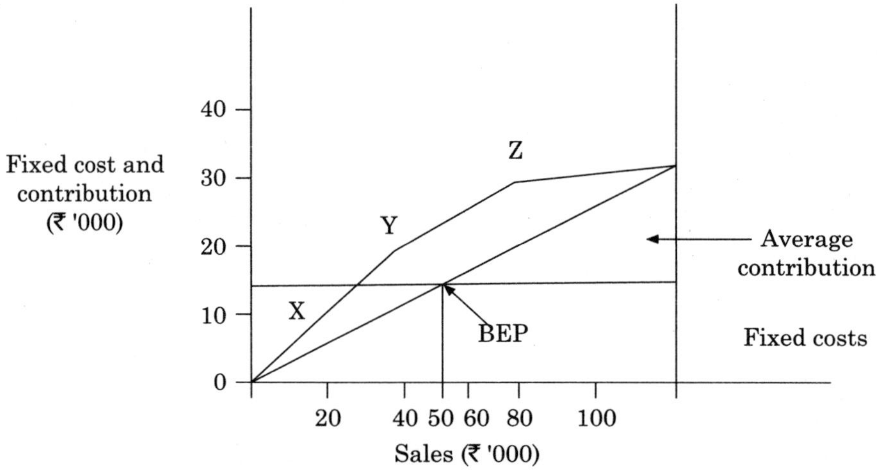

Figure 14.4 Multiple Break-even Chart.

Thus, BEP sale is ₹ 50000.

Check

$$\text{BEP sales} = \frac{\text{Fixed cost} \times \text{Total sales}}{\text{Total contribution}}$$

$$= \frac{18500 \times 100000}{37000} = ₹\ 50000$$

14.5 COST-VOLUME-PROFIT (C-V-P) ANALYSIS

Cost-volume-profit analysis is a systematic method of analysis of relationship between selling price, cost, volume, and profitability. In the short run, profitability is sensitive to volume of sales. It involves study of four variables as follows:

(i) Selling price
(ii) Variable costs
(iii) Fixed costs
(iv) Volume

Cost-Volume-Profit analysis is used for studying the results of various changes in factors, they are:

(i) Changes in fixed costs
(ii) Changes in variable costs
(iii) Changes in selling price
(iv) Changes in sales mix

There is an effect of the above changes on the following:

(i) Break even point
(ii) Margin of safety
(iii) Profit volume ratio

Change in fixed costs

A change in fixed costs will bring change in BEP by an equal percentage provided variable costs and selling price remain constant. Once BEP is changed it will affect M/S, but the effect will be reversed as compared to BEP, which means if BEP goes down it will increase M/S and vice versa.

Change in variable costs

A change in variable costs without a corresponding change in selling price and fixed costs will change the BEP, M/S, and P/V ratio.

Change in selling price

A change in selling price without a corresponding change in variable costs and fixed costs will change the BEP, M/S, and P/V ratio.

Change in sales mix

The overall P/V ratio will change with changes in sales mix. In such case although budgeted sales volume is met, but the actual profit will be lower than that budgeted if the proportion of low margin product sold exceeds that anticipated. So, change in sales mix will result in change in BEP and M/S.

The above analyses can be shown graphically in the following manner:

	P/V	MOS	BEP	P
Increase in selling price	↑	↑	↓	↑
Decrease in selling price	↓	↓	↑	↓
Increase in variable cost	↓	↓	↑	↓
Increase in volume	–	↑	–	↑
Increase in fixed cost	–	↓	↑	↓

Another important area of C-V-P analysis is to find out the volume necessary to achieve a desired profit.

$$\text{Desired sales volume (in quantity)} = \frac{\text{Fixed costs + Desired profit}}{\text{Unit contribution}}$$

$$\text{Desired sales volume (in ₹)} = \frac{\text{Fixed costs + Desired profit}}{\text{P/V ratio}}$$

Example 4

The following details are obtained from ABC Co. Ltd. for a financial year:

Present production and sales = 8000 units

Selling price per unit = ₹ 20

Variable cost per unit: Direct material = ₹ 5.00

Direct labour = ₹ 2.50

Variable overhead = ₹ 100% of direct labour cost

Fixed cost (total) = ₹ 40000.

Calculate

(i) P/V ratio,

(ii) BEP,

(iii) margin of safety,

(iv) find out the effect on P/V ratio, BEP, and M/S, of changes in each of the following situations:

(a) 10% increase in selling price

(b) 10% increase in variable costs

(c) 10% decrease in fixed cost

(d) 10% decrease in sales volume.

Solution:

(i) $\text{P/V ratio} = \dfrac{\text{Contribution}}{\text{Sales}}$

$$= \frac{S - V}{S} = \frac{20 - (5.00 + 2.50 + 2.50)}{20} \times 100$$

$$= 50\%$$

(a) $= \dfrac{(20 + 2) - 10}{(20 + 2)} = \dfrac{12}{22} \times 100 = 54.55\%$

(b) $= \dfrac{20 - (10 + 1)}{20} = \dfrac{9 \times 100}{20} = 45\%$

(c) = No effect on P/V ratio

(d) = No effect on P/V ratio

(ii) BEP sales = $\frac{\text{Fixed cost}}{\text{P/V ratio}}$

$$= \frac{₹\ 40000}{50\%} = ₹\ 80000$$

(a) $= \frac{₹\ 40000}{54.55\%} = ₹\ 73328$

(b) $= \frac{₹\ 40000}{45\%} = ₹\ 88888$

(c) $= \frac{₹\ 40000 - (10\%\ \text{of}\ 40000)}{50\%} = \frac{36000}{50\%} = ₹\ 72000$

(d) = No effect on BEP

(iii) Margin of safety (M/S) = Total sales – BEP sales

$(8000 \times 20) - 80000 = ₹\ 80000$ or 50%

(a) $= (8000 \times 22) - 73328 = ₹\ 102672$ or 58.34%

(b) $= (8000 \times 20) - 88888 = ₹\ 71112$ or 44.44%

(c) $= (8000 \times 20) - 72000 = ₹\ 88000$ or 55%

(d) $= [(8000 - 10\%\ \text{of}\ 8000 \times 20) - 80000]$

$= ₹\ 64000$ or 44.44%

Example 5

The following data are obtained from the records of a company:

Particulars	1st year (₹)	2nd year (₹)
Sales	80000	90000
Profit	10000	14000

Calculate: (i) P/V ratio, (ii) BEP sales, (iii) Profit or loss when sales amount to ₹ 50000, (iv) Sales required to earn a profit of ₹ 19000.

Solution:

(i) P/V ratio

Year	Sales (₹)	Profit (₹)
2nd	90000	14000
1st	80000	10000
Change	10000	4000

$$P/V = \frac{\text{Change in profit} \times 100}{\text{Change in sales}}$$

$$= \frac{4000 \times 100}{10000} = 40\%$$

(ii) BEP sales

We know

$$\text{Fixed cost} = \text{Contribution} - \text{Profit.}$$

$$\text{Fixed cost (1st year)} = (40\% \text{ of } 80000) - 10000 = 32000 - 10000 = ₹\ 22000$$

$$\text{Fixed cost (2nd year)} = (40\% \text{ of } 90000) - 14000 = 36000 - 14000 = ₹\ 22000$$

$$BEP = \frac{\text{Fixed cost}}{\text{P/V ratio}} = \frac{22000}{40\%}$$

$$= ₹\ 55000$$

(iii) Profit/loss calculation at sales value of ₹ 50000

$$\text{Sales} = ₹\ 50000.$$

$$\text{P/V ratio} = 40\%.$$

$$\text{Contribution} = 40\% \text{ of } 50000 = ₹\ 20000.$$

$$\text{Profit} = \text{Contribution} - \text{Fixed cost}$$

$$= ₹\ 20000 - 22000 = \text{(loss) } ₹\ 2000.$$

(iv) Sales required to earn profit of Rs 19000

$$\text{Desired sales} = \frac{\text{Fixed cost + Profit}}{\text{P/V ratio}} = \frac{22000 + 19000}{40\%}$$

$$= ₹\ 102500$$

Example 6

The following information relates to three months' activities of a company which produces a single product:

Year 2010	Production (units)	Total cost (₹)
May	12500	115000
June	14000	124000
July	16400	138400

Calculate:

(i) Variable cost per unit
(ii) Total fixed cost

Solution:

Calculation of Variable Cost per unit

Year/Month	Units produced	Monthly change in units	Total cost (₹)	Monthly change in costs (₹)	Variable cost per unit (₹)
2010/May	12500	–	115000	–	–
June	14000	1500	124000	9000	6
July	16400	2400	138400	14400	6

Calculation of Fixed Costs

Fixed cost = Total cost – Variable cost

For June ₹ 124000 – (14000 × ₹ 6) = ₹ 40000

For July ₹ 138400 – (16400 × ₹ 6) = ₹ 40000.

Example 7

The annual profit plan of ABC Ltd. is given below. From the data given, calculate the break-even point?

Annual Profit Plan of ABC Ltd.

Particulars	Fixed cost (₹)	Variable cost (₹)	Total (₹)
Budgeted sales			400000
(20000 units @ ₹ 20 each)			
Budgeted cost:			
Direct labour		70000	
Direct material		100000	
Factory overhead	64000	20000	
Administrative expenses	50000	10000	
Distribution expenses	30000	20000	
	144000	220000	364000
Budgeted profit			36000

Capacity of production: 25000 units.

Solution:

Sales	₹ 400000
Less: Variable cost	₹ 220000
Contribution	₹ 180000

$$\text{Contribution per unit} = \frac{₹\,180000}{20000} = ₹\,9.$$

$$\text{Break-even point in units} = \frac{\text{Fixed cost}}{\text{Contribution per unit}} = \frac{₹1440000}{9} = 16000 \text{ units.}$$

Break-even point in sales value = Break-even units × Selling price
= 16000 × ₹ 20 = ₹ 320000.

Alternatively:

$$\text{Break-even point in sales value} = \frac{\text{Fixed cost}}{\text{Sales/contribution}}$$

$$= ₹\ 144000 \times \frac{₹\ 400000}{₹\ 180000} = ₹\ 320000.$$

Example 8

A company produces 200 units of a product and incurs the following expenditures:

(i) Materials ₹ 30000
(ii) Labour ₹ 20000
(iii) Factory overhead ₹ 4000
(iv) Administrative overhead ₹ 5754
(v) Selling and Distribution overhead ₹ 1500.

The products are sold at a price of ₹ 400 per unit.

The above expenditures are classified into fixed variable as follows:

Expenditures	Fixed	Variable
Materials	Nil	100%
Labour	50%	50%
Factory overhead	25%	75%
Administrative overhead	100%	Nil
Selling and Distribution overhead	60%	40%

From the above information, determine:

(i) Total variable cost and fixed costs
(ii) Contribution
(iii) P/V ratio
(iv) Break-even point in units
(v) Break-even point in sales value

Solution:

(i) Calculation of Total Variable costs and Fixed costs

Particulars	Fixed (₹)	Variable (₹)
Materials	–	30000
Labour	10000	10000
Factory overhead	1000	3000
Administrative overhead	5754	–
Selling and Distribution overhead	900	600
Total	17654	43600

Calculation of Contribution

	Particulars	Total (₹)	Per unit (₹)
	Sales (200 × ₹ 400)	80000	400
	Less: Variable cost	43600	218 (₹ 43600/200)
(ii)	Contribution	36400	182

(iii) $\text{P/V ratio} = \dfrac{\text{Contribution}}{\text{Sales}} \times 100 = \dfrac{₹\ 36400}{80000} \times 100 = 45.5\%.$

(iv) $\text{Break-even point in units} = \dfrac{\text{Fixed cost}}{\text{Contribution per unit}} = \dfrac{₹\ 17654}{₹\ 182} = 97 \text{ units.}$

(v) $\text{Break-even point in sales value} = \dfrac{\text{Fixed cost}}{\text{P/V ratio}} = \dfrac{₹\ 17654}{45.5\%} = ₹\ 38800.$

Example 9

Suchitra Industries manufactures small capacity motors. The cost structure of a motor is as under:

Material	₹ 50
Labour	₹ 80
Variable overhead	75% of labour cost

Fixed overhead of the company amount to ₹ 240000 per annum. The sale price of the motor is ₹ 230 each.

(i) Determine the number of motors that have to be manufactured and sold in a year in order to break-even?

(ii) How many motors have to be made and sold to make a profit of ₹ 100000 per year?

(iii) If the sale price is reduced by ₹ 15 each, how many motors have to be sold to break-even?

Solution:

Particulars	₹	₹
Selling price per motor		230
Less: Variable costs per motor:		
Material	50	
Labour	80	
Variable overhead @ 75% of labour cost	60	
		190
Contribution per unit		40

(i) Number of motors to be manufactured and sold in a year to break-even:

$$\text{Break-even in units} = \frac{\text{Fixed cost}}{\text{Contribution per unit}} = \frac{₹\ 240000}{₹\ 40} = 6000 \text{ units.}$$

(ii) Required sales for target profit of ₹ 100000 per year:

$$\text{Sales in units} = \frac{\text{Fixed cost + Profit}}{\text{Contribution per unit}} = \frac{₹\ 240000 + 100000}{₹\ 40} = 8500 \text{ units.}$$

(iii) Number of motors to be sold to break-even when price is reduced by ₹ 15 each:

Particulars		₹
Selling price per motor	(₹ 230 – ₹ 15)	215
Less: Variable costs per motor		190
Contribution per unit		25

$$\text{Break-even in units} = \frac{\text{Fixed cost}}{\text{Contribution per unit}} = \frac{₹\ 240000}{₹\ 25} = 9600 \text{ units.}$$

Example 10

A company manufacturing one type of commodity, selling at ₹ 20 per unit, has the capacity to produce 40000 units. The budget for the year ending 31st December 2009 predicts sales of 32000 units. The costs of each unit are expected to be as follows:

	₹
Materials	6
Wages	4
Overheads	2

Fixed costs for the year are expected to be ₹ 240000.

(i) Calculate the break-even point for the year?

(ii) What profit can be expected during the year, assuming that the opening and closing stocks remained constant?

(iii) If management are willing to invest ₹ 200000 with an expected return of 20%, how many units must be produced to achieve this?

(iv) If, by reducing the selling price to ₹ 19, extra sales can be expected, what must be the volume of production and sales to achieve the same profits as in (iii) above?

Solution:

Particulars	₹	₹
Selling price per motor		20
Less: Variable costs per unit:		
Material	6	
Wages	4	
Variable overhead	2	
		12
Contribution per unit		8

(i) Break-even point:

$$\text{Break-even in units} = \frac{\text{Fixed cost}}{\text{Contribution per unit}} = \frac{₹\,240000}{₹\,8} = 30000 \text{ units.}$$

Break-even in sales value = Break-even units × Selling price
= 30000 × ₹ 20 = ₹ 600000.

Alternatively,

$$\text{Break-even in sales value} = \frac{\text{Fixed cost} \times \text{Sales}}{\text{Contribution}} = \frac{₹\,240000 \times ₹\,20}{₹\,8} = ₹\,600000.$$

(ii) Expected profit for the year:

Particulars	₹
Total contribution from sale of 32000 units = (32000 × ₹ 8)	256000
Less: Fixed costs	240000
Profit	16000

(iii) Required sale for desired profit (20% of ₹ 200000) = ₹ 40000:

$$\text{Sales in units} = \frac{\text{Fixed cost} + \text{Profit}}{\text{Contribution per unit}} = \frac{₹\,240000 + 40000}{₹\,8} = 35000 \text{ units.}$$

(iv) Required sale at reduced price for same profit:
If the price falls to ₹ 19, the contribution per unit will be (₹ 19 – 12) = ₹ 7.

$$\text{Required units} = \frac{₹\,280000}{₹\,7} = 40000 \text{ units.}$$

Example 11

Cookwell Ltd. manufactures pressure cookers, the selling price of which is ₹ 300 per unit. Currently, the capacity utilisation is 60% with a sales turnover of ₹ 18 lakh. The company proposes to reduce the selling price by 20%, but desires to maintain the same profit position by increasing the output. Assuming that the increased output could be made and sold, determine the level at which the company should operate to achieve the desired objective.

The following further data are available:

(a) Variable cost per unit ₹ 60
(b) Semi-variable cost (including a variable element of ₹ 10 per unit) ₹ 180000.
(c) Fixed cost of ₹ 300000 will remain constant upto 80% level. Beyond this, an additional amount of ₹ 60000 will be incurred.

Solution:

Profitability at 60% capacity level:

$$\text{No. of units sold} = \frac{₹\,1800000}{₹\,300} = 6000 \text{ units.}$$

Sales per unit	₹ 300
Less: Variable cost (₹ 60 + 10)	₹ 70
Contribution per unit	₹ 230

Total contribution from sale of 6000 units	= 6000 × ₹ 230 = ₹ 1380000	
Less: Fixed costs	= ₹ 300000	
Fixed portion of semi-variable cost		
₹ 180000 – (6000 × ₹ 10)	= ₹ 120000	
		= ₹ 420000
Profit		₹ 960000

Operating level at revised selling price:

Revised selling price per unit = (₹ 300 – 20% of 300)	₹ 240
Less: Variable cost per unit	₹ 70
Revised contribution per unit	₹ 170

$$\text{Sales in units} = \frac{\text{Fixed cost + Profit}}{\text{Contribution per unit}}$$

$$= \frac{420000 + 960000}{170} = 8118 \text{ units i.e. } 81.18\% \text{ capacity level.}$$

Since the capacity level exceeds 80%, an additional amount of ₹ 60000 will be incurred towards fixed costs. Hence, the total fixed costs will be (₹ 420000 + 60000) = ₹ 480000. Therefore, the required sales in units = (480000 + 960000)/170 = 8471 units, i.e. 84.71% capacity level.

Example 12

X Ltd. sells 8000 units of its products at a loss of ₹ 16000. Variable cost per unit is ₹ 12 and total fixed cost is ₹ 48000.

Calculate:

(i) Profit-volume ratio
(ii) Number of units to be sold to earn a profit of ₹ 10000
(iii) The amount of profit from sale of 20000 units.

Solution:

	₹
Total variable cost = 8000 × ₹ 12	96000
Total fixed cost	48000
Total cost	144000
Less: Loss	16000
Total sales	128000

$$\text{Selling price per unit} = \frac{₹\ 128000}{8000} = ₹\ 16.$$

Contribution = Sales – Variable cost
Contribution per unit = (₹ 16 – 12) = ₹ 4.

(i) P/V ratio = Contribution per unit/Selling price per unit = ₹ 4/₹ 16 = 1/4 = 25%.

(ii) Required sales for target profit of ₹ 10000 = (Fixed cost + Profit)/Contribution per unit

No. of units = (₹ 48000 + 10000)/₹ 4 = 14500 units.

(iii) Amount of profit from sale of 20000 units:

	₹
Contribution from 20000 units = (20000 × ₹ 4)	80000
Less: Fixed cost	48000
Profit	32000

Example 13

A company is able to sell its product for ₹ 12 per unit. Variable costs of production are ₹ 7 per unit. Fixed costs total to ₹ 80000 per annum.

Calculate:

(i) Number of units to break-even
(ii) Sales at break-even point
(iii) C/S ratio
(iv) What number of units will need to be sold to earn a profit of ₹ 30000
(v) What level of sales will achieve a profit of ₹ 30000 per annum
(vi) Because of increasing costs, variable costs are expected to rise by ₹ 2 per unit and fixed costs by ₹ 10000 per annum. If the selling price cannot be increased what will be the number of units required to be sold to maintain a profit of ₹ 30000 per annum?
(vii) If the taxation rate is 40%, how many units will need to be sold to make a profit of ₹ 30000 per annum?

Solution:

Contribution = Sales – Variable costs

Contribution per unit = (₹ 12 – 7) = ₹ 5.

(i) Break-even point in units $= \dfrac{\text{Fixed cost}}{\text{Contribution per unit}} = \dfrac{₹\ 80000}{₹\ 5} = 16000$ units.

(ii) Break-even point in sales value = 16000 units × ₹ 12 = ₹ 192000.

(iii) C/S ratio $= \dfrac{\text{Contribution per unit}}{\text{Selling price per unit}} = \dfrac{5}{12} = 41.67\%$.

(iv) Required sales for target profit:

Sales in units $= \dfrac{\text{Fixed cost + Profit}}{\text{Contribution per unit}} = \dfrac{(₹\ 80000 + 30000)}{₹\ 5} = 22000$ units.

(v) Required sales in rupees for target profit = 22000 units × ₹ 12 = ₹ 264000.

(vi) Required sales in units for target profit when variable costs and fixed costs increase:

Contribution per unit = (₹ 12 – 9) = ₹ 3.

Fixed costs = (₹ 80000 + 10000) = ₹ 90000.

$$\text{Sales in units} = \frac{\text{Fixed cost + Profit}}{\text{Contribution per unit}} = \frac{(₹\ 90000 + 30000)}{₹\ 3} = 40000 \text{ units.}$$

(vii) Required sales in units for target profit after tax:

	₹
Net profit required after tax	30000
Add: Income tax (40 × ₹ 30000/60)	20000
Net profit required before tax	50000

$$\text{Sales in units} = \frac{\text{Fixed cost + Profit}}{\text{Contribution per unit}} = \frac{(₹\ 80000 + 50000)}{₹\ 5} = 26000 \text{ units.}$$

Example 14

AB Ltd. has a maximum capacity of producing 200000 units per year. The cost sheet on the basis of full capacity utilisation is as follows:

Cost per unit	₹
Variable manufacturing cost	12
Variable overhead	5
Fixed overhead	3
Total cost	20

Current selling price is ₹ 23 per unit.

Answer the following questions considering each situation independently:

(i) What is the break-even point in (a) units, (b) rupee sales?

(ii) How many units must be sold to earn a net return of ₹ 240000 per year?

(iii) Assume that the sale for the year just ended was 185000 units. A strike at a major supplier's plant has caused shortage of material, and so the current year's sales will reach 160000 units only. Top management is planning to decrease fixed costs in the current year by ₹ 59000. Management is also thinking of either increasing the selling price or reducing variable costs, or both, in order to earn last year's target net income. The company has already sold 30000 units this year at a selling price of ₹ 23 per unit with variable costs unchanged. What contribution margin per unit is needed on the remaining 130000 units in order to reach the target net income?

Solution:

	₹
Selling price per unit	23
Variable cost per unit	17
Contribution per unit	6

Total fixed overhead = 200000 × ₹ 3 = ₹ 600000.

(i) Break-even point:

(a) Break-even in units = Fixed cost/Contribution per unit = ₹ 600000/₹ 6 = 100000 units.

(b) Break-even in rupee sales = 100000 × ₹ 23 = ₹ 2300000.

Alternatively:

$$\text{Break-even in rupee sales} = \text{Fixed cost} \times \frac{\text{Sales}}{\text{Contribution}} = ₹\,600000 \times \frac{₹\,23}{₹\,6}$$

$$= 2300000$$

(ii) Required sales for target profit:

$$\text{Sales in units} = \frac{\text{Fixed cost + Profit}}{\text{Contribution per unit}} = \frac{(₹\,600000 + 240000)}{₹\,6} = 140000 \text{ units.}$$

(iii) Required contribution margin on the remaining units for target profit:

	₹
Contribution on 185000 units @ ₹ 6	1110000
Less: Fixed costs	600000
Profit earned in the last year	510000
Fixed costs = ₹ 600000 – ₹ 59000	541000
Desired profit	510000
Desired contribution for current year	1051000
Less: Contribution from 30000 units already sold (30000 × ₹ 6)	180000
Required contribution from the remaining 130000 units	871000

Contribution per unit = ₹ 871000/₹ 130000 = ₹ 6.70.

14.6 COMPARISON OF ABSORPTION COSTING AND MARGINAL COSTING

The distinction between absorption costing and marginal costing relates to the treatment of fixed costs. In absorption costing, the fixed costs are considered as a valid part of the cost of output produced during a period. Therefore, the unit cost contains both variable costs and an apportionment of total fixed costs whether the unit is sold or is taken into inventory.

On the contrary, marginal costing uses only variable costs to derive a unit cost. The fixed costs are treated as the cost of providing facilities for business operations, and hence, are considered as a period cost rather than a cost of the products produced.

Let us consider an example to understand the above distinction.

Example 15

The budget of XYZ Ltd. provides for the manufacture and sale of 10000 units per month, the standard cost per unit being ₹ 12, made up as follows:

	₹
Direct material	7
Direct labour	1
Fixed overhead	4

The selling price per unit is ₹ 16.

Production and sales in quantities for 2009 and 2010 were as follows:

	2009	2010
Production	10000	10000
Sales	8000	12000

You are required to:

(i) prepare operating statements for each of the two periods assuming that:
  (a) the company uses marginal costing
  (b) the company uses absorption costing, and

(ii) comment on the differences of the two systems as regards:
  (a) stock valuation
  (b) period profit.

Solution:

(i)

Statement of Profit
(under Absorption Costing)

Particulars	Per unit	2009			2010		
	(₹)	Units	₹	₹	Units	₹	₹
Sales	16	8000		128000	12000		192000
Direct costs:							
(Direct material +							
Direct labour)	8	10000	80000		10000	80000	
Fixed overhead	4	10000	40000		10000	40000	
		10000	120000		10000	120000	
Add: Opening stock	12	–	–		2000	24000	
		10000	120000		12000	144000	
Less: Closing stock	12	2000	24000		–	–	
Cost of sales		8000	96000	96000	12000	144000	144000
Profit				32000			48000

Statement of Profit
(under Marginal Costing)

Particulars	Per unit	2009			2010		
	(₹)	Units	₹	₹	Units	₹	₹
Sales	16	8000		128000	12000		192000
Direct costs: (Direct material + Direct labour)	8	10000	80000		10000	80000	
Add: Opening stock	8	–	–		2000	16000	
		10000	80000		12000	96000	
Less: Closing stock	8	2000	16000		–	–	
Marginal cost of sales	8	8000	64000	64000	12000	96000	96000
Contribution	8	8000		64000	12000		96000
Fixed overhead				40000			40000
Profit				24000			56000

(ii) Under absorption costing, fixed and variable costs are absorbed at the point of manufacture, and a portion of all costs, including fixed, will be included in the valuation of stock. Under marginal costing, only variable costs are charged to cost units. Fixed costs are written-off against the sales of the period in which they occur. Consequently, fixed costs are not included in valuation of stock.

Because of the fact that a higher stock valuation will result in a higher profit figure, the use of absorption costing will show higher profits in those years when production is greater than sales. On the contrary, when sales during the periods are greater than production, marginal costing will show higher profits.

14.7 CONCLUSION

In this chapter we learnt another important technique of costing, i.e. marginal costing. The definition of marginal cost, marginal costing, the concept of sales, cost and profit was explained. The concept of break-even point, break-even chart, margin of safety, profit-volume ratio, angle of incidence, profit-volume graph, multiproduct break-even chart, etc. were explained with graphical representations and examples.

This chapter also analyzed in details and with various examples, the impact of multiple changes in factors viz. (a) change in the fixed costs, (b) change in variable costs, (c) change in selling price, and (d) change in sales mix on (i) break-even point, (ii) margin of safety, (iii) P/V ratio, and (iv) profit. The distinctions between the absorption costing and marginal costing were also discussed with a practical example.

It is needless to say that marginal costing is an important tool in the hands of management for decision-making. Further discussions on managerial decision-making where marginal costing technique has been applied are made in the Chapter 15.

REVIEW QUESTIONS

14.1 What is marginal costing? Explain the concept of marginal costing?

14.2 What is Profit/Volume (P/V) ratio? How the P/V ratio can be improved by the management?

14.3 What is a Break Even Chart (BEC)? Explain what information does this chart show to the management, with diagram?

14.4 What is Margin of Safety (M/S)? What is the impact of M/S on profitability of a company?

14.5 Define angle of incidence? What does it indicate to the management?

14.6 Write short notes on:

(a) Opportunity costs

(b) Sunk cost

(c) Relevant costs.

14.7 Explain the concept of Cost-Volume-Profit (C-V-P) analysis?

14.8 Two firms XYZ Ltd. and PQR Ltd. sell the same type of product in the same market. Their budgeted Profit and Loss Accounts for the year ended 2009 are as follows:

Particulars	XYZ Ltd.		PQR Ltd.	
Sales (₹)		150000		150000
Less: Variable cost	(₹) 120000		100000	
Fixed costs	(₹) 15000	135000	35000	135000
Net budgeted profit	(₹)	15000		15000

Calculate:

(a) The break-even point of each business firm

(b) State which firm is likely to earn greater profits in conditions of:

(i) heavy demand for the product;

(ii) low demand for the product.

14.9 The following data are related to sales and costs of a manufacturing company for the two years:

	2009	2010
Sales @ ₹ 20 per unit	10000 units	10000 units
Production	12000 units	8000 units
Production costs:	(₹)	(₹)
Material	4 per unit	4 per unit
Labour	6 per unit	6 per unit
Variable overhead	2 per unit	2 per unit
Fixed overhead	₹ 36000 per year	₹ 36000 per year

You are required:

(a) To calculate for each of the two years the gross profits under both absorption costing and marginal costing principles, and

(b) To explain why the calculated profits differ each year under absorption costing from those shown by marginal costing.

15

Managerial Decision-Making

15.1 INTRODUCTION

Managerial decision-making is the process of choosing among alternative courses of action. Some decisions are routine in nature and take very little of a manager's time due to little uncertainty or because the cost is insignificant. At times, the managers have to take some crucial decisions for which considerable amount of time and thought are spent, because these decisions involve huge uncertainty and large sum of money. Alternative, choice decisions involve situations with two or more courses of action from which the decision maker must select the best alternative. A decision involving more than two alternatives is called a multiple-alternative choice decision. In this chapter, the cost and financial aspects of decision-making process is dealt with for clear understanding of the managers.

15.2 IMPORTANCE OF DECISION-MAKING

Decision-making is a complex subject in the management process. Every decision taken by a manager has cost impact, and ultimately reflects in the overall profitability of the firms. The manager has to take a decision as it is a part of his basic function. He decides what should be done today to get effective results tomorrow. Tomorrow is always uncertain. Therefore, he is expected to be careful and use abundant caution in taking decision.

An efficient and effective manager is expected to possess requisite ability to take decision. Manager's ability depends on his understanding of the subject that he deals with. This includes technical aspect or result he intends to achieve as also the cost impact and ultimate reflection in overall profitability of his department and the company. A manager who does not take decision may be a failure. Similarly, a manager who takes wrong decision is also considered as a failure. Therefore, it is imperative for the manager to acquire skill for taking decision.

The decision-making process gets influenced by the various factors viz.

(i) Customers' need
(ii) Competition in the market place
(iii) Production processes
(iv) Technology used
(v) Industrial relations
(vi) Cost and financial impact
(vii) Internal and external environment etc.

However, the decision is not always taken based on cost or financial considerations. The other aspects of decision-making are necessarily kept in mind. Nevertheless, it is essential for a manager to be aware of the cost implication of the decision.

15.3 STEPS IN DECISION-MAKING

Following steps are normally taken by the management of a company before arriving at the final decision:

(i) Define the problem
(ii) Develop alternative solutions
(iii) Evaluate the alternatives
(iv) Arrive at a decision

15.4 COSTS AND REVENUES FOR DECISION-MAKING

15.4.1 Relevant Cost

The relevant cost is the future cost which has not been incurred. For a cost to be relevant, it must have two characteristics:

(i) It must be a future cost.
(ii) It must be affected by the decision being taken or not taken.

15.4.2 Sunk Cost

Sunk cost is the economic resource which has been committed or spent and cannot be recovered. Sunk cost is already incurred and nothing can be done now. This is a past cost and not relevant for deciding the cost impact of the present or future. For example, XYZ Co. Ltd. invested ₹ 1 crore in a research project to develop bio-degradable fertilizers. The project failed because the fertilizers developed by the company were not of acceptable quality in the market. The investment of XYZ Co. Ltd. in this project is a sunk cost as nothing can be done at this stage.

15.4.3 Differential Cost

Differential cost is the additional cost incurred or to be incurred arising out of a decision taken by the management. It is also called incremental cost which is the result of a management decision as compared to not taking such decision. However, the increase in normal or routine cost is not considered as differential cost. For example, the management of XYZ Co. Ltd. decided to introduce in-house secretarial department and accordingly appointed 1 company secretary, 1 legal officer, and 2 office assistants. The cost incurred on secretarial department is the differential cost for the company.

15.4.4 Variable Cost

Variable costs are those which vary proportionately with the output.

15.4.5 Opportunity Cost

They represent the benefit foregone in sacrificing the best alternative. In other words, the cost attached to the opportunities lost is called the opportunity cost. It is the economic benefit which is lost due to adoption of different alternatives. Opportunity cost is not derived in cash. Therefore, it is not recorded in the books of accounts or cost accounts. But it is very much in the reckoning for decision-making purposes. For example, a manager has ₹ 100000 cash in his disposal. He has options to invest the money in (a) bank as fixed deposit, (b) tax-free bonds of RBI, (c) shares of a good company. If he decides to invest in fixed deposit, then he cannot invest in RBI bonds or in shares. The opportunity cost in investing in fixed deposit of a bank is the tax-free interest of RBI bonds and high dividend on shares, which is foregone by deciding in investment in bank.

Opportunity cost provides the benefit or cost being foregone by adopting an alternative in preference to other available alternatives.

15.4.6 Depreciation

It is the nature of a recovery of sunk cost due to the past decision. Hence, depreciation charges are totally irrelevant for decision-making process.

15.4.7 Fixed Cost

Fixed costs in a business do not change. They remain constant for a period or capacity. Fixed costs may be either relevant or irrelevant. When a fixed cost is incurred only if a certain decision is taken, it is relevant. If a fixed cost is incurred irrespective of whatever decision is taken in a certain situation, it is an irrelevant cost.

15.4.8 Replacement Cost

The value of an asset appears in the books of accounts at cost. The cost reflected in the books is called historical cost. The cost at which the asset was acquired less depreciation is the present written down value of the asset. In case the asset is replaced the historical cost is not relevant. The current value of the asset in the market is relevant as the buyer has to pay money equivalent to the current value of the asset. The current value of the asset is called replacement cost. In the decision-making process historical cost is not important. What is important is the replacement cost as money equivalent of replacement cost is required if the management decides to replace the asset.

For example, a machine was purchased in 1996 for ₹ 2000000. The depreciated value of the asset as on 1.4.2006 is say, 1000000, i.e. the asset has suffered depreciation of ₹ 1000000 from 1996 to 31.3.2006. The present market value of the asset is ₹ 2500000. This is the replacement cost of the asset.

15.4.9 Incremental Profit

It represents the contribution to the total profit of the firm which is specifically traceable to the alternative. Generally, we apply the following formulae to find out the incremental cost, revenue and profit while taking managerial decisions:

Incremental Revenues = Revenues directly flowing from the decision
+ Increase in revenues from other activities
– Decrease in revenues from other activities due to decision

Incremental Costs = Costs directly related to the decision
+ Increase in costs of other activities
– Decrease in costs of other activities due to decision

Incremental profit = Incremental revenues – Incremental costs

15.5 APPLICATION OF MARGINAL COSTING FOR MANAGERIAL DECISION-MAKING

Marginal costing technique may be applied by a company in taking various management decisions as follows:

(i) Diversification of products/Introduction of new product
(ii) Selection of profitable product mix/sales mix
(iii) Problem of limiting factor
(iv) Make or buy decision
(v) Closing down of a plant or division, outsourcing or suspending activities, etc.
(vi) Acceptance of additional order at lower price etc.

15.5.1 Diversification of Products/Introduction of New Product

Sometimes, a new product may be proposed to be introduced by the management to the existing product line to utilize idle facilities, to capture a new market. A new product can be manufactured if it is capable of contributing something towards fixed costs and profit after meeting its variable costs of sales. Fixed costs however, will not change on the assumption that the new product can be manufactured by the existing resources and manpower.

Example 1

The following data are available in respect of product X, from the records of ABC Ltd.:

Sales = ₹ 50000
Direct materials = ₹ 20000
Direct labour = ₹ 10000
Variable overhead = ₹ 5000
Fixed overhead = ₹ 10000

The company now proposes to introduce a new product Y so that sales may be increased by ₹ 10000. There will be no increase in fixed costs. The estimated variable costs of the new product Y are:

Direct materials = ₹ 4800
Direct labour = ₹ 2200
Variable overhead = ₹ 1400

Advise management whether product Y will be profitable or not?

Solution:

Calculation of profitability under absorption costing method

Direct materials	₹ 20000
Direct labour	₹ 10000
Variable overhead	₹ 5000
Fixed overhead	₹ 10000
Total cost	₹ 45000
Sales	₹ 50000
Profit	₹ 5000

Proposed position (in ₹)

Particulars	Product X	Product Y	Total
Direct materials	20000	4800	24800
Direct labour	10000	2200	12200
Variable overhead	5000	1400	6400
Fixed overhead (apportioned on sales value)	8333	1667	10000
Total cost	43333	10067	53400
Sales	50000	10000	60000
Profit (+)/Loss (–)	6667	(–) 67	6600

From the table it is clear that product X is more profitable due to reduction of total costs from ₹ 45000 to ₹ 43333. The entire profit is earned by product X, whereas product Y incurs a loss of ₹ 67. But the position will be quite different if the data are presented under marginal costing technique.

Calculation of profitability under marginal costing technique (in ₹)

Particulars	Product X	Product Y	Total
Direct materials	20000	4800	24800
Direct labour	10000	2200	12200
Prime cost	30000	7000	37000
Variable overhead	5000	1400	6400
Marginal cost	35000	8400	43400
Sales	50000	10000	60000
Contribution	15000	1600	16600
Fixed overhead			10000
Profit			6600

It is now clear that with the introduction of new product Y, there will be no change in the profitability of product X. On the contrary, product Y is also yielding a contribution of ₹ 1600 towards fixed and profit. So, product Y should be introduced assuming that the capacity to be utilized for the new product Y cannot otherwise be more profitably utilized.

15.5.2 Selection of Profitable Product Mix/Sales Mix

Suitable product mix or sales mix will denote the ratios in which various products are produced and/or sold. In absence of the limiting factor contribution of each mix will be considered and the nix which will give the highest contribution will be the most profitable one, provided the fixed costs remain constant. But when the changes in product mix are associated with changes in fixed costs, then relative profitability of 'mixes' will be assessed on the basis of net profit and not on contribution basis.

Example 2

The directors of a company are considering sales budget for the next budget period. From the following information advise the management clearly:

(i) The marginal product cost and the contribution per unit

(ii) The total contribution resulting from each of the following sales mix

	Product A (₹/unit)	Product B (₹/unit)
Direct material	10	9
Direct wages	3	2
Fixed expenses (total) ₹ 800		
Variable expenses (allocated to products as 100% of direct wages).		
Selling price	20	15

Sales mix

(a) 100 units of product A and 200 units of product B

(b) 150 units of product A and 150 units of product B

(c) 200 units of product A and 100 units of product B

Recommend which of the sales mix should be adopted?

Solution:

Particulars	Product A (₹/unit)	Product B (₹/unit)
Direct material	10	9
Direct wages	3	2
Variable expenses	3	2
Marginal cost	16	13
Selling price	20	15
Contribution	+4	+2

$$\text{P/V ratio} = \frac{(C \times 100)}{s}$$

$$= \frac{(4 \times 100)}{20} = 20\% \text{ (Product A)}$$

$$= \frac{(2 \times 100)}{15} = 13.3\% \text{ (Product B)}$$

It is evident from the above that since P/V ratio of product A is higher than that of product B, product A is more profitable. So, the product/sales mix which takes into account the maximum number of product A would be the most profitable. This is proved from the following:

Sales mix		(a)		(b)		(c)	
Product	Contribution (₹ per unit)	Units	Contribution (₹)	Units	Contribution (₹)	Units	Contribution (₹)
A	4	100	400	150	600	200	800
B	2	200	400	150	300	100	200
		300	800	300	900	300	1000

Sales mix C will give highest contribution. So, this should be adopted.

Example 3

A company produces three products A, B, and C. The budgets are now prepared for 2012. The estimates have been submitted by the respective departments for sales, cost and output. From the information given below, prepare the appropriate statements to place before the board showing:

(i) the expected profit if original budget is followed

(ii) the expected profit at maximum sales demand

The standard cost per unit:

Product	A (₹)	B (₹)	C (₹)
Direct material X:	8	6	6
Y:	2	4	2
Z:	6	2	4
Direct wages	8	10	12
Variable overhead	6	8	8
Fixed overhead	12	15	18

Fixed overhead is absorbed as a percentage of direct wages i.e. 150% and is based on the original budget.

Budgeted output (units)	8000	6000	10000
Maximum estimated sales demand	10000	7500	12500
Selling price (₹)	40	50	60

Solution:

Original Budget (2012)

	A	B	C	Total
Selling price (₹)	40	50	60	
Marginal cost (₹)	30	30	32	
Contribution per unit (₹)	10	20	28	
Sales (units)	8000	6000	10000	24000
Total contribution (₹)	80000	120000	280000	480000
Fixed overhead (₹)				
12 × 8000 = 96000				
15 × 6000 = 90000				
18 × 10000 = 180000				366000
Profit (₹)				114000

Budget at Maximum Sales Demand

	A	B	C	Total
Contribution per unit (₹)	10	20	28	
Sales (units)	10000	7500	12500	30000
Total contribution (₹)	100000	150000	350000	600000
Fixed overhead (₹)				366000
Profit (₹)				234000

Example 4

XYZ Ltd. manufactures two products A and B. Following information is available from their books:

	A (₹)	B (₹)
Direct material per unit	20	18
Direct wages per unit	6	4

Fixed expenses during the period are expected to be ₹ 1600.
Variable expenses are allocated to products @ 100% of direct wages.

Selling price per unit	40	30

Sales mixes proposed are:

(i) 100 units of A and 200 units of B
(ii) 150 units of A and 150 units of B
(iii) 200 units of A and 100 units of B

Present the following to the management of the company:

(i) The unit marginal cost and unit contribution
(ii) The total contribution and resultant profit from each of the above sales mixes
(iii) The proposed sales mix to achieve a profit of ₹ 300 and ₹ 600 when the total sales of A and B are 300 units?

Solution:

(i) Statement of Marginal Cost and Contribution per unit

	A (₹)	B (₹)
Direct material	20	18
Direct wages	6	4
Variable overhead (100% of direct wages)	6	4
Marginal cost	32	26
Selling price	40	30
Contribution	8	4

(ii) Statement of Profitability

Sales mix	Contribution (₹)	Total contribution (₹)	Fixed cost (₹)	Profit (₹)
(i) A 100 units @ ₹ 8	800			
B 200 units @ ₹ 4	800	1600	1600	–
(ii) A 150 units @ ₹ 8	1200			
B 150 units @ ₹ 4	600	1800	1600	200
(iii) A 200 units @ ₹ 8	1600			
B 100 units @ ₹ 4	400	2000	1600	400

(iii) Proposed Sales Mix to earn desired profit

	1st Situation (₹)	2nd Situation (₹)
Desired profit	300	600
Fixed expenses	1600	1600
Required contribution	1900	2200

1st Situation

Let x units of A are sold, then $(300 - x)$ units of B are to be sold.

Therefore, $8x + 4(300 - x) = 1900$
or, $8x + 1200 - 4x = 1900$
or, $4x = 700$
or, $x = 175$

Proposed sales mix:
A = 175 units
B = 300 − 175 = 125 units

2nd Situation

Let y units of A are sold, then $(300 - y)$ units of B are to be sold.

Therefore, $8y + 4(300 - y) = 2200$
or, $8y + 1200 - 4y = 2200$
or, $4y = 1000$
or, $y = 250$

Proposed sales mix:
A = 250 units
B = 300 − 250 = 50 units

15.5.3 Problems of Limiting Factor

The problem of product mix or sales mix is generally linked up with the problem of limiting factor. Limiting factor or key factor is a factor that limits production and/or sales factors. When resources are scarce, selection of profitable product will be on the basis of contribution per unit of the limiting factor. The higher the contribution per unit of the limiting factor, the more profitable is the product or product line and vice versa. When an optimum sales mix has to be determined in the context of limiting factor, the product preference for the purpose of sales mix should be strictly according to relative profitability of products based on contribution in relation to the limiting factor.

Example 5

The following particulars are extracted from the records of a firm:

Particulars	Product A (₹ per unit)	Product B (₹ per unit)
Sales	100	120
Consumption of material per unit	2 kg	3 kg
Material cost	10	15
Direct wages cost	15	10
Direct expense	5	6
Machine hours used per unit	3 hr	2 hr
Fixed overhead expenses	5	10
Variable overhead expenses	15	20

Direct wages per hour is ₹ 5. Comment on the profitability of each product using same raw material when:

(i) Total sales potential in units is limited
(ii) Total sales potential in value is limited
(iii) Raw material is in short supply
(iv) Production capacity (in machine hours) is the limiting factor

Assuming raw material as the key factor, availability of which is 10000 kg and maximum sales potential of each product being 3500 units, find out the product mix which will yield the maximum profit?

Solution:

Particulars	Product A (₹ per unit)	Product B (₹ per unit)
Material cost	10	15
Direct wages cost	15	10
Direct expense	5	6
Prime cost	30	31
Variable overhead expenses	15	20
Marginal cost	45	51
Sales	100	120
Contribution	55	69
P/V ratio or C/S ratio	0.55	0.575

Contribution per kg of material: ₹ 55/2 kg = ₹ 27.50 ₹ 69/3 kg = ₹ 23.00

Contribution per machine hour: ₹ 55/3 hr = ₹ 18.33 ₹ 69/2 hr = ₹ 34.50

The profitability of each product will be determined based on the principle: the higher the contribution per unit of limiting factor, the more profitable is the product.

Statement of profitability under different conditions

Limiting factor	Ranking of products	Ranking based on
(i) Sales volume	B A	Unit contribution
(ii) Sales value	B A	P/V ratio
(iii) Raw materials	A B	Contribution per kg
(iv) Production capacity (machine hrs)	B A	Contribution per machine hour

Therefore, product preference will be in the same order as (iii) above, subject to the condition that maximum demand for each of the two products is 3500 units. So, 3500 units of more profitable product will be produced first. The balance quantity of available raw materials will then have to be utilized to produce less profitable product. Thus, the optimum product mix would be:

Product	Units	Raw materials per unit	Total raw materials required
A	3500	2 kg	7000 kg
B	1000*	3 kg	3000 kg
			10000 kg

[10000 kg – 7000 kg = 3000 kg/3 kg per unit of B = 1000* units of B].

Example 6

XYZ Ltd. is reviewing its product range as the basic raw material used in all its products has recently increased its price. The board would like to make the best use of the company's capacity and resources. Following budget data for the coming year are available:

Product	A	B	C	D
Maximum production (units)	5000	5000	5000	5000
	₹	₹	₹	₹
Selling price per unit	25	33	43	56
Variable cost:				
Material	9	12	17	20
Labour	8	10	12	18
Overhead	4	5	6	9

The total amount of raw material available to the company is limited by the supplier's production capacity limited to ₹ 200000. The budgeted fixed cost amounts to ₹ 80000.

Advice the board on the optimum product mix which would ensure maximum profit?

Solution:

Statement showing the Contribution

Product	A	B	C	D
	₹	₹	₹	₹
Selling price per unit	25	33	43	56
Variable cost:				
Material	9	12	17	20
Labour	8	10	12	18
Overhead	4	5	6	9
Total marginal cost	21	27	35	47
Contribution per unit	4	6	8	9
Contribution per ₹ of material:	₹ 0.44	₹ 0.50	₹ 0.47	₹ 0.45

Since raw material is a limiting factor we have to maximise the contribution to the limiting factor. Therefore, production priorities should be B, C, D, A. Another limiting factor is the production capacity. Therefore, B should be produced upto the limit of its production capacity, followed by C and so on till the available raw material limit is reached. So, the optimum product mix would be:

Product	Units	Contribution per unit	Contribution	Material per unit	Material limit value
		₹	₹	₹	₹
B	5000	6	30000	12	60000
C	5000	8	40000	17	85000
D	2750 (working)	9	24750	20	55000
			94750		200000
Less: Fixed cost			80000		
Profit			14750		

Working:

55000/20 = 2750 units

Example 7

A company produces three products M, N, and O by using the same raw material. Following information has been obtained for the year 2010–2011:

	M	N	O
Selling price per unit (₹)	20	15	10
Profit volume ratio (%)	10	20	40
Maximum sales potential (units)	8000	5000	2000
Raw material content as percentage of variable cost (%)	50	50	50

The fixed costs are estimated at ₹ 12000. Raw material is in short supply. The total amount of raw material available to the company is limited by the supplier's production capacity limited to ₹ 72000 for the year 2010–2011.

Advice the board on the optimum product mix which would ensure maximum profit?

Solution:

Statement showing the Contribution

Product	M	N	O
	₹	₹	₹
Selling price per unit	20	15	10
Profit volume ratio (%)	10	20	40
Variable cost as % of selling price (100 – P/V ratio %)	90	80	60
Variable cost per unit (₹)	18	12	6
Material content per unit: 50% of variable cost	9	6	3
Contribution per unit (₹)	2	3	4
Contribution as % of material content (for M = 2/9 × 100, N = 3/6 × 100 and O = 4/3 × 100)	22.2%	50%	133.3%
Ranking as per limiting factor	3	2	1

Product	Units	Contribution per unit	Contribution	Material per unit	Material limit value
	₹	₹	₹	₹	₹
O	2000	4	8000	3	6000
N	5000	3	15000	6	30000
M	4000	2	8000	9	36000
			31000		72000
Less: Fixed cost			12000		
Profit			19000		

Example 8

XYZ Ltd. manufactures two products M and O. Raw material for both products is of the same type but of different qualities. The machine used in the manufacture of both products is the same. Following cost data are available:

	M	N
Budgeted output (units)	10000	8000
Budgeted consumption of raw material (kg)	12000	10000
Budgeted machine hours	50000	32000
Budgeted cost per unit of finished product:	(₹)	(₹)
Raw material	300	200
Direct labour	100	75
Factory overhead @ ₹ 15 per machine hour (50% fixed)	75	60
Administration overhead (25% of direct labour) [75% fixed]	20	15
Total budgeted cost per unit	495	350

Owing to recent scarcity of raw material, the company has to restrict the consumption of raw material to 18000 kg annually. The selling price of M and N is ₹ 600 and ₹ 466.25 per unit, respectively.

Advise the management in which of the two products would you recommend restriction of production and why?

Solution:

Statement showing the Contribution

Product/per unit	M	N
	₹	₹
Selling price	600.00	466.25
Variable costs:		
Raw material	300.00	200.00
Direct labour	100.00	75.00
Factory overhead (50%)	37.50	30.00
Administration overhead (25%)	5.00	3.75
Total variable cost	442.50	308.75
Contribution per unit (₹)	157.50	157.50
Consumption of raw material per unit	1.20 kg	1.25 kg
Contribution per kg of raw material (₹)	131.25	126.00

Since the raw material is the limiting factor, production of M should be made in full as its contribution per kg of material is more than the product N. This will maximize the total contribution and the total profit of the company. Therefore, 12000 kg of material should be utilised for production of M at the current level output, i.e. 10000 units and the balance quantity of material, i.e. 6000 kg should be utilized for production of N at 4800 units (6000/1.25).

15.5.4 Make or Buy Decision

A company may have unused capacity which may be utilized in making parts or similar items instead of buying them from market. In taking such decision the marginal cost of manufacturing the component/parts should be compared with price quoted by outside vendors. If the variable or marginal costs are lower than purchase price, then it will be profitable more to produce the components/parts in the factory. If manufacture involves increase in fixed costs (available), then it is necessary to include them in product cost. Under such situation it is necessary to ascertain the minimum volume which would justify 'making' as compared to 'buying'. This volume is determined as follows:

$$\text{Volume} = \frac{\text{Increase in fixed costs}}{\text{Contribution per unit}}$$

Note: Here, Contribution = Purchase price less variable cost of production

Example 9

A manufacturing company traditionally purchases its component part A for its final product. During any one year the company will require 10000 units which are purchased at ₹ 30 per unit. Currently, the company has an underutilized capacity which can be used to produce the component part A. Total manufacturing costs of ₹ 32 per unit include ₹ 16 as raw material, ₹ 6 as direct labour, ₹ 3 as variable overhead, ₹ 3 as fixed overhead (available), and ₹ 4 as other fixed overheads.

Find out whether the company should make or buy the part A? Also determine the range of production at which one is more profitable than the other?

Solution:

Particulars	Amount (in ₹) per unit
Purchase price of component part A	30
Cost of manufacture of component part A:	
Direct material	16
Direct labour	6
Prime cost	22
Variable overhead	3
Marginal cost	25
Fixed overhead (available)	3
Total relevant cost	28

The company should make component A as the cost of manufacture per unit of part A is lower than its purchase price.

	Amount (in ₹) per unit
Purchase price of component part A	30
Less marginal cost	25
Savings	5

On comparison of purchase price and the marginal cost of manufacture it appears that making is, as if, more profitable than buying, thereby causing a saving of ₹ 5 per unit. But making will involve an additional fixed overhead (available) of ₹ 3 per unit i.e., (₹ 3 × 10000) = ₹ 30000 in total. So, if the fixed overhead (available) is included in the cost of manufacture, the profitability will definitely change i.e., buying will be more profitable than manufacture until additional fixed overhead is recovered. Once this is recovered, then making will be more profitable than buying.

Let us determine the volume at which both alternatives are equally profitable.

$$\text{Volume} = \text{Increase in fixed overhead (available)/savings per unit}$$

$$= \frac{30000}{5} = 6000 \text{ units}$$

Hence, below the above volume buying will be more profitable and above it, making will be more profitable. So the product range from 1 to 5999 units, the buying will be more profitable and from 6001 to 10000 units, the making will be more profitable.

When there is only one resource which is in limited supply, the selection for manufacture should be based on the 'contribution' made by each product per unit of limiting factor of output.

Example 10

Four types of components are currently being produced using a company's own facilities. However, the company is working in full capacity and is considering buying one or more type of component from an outside supplier. The total fixed cost will remain unaffected for the company as a whole while making or buying the component. Relevant data per unit of component are given below:

Components	A	B	C	D
Time per unit: Labour hours	0.40	0.50	0.50	0.30
Machine hours	0.10	0.20	0.40	0.50
Cost per unit: Marginal cost (₹)	10	12	15	15
Fixed cost (allocated) (₹)	2	4	5	15
Total cost per unit (₹)	12	16	20	30
Bought out (purchase) price (₹)	9	17	22	24

Advise management which component or components would you recommend to be bought out or purchased when: (a) labour time is the limiting factor? and (b) machine time is the limiting factor?

Solution:

Components	A	B	C	D
Bought out (purchase) price (₹)	9	17	22	24
Less marginal costs (₹)	10	12	15	15
Contribution per unit (₹)	(–) 1	5	7	9
Contribution: Per labour hour (₹)	(–) 2.5	10	14	30
Per machine hour (₹)	(–) 10	25	17.5	18

Fixed costs have not been given any consideration as they do not change for the company as a whole in regard to making or buying components. As A shows negative contribution while making, therefore, A should be bought out.

If there is still a limitation of resource after removing A, then selection of components for buying out should be considered as per lower contribution per unit of limiting factor. Therefore, when labour time is the limiting factor the order of selection of components for buying if required, would be B, C, D. When machine hour is the limiting factor, the same order would be changed to C, D, B.

When there is no idle capacity, and accordingly when making the components in the factory involve putting aside other work, the loss of contribution from displaced work should also be considered along with the marginal cost of production. It means that the contribution foregone is an opportunity cost of making and should be added to marginal cost in order to find out 'relevant cost' of making. So long as purchase price will be higher than the marginal cost plus traceable fixed cost plus the loss of contribution, it would be more beneficial to manufacture.

Example 11

A company produces a variety of products each having a number of component parts. Product Y takes 10 hours to process on a machine working to full capacity. Y has a selling price of ₹ 80 and a marginal cost of ₹ 40. A component of another product Z, Z – 5 could be made on the same machine in 2 hours with a marginal cost of ₹ 10 per unit. The bought out price of the component Z–5 is ₹ 15 per unit. Advise the management whether the company should make or buy Z–5?

Solution:

Contribution of Y per unit = ₹ 80 – ₹ 40 = ₹ 40.
Contribution per machine hour = ₹ 40/10 hr = ₹ 4.
Purchase price per unit of Z–5 = ₹ 15
Cost of manufacture per unit:

Marginal cost	₹ 10
Plus opportunity cost, i.e.	
Contribution foregone (₹ 4 × 2 hr) =	₹ 8
Total (relevant) cost of manufacture =	₹ 18

Thus, buying will be more profitable than making Z–5.

Management of a firm may prefer to make rather than buy even if the marginal contribution is nil or very low under following circumstances:

(i) Manufacturing ensures better control on deliveries of stock.
(ii) There are transport bottlenecks which may result in delay in deliveries.
(iii) The design or process may be a trade secret which a firm may not like to pass on to the suppliers.
(iv) As a matter of policy management may decide to manufacture and not to depend on a single source of supply.

However, buying may be preferred rather than making under the following situations:

(i) Proper facilities for manufacture, e.g., equipments, skill, time, etc., may not be readily available.
(ii) Market trends for the item to be manufactured may be seasonal, cyclical or risky.

(iii) Small return on capital employed may make further investment on manufacture unattractive.

(iv) Special technique may be required for manufacturing.

Example 12

An electronic goods manufacturing company finds that while it costs ₹ 6.25 to make a component X, the same is available in the market at ₹ 5.75 each, with an assurance of continued supply. The break-up of cost is given below:

	₹/each
Materials	2.75
Labour	1.75
Other variable cost	0.50
Fixed cost	1.25
	6.25

(i) Should you make or buy?

(ii) What would be your decision if the supplier offers the component at ₹ 4.85?

Solution:

Let us first find out the marginal cost per unit of component X.

	₹
Materials	2.75
Labour	1.75
Other variable cost	0.50
Marginal cost	5.00

(i) The decision to make or buy is influenced by the fact whether the capacity to be released by way of stopping manufacture of the component can be utilised in producing some other profitable product or not. If the released capacity can be utilised profitably elsewhere, buying is preferable to making.

If the released capacity cannot be utilised profitably elsewhere, the fixed cost of ₹ 1.25 will have to be incurred, and hence, the saving in cost will be the marginal cost of ₹ 5 only. The net cost of buying will be ₹ 7 (i.e. purchase price ₹ 5.75 + unrecovered fixed cost ₹ 1.25). So, buying from the market will mean an extra cost of ₹ 2 (i.e. ₹ 7 – 5).

(ii) If the price offered by the supplier is ₹ 4.85 which is less than the marginal cost of ₹ 5, it will be economical to buy the component X even if the capacity released cannot be utilised profitably elsewhere. This will result in a saving of ₹ 0.15 per unit (i.e. ₹ 5 – 4.85). However, the saving will be more if the released capacity can be utilised profitably elsewhere.

15.5.5 Closing Down of a Plant or Division, Outsourcing or Suspending Activities

This may relate to a product, department, division, or even the firm itself. A proposal to suspend, drop or outsource, or close down a part of the business activity may arise due to circumstances like unprofitable operation, trade recession, etc. If a product or division or plant earns negative contribution, i.e. marginal costs exceeding sales then it would be desirable to shut down the product unless, of course, there is other special reason to do so.

In a shut down decision the fixed cost should be analyzed and divided into two groups—(i) specific, identifiable or associated fixed cost, and (ii) general fixed cost.

The specific fixed cost will be directly affected by the decision, and hence, this should be taken into account along with marginal costs. The general fixed cost may or may not remain constant. When general fixed costs remain constant a product may be shut down or suspended if its total contribution is less than the fixed costs associated with it. When general fixed costs are likely to come down in the event of closure or suspension of a product, the excess of contribution over specific fixed costs will have to be compared with savings or reduction in general fixed costs. If the excess of contribution is more than the general fixed costs, it would be more beneficial to close down the product and vice versa.

Example 13

A company has three branches. Their summarized accounting particulars for a period are given below:

Branches	Mumbai (₹)	Kolkata (₹)	Chennai (₹)
Sales	450000	400000	700000
Branch expenses:			
Salaries, commission and travelling expenses	41000	40000	60000
Advertisement expenses	9000	10000	11000
Other expenses	10000	11000	12000

Head office expenses of ₹ 155000 are apportioned to branches on the basis of sales. However 25% of the sales value is taken as gross profit. Prepare a comparative profit and loss statement for these branches. Offer your comments on the contemplated closure of the branch which shows a loss assuming that in the event of closure of a branch, Head office expenses (i) will remain unaffected, (ii) can be reduced by 30%?

Solution:

Calculation of Branch Profitability

Particulars	Mumbai (₹)	Kolkata (₹)	Chennai (₹)	Total (₹)
Sales	450000	400000	700000	1550000
Gross profit (25% of sales)	112500	100000	175000	387500
Branch expenses:				
Salaries, commission and travelling expenses	41000	40000	60000	141000
Advertisement expenses	9000	10000	11000	30000
Other expenses	10000	11000	12000	33000
	60000	61000	83000	204000

Contribution:				
(Gross profit – Branch expenses)	52500	39000	92000	183500
Head office expenses				
(Apportioned on sales value)	45000	40000	70000	155000
Branch profit (+)/loss (–)	(+) 7500	(–) 1000	(+) 22000	(+) 28500

Since Kolkata branch is showing a loss of ₹ 1000, it is proposed to close down this branch. However, the proposal should be evaluated in the light of two alternative situations as follows:

(i) *When there is no reduction of head office expenses*

In this situation closure of Kolkata branch will result in a loss of contribution by ₹ 39000, whereas the entire head office expenses will have to be borne by Mumbai and Chennai branches. It means that head office expenses remaining constant, the overall profit will come down by ₹ 39000 due to the loss of contribution. It is evident from the following statement:

Contribution from Mumbai and Chennai = ₹ 52500 + ₹ 92000	= ₹ 144500
Less head office expenses (unaffected)	= ₹ 155000
Net loss	= ₹ (–) 10500

Thus, Kolkata branch should not be closed down.

(ii) *When head office expenses are reduced by* 30%

$$30\% \text{ of ₹ } 155000 = \frac{(\text{₹ } 30 \times 155000)}{100} = \text{₹ } 46500$$

Revised Head Office expenses = ₹ 155000 – ₹ 46500 = ₹ 108500.

In this situation if the reduction in head office expenses exceeds the loss of contribution, then closing down of a branch would be a better proposition in order to improve overall profit position. If Kolkata branch is closed down profit will increase by ₹ 7500 i.e., (₹ 46500 – ₹ 39000) = ₹ 7500. It is evident from the following:

Contribution from Mumbai and Chennai = ₹ 52500 + ₹ 92000	= ₹ 144500
Less: head office expenses (revised)	= ₹ 108500
Net profit	= ₹ 36000

Therefore, a decision to close down Kolkata branch would be prudent and more beneficial to the company.

While it is a fact that suspension or temporary closure of a firm will help avoid certain fixed costs but there are some additional costs which may have to be incurred for redundancy payments, maintenance of plants, training of new personnel, etc. All these costs are associated with temporary closing down of a firm and should be taken into consideration in arriving at a decision. Besides, certain other factors to be taken into account are as follows:

(i) Obsolescence of plant
(ii) Retaining the customers

(iii) Relationship with workers
(iv) Relationship with the suppliers
(v) Non-collection of dues from customers
(vi) Operations carried based on overdraft system

Example 14

The annual flexible budget of a firm is as follows:

Production capacity	40%	60%	80%	100%
Costs	(₹)	(₹)	(₹)	(₹)
Direct labour	16000	24000	32000	40000
Direct material	12000	18000	24000	30000
Production overhead	11400	12600	13800	15000
Administration overhead	5800	6200	6600	7000
Selling and distribution overhead	6200	6800	7400	8000
Total cost	51400	67600	83800	100000

Owing to the business recession the firm is presently operating at 50% capacity. The selling price had to be lowered to such an extent that the directors are considering seriously whether or not their factory should be closed down temporarily until trade recession has passed.

A market research team advised to the firm that there will be an increase of sales to 75% of normal capacity and the sales revenue in the second year would be expected at ₹ 90000. The present sales revenue at 50% capacity level is amounted to ₹ 49500 throughout the year. If the directors decide to close down the factory for a year, it is estimated the following:

(i) the present fixed costs would be reduced to ₹ 11000 per annum;
(ii) close-down costs would amount to ₹ 7500;
(iii) necessary plant maintenance would cost ₹ 1000;
(iv) on reopening the factory the cost of plant overhauling, training etc. of new personnel would amount to ₹ 4000.

Prepare a statement for the directors in appropriate manner and advise the management whether or not it is desirable to close the factory.

Solution:

Calculation of marginal costs and fixed costs

At 50% capacity operation

At 60% the total cost	= ₹	67600
At 40% the total cost	= ₹	51400
Difference 20%, cost difference	= ₹	16200

The cost difference is due to the variable costs only.

$$\text{Variable costs at 40\% would be} = \frac{(16200 \times 40)}{20} = ₹\ 32400$$

$$\text{Fixed costs} = \text{Total costs} - \text{Variable costs}$$

$$= ₹\ 51400 - ₹\ 32400 = ₹\ 19000$$

$$\text{Variable costs at 50\% would be} = \frac{(16200 \times 50)}{20} = ₹\ 40500$$

At 75% capacity operation

At 80% the total cost = ₹ 83800
At 60% the total cost = ₹ 67600
Difference 20%, cost difference = ₹ 16200

$$\text{Variable costs at 75\% would be} = \frac{(16200 \times 75)}{20} = ₹\ 60750$$

The fixed costs remain the same at ₹ 19000

$$\text{Variable costs at 60\% would be} = \frac{(16200 \times 60)}{20} = ₹\ 48600$$

Calculation of special costs for close down i.e., at '0' capacity operation

Close down costs = ₹ 7500
Plant maintenance cost = ₹ 1000
Overhauling, training, etc. = ₹ 4000
Total = ₹ 12500

Statement of profit and loss for expected levels of operations

Levels of operations	0%	50%	75%
Particulars	(₹)	(₹)	(₹)
Sales	0	49500	90000
Less marginal costs	0	40500	60750
Contribution	0	9000	29250
Less fixed costs	11000	19000	19000
Profit (+)/loss (–)	(–) 11000	(–) 10000	(+) 10250
Add special costs	12500	–	–
Total profit (+)/loss (–)	(–) 23500	(–) 10000	(+) 10250

Comment

It is clear from the statement that the loss of the firm will reduce from ₹ 23500 to ₹ 10000, if it is allowed to continue its operation. Further, in the second year there will be an estimated profit of ₹ 10250 at 75% operation. So, closing down of the plant is undesirable.

Example 15

ABC Ltd. manufactures three different products X, Y and Z. The company's budgeted profit & loss statement for 2010 are as follows:

Particulars	Total (₹)	X (₹)	Y (₹)	Z (₹)
Sales	300000	45000	225000	30000
Production cost:				
Variable	180000	24000	144000	12000
Fixed	60000	3000	48000	9000
Factory cost	240000	27000	192000	21000
Administration and Selling cost:				
Variable	24000	8100	8100	7800
Fixed	6000	2100	1800	2100
Total cost	270000	37200	201900	30900
Profit (Loss)	30000	7800	23100	(900)

Based on the above information the board is inclined to eliminate product Z, on which a loss was budgeted. Advise the board members with your considered opinion?

Solution:

Comparative Profitability Statement

Particulars	X (₹)	Y (₹)	Z (₹)	Total (₹)
Sales	45000	225000	30000	300000
Variable cost:				
Production cost	24000	144000	12000	180000
Administration & Selling cost	8100	8100	7800	24000
Total variable cost	32100	152100	19800	204000
Contribution	12900	72900	10200	96000
Fixed cost (₹ 60000 + 6000)				66000
Profit				30000

It is evident from the above statement that product Z provides a contribution of ₹ 10200. If the product is eliminated, the total contribution and the consequent total profit will be reduced by ₹ 10200. Therefore, product Z should be continued.

Example 16

ABC Ltd. manufactures three different products X, Y and Z in three different locations. The budgeted figures for the year 2011 are as follows:

Factories	Kanpur (₹)	Himachal Pradesh (₹)	Fatepur (₹)
Sales	440000	400000	700000
Branch expenses:			
Salaries	42000	38000	62000
Advertisement	8000	15000	10000
Miscellaneous	10000	8000	11000

There is a Head Office in Mumbai, the estimated cost of which is ₹ 154000 and this cost is to be apportioned to three factories on the basis of their sales figures. Variable costs amount to 75% of the sales of each factory.

You are required to:

(i) Prepare a comparative profit & loss statement for the year 2011

(ii) Advise whether the Himachal Pradesh factory should be closed if that would save the Himachal Pradesh branch expenses and reduce the Head Office expenses from ₹ 154000 to ₹ 124000.

Solution:

Budgeted Profit & Loss Statement

	Kanpur (₹)	Himachal Pradesh (₹)	Fatepur (₹)	Total (₹)
Sales	440000	400000	700000	1540000
Variable costs: 75%	330000	300000	525000	1155000
Contribution: 25%	110000	100000	175000	385000
Branch expenses	60000	61000	83000	204000
Head Office expenses	44000	40000	70000	154000
Fixed costs	104000	101000	153000	358000
Profit (Loss)	6000	(1000)	22000	27000

From the above statement it is observed that Himachal Pradesh branch provides a contribution of ₹ 100000. If the branch is closed down there will be a saving of ₹ 91000 [i.e. ₹ 61000 + (₹ 154000 – 124000)] only in fixed cost. Therefore, profit will come down by ₹ 9000 (i.e. ₹ 100000 – 91000). Hence, it is advisable not to close down Himachal Pradesh factory.

Example 17

The following data relates to a company which produces three products X, Y, and Z.

	X	Y	Z
Production (units)	2000	2400	3000
Cost per unit:	₹	₹	₹
Materials	5	8	12
Labour	2	4	3
Variable overhead	1	2	1
Fixed overhead	6	5	6
	14	19	22
Selling price per unit	20	25	30
Profit per unit	6	6	8

The works manager suggests that one production line should be discounted and the current production may be doubled in the remaining two lines.

Evaluate the proposal and advise the management whether the proposal is acceptable? Which product line should be discontinued?

Solution:

Fixed overhead:

Product	₹
X = 2000 × ₹ 6	= 12000
Y = 2400 × ₹ 5	= 12000
Z = 3000 × ₹ 6	= 18000
Total fixed cost	= 42000

Contribution per unit:	X	Y	Z
	₹	₹	₹
Materials	5	8	12
Labour	2	4	3
Variable overhead	1	2	1
Variable cost	8	14	16
Selling price	20	25	30
Contribution	12	11	14

Profitability under alternative arrangements

(i) *If all the products are continued:*

Contribution

Product	₹
X = 2000 × ₹ 12	= 24000
Y = 2400 × ₹ 11	= 26400
Z = 3000 × ₹ 14	= 42000
	= 92400
Fixed overhead	= 42000
Profit	50400

(ii) *If product X is eliminated:*

Contribution

Product	₹
Y = 4800 × ₹ 11	= 52800
Z = 6000 × ₹ 14	= 84000
	136800
Fixed overhead	= 42000
Profit	94800

(iii) *If product Y is eliminated:*

Contribution

Product	₹
X = 4000 × ₹ 12	= 48000
Z = 6000 × ₹ 14	= 84000
	132000
Fixed overhead	= 42000
Profit	90000

(iv) *If product Z is eliminated:*

Contribution

Product	₹
X = 4000 × ₹ 12	= 48000
Y = 4800 × ₹ 11	= 52800
	100800
Fixed overhead	= 42000
Profit	58800

From the above calculation it is clear that if any of the products is eliminated, the position will be better than the current position. The best position will be achieved with a profit of ₹ 94800 as against the current profit of ₹ 50400, provided product X is eliminated.

However, this decision is entirely based on profitability analysis. The management may consider the following aspects before taking final decision:

(i) Whether other product lines will have adverse effects if one product line is eliminated

(ii) Whether market will be in a position to absorb the entire additional productions of the other two product lines.

15.5.6 Acceptance of Additional Order at Lower Price

When additional orders are quoted by the firm below normal selling price, management should ensure that these will not adversely affect the normal market and the goodwill of the firm. As regards the foreign markets, the effect of benefits viz. import entitlements, subsidies etc. from the government should be taken into account while fixing up the export price. It is of course, assumed that the capacity proposed to be utilised for this purpose cannot be more profitably utilised elsewhere.

Example 18

ABC & Co. Ltd. has a capacity to produce 20000 units at a cost of ₹ 20 per unit by utilising 50% of the capacity. Put of which, 40% of the total cost is fixed, and 60% is variable. A purchaser offers to buy 8000 additional units at ₹ 18. Can this offer be accepted by the company?

Solution:

Variable cost per unit = 60% of ₹ 20 = ₹ 12
Existing production at 50% capacity = 10000 units
Idle capacity = 10000 units

Therefore, the company can produce 10000 additional units without incurring any additional fixed cost. Let us now find out the contribution per unit at an offered price of ₹ 18 per unit.

Contribution per unit = (Offered price ₹ 18 – Variable cost ₹ 12) = ₹ 6

Acceptance of the offer will increase the total contribution as also the total profit by ₹ 48000 (₹ 6 × 8000). The company is therefore advised to accept the offer.

Example 19

XYZ Co. Ltd. is currently running its plant at 50% capacity level. The following information is available from the books of the company:

	Cost of production per unit (₹)
Direct material	4
Direct labour	2
Variable overhead	6
Fixed overhead (fully absorbed)	4
	16

Production per month = 40000 units
Selling price per unit = ₹ 14

An exporting company offers to buy 10000 units per month @ ₹ 13 per unit. The company is not sure as to whether the offer should be accepted due to the reason that it will further increase its current operating loss.

Advise the management whether the company should accept the offer or reject?

Solution:

Existing production at 50% capacity = 40000 units

Idle capacity = 40000 units

The production of 10000 additional units for export market will not require any additional fixed cost.

Variable cost per unit (₹)	
Direct material	4
Direct labour	2
Variable overhead	6
	12

Profit/Loss Statement

	Without export order	With export order
Level of sales (units)	40000	50000
Sales revenue: 40000 × ₹ 14 =	₹ 560000	₹ 560000
10000 × ₹ 13 =	–	130000
	560000	690000
Less: Variable cost @ ₹ 12	480000	600000
Contribution	80000	90000
Less: Fixed cost: 40000 × ₹ 4	160000	160000
Loss	80000	70000

From the above Profit/Loss Statement it is observed that acceptance of the offer will increase the total contribution by ₹ 10000 which means that the company will be able to recover ₹ 10000 more of its fixed cost. Therefore, the total loss will be reduced by ₹ 10000, i.e. from ₹ 80000 to ₹ 70000. The management should be advised to accept the offer. It is assumed that reduction of price in the export market is not likely to affect domestic sales unless the goods are re-exported for sale in the domestic market.

Example 20

ABC Ltd. has been operating at 60% of its potential capacity. The following particulars for the year ended 31st March 2010 are available:

Units produced and sold	10000
Cost incurred:	₹
Materials	50000
Direct labour	30000
Production overhead (60% variable)	20000
Administration overhead (fixed)	10000
Selling and distribution overhead (50% fixed)	30000

The current selling price per unit is ₹ 16. In order to utilise idle capacity the sales manager recommends accepting an export order for 5000 units at ₹ 13 per unit. The export order will entail an additional expense of 0.30 per unit for special packing.

Advise the management with your recommendation whether it is worthwhile to accept the export order?

Solution:

Profitability of Export Order

	Per unit (₹)	For 5000 units (₹)
Materials	5.00	25000
Direct labour	3.00	15000
Variable overhead:		
Production	1.20	6000
Selling and distribution	1.50	7500
Additional expenses for packing	0.30	1500
Variable cost	11.00	55000
Sales	13.00	65000
Contribution	2.00	10000

It is evident from the above statement that the export order at a lower price will yield an additional contribution of ₹ 10000 and will increase the profit by the same amount as the company is currently operating above the break-even point. The order should therefore be accepted. However, following additional points should be taken into consideration before taking a decision:

1. The cost of additional working capital
2. Can the idle capacity be utilised more profitably for producing some other products?
3. Will there be any risk of dumping?
4. The effect of rnduced export price on the domestic market.

Example 21

The variable cost of a product X manufactured by a company is ₹ 4 and the selling price is ₹ 10 per unit. The company accepts its net profit for the current year to be ₹ 275000 after charging fixed cost of ₹ 85000.

The company's production capacity is not fully utilised. Its market research department recommends three alternative strategies for the next year, viz:

Strategy	Reduce selling price by	Sales volume expected to be increased by
1	5%	10%
2	7%	20%
3	10%	25%

(i) Assuming that the same cost structure will prevail as in the current year, evaluate the alternative strategies available to the company and recommend which one is the most profitable?

(ii) Suggest other considerations which should be taken into consideration before taking the decision by the management?

Solution:

(i) We know, Contribution = Fixed cost + Profit = ₹ 85000 + ₹ 275000 = ₹ 360000
So, contribution per unit = ₹ 10 – ₹ 4 = ₹ 6

$$\text{Expected sales} = \frac{₹\ 360000}{₹\ 6} = 60000 \text{ units}$$

Evaluation of Strategies

Strategy	Selling price per unit ₹	Contribution per unit ₹	Estimated sales units	Total contribution ₹
1	9.50	5.50	66000	363000
2	9.30	5.30	72000	381600
3	9.00	5.00	75000	375000

From the above statement it is apparent that Strategy 2 with the highest total contribution is the most profitable.

(ii) Following additional points should be taken into consideration before taking a decision by the management:

(a) The cost of additional working capital particularly fixed cost.

(b) Accuracy and reasonableness of the demand estimates.

(c) Can the idle capacity be utilised more profitably for producing some other products?

(d) Reaction of the competitors to the projected price reduction.

Example 22

A company has prepared a draft budget for the next year based on 3 items produced, the details of which is given below:

Product	X	Y	Z
Budgeted sales (units)	20000	15000	8000
Sale price per unit (₹)	30	40	50
Variable cost per unit (₹):			
Material	10	20	5
Labour	12	6	30
Sales	3	6	5

Fixed labour cost is ₹ 110000.

Three members of the board of directors have each put forward their own recommendations to improve profitability. Their recommendations are:

Sales director: A special advertisement campaign costing an additional amount of ₹ 65000 would increase sales of all products by 25% for the year.

Personnel director: A labour incentive scheme would increase variable labour cost by one-sixth, but would eliminate the fixed labour cost for the year.

Finance director: Introduce a sales commission scheme which would increase the sales volume by 50% for the year, but would also increase variable selling cost by ₹ 2 per unit.

Evaluate these three unrelated recommendations, showing the effect of each on the budgeted profit? Give your recommendation with reasons?

Solution:

	X (₹)	Y (₹)	Z (₹)
Sale price per unit	30	40	50
Variable cost:			
Material	10	20	5
Labour	12	6	30
Sales	3	6	5
	25	32	40
Contribution per unit	5	8	10
Budgeted sales (units)	20000	15000	8000
Total contribution (₹)	100000	120000	80000

	(₹)
Total contribution	300000
Fixed labour cost	110000
Budgeted profit	190000

Suggestions

Sales director

	(₹)
Revised contribution = ₹ 300000 + 25%	= 375000
Fixed cost = 110000 + 65000	= 175000
Budgeted profit	= 200000

Personnel director

Current contribution		= 300000
Less: Increase in variable cost:		
Product X = 20000 × 1/6 × ₹ 12 =	40000	
Product Y = 15000 × 1/6 × ₹ 6 =	15000	
Product Z = 8000 × 1/6 × ₹ 30 =	40000	95000
Revised contribution		205000
Fixed cost		= –
Budgeted profit		205000

Finance director

Budgeted sales × Contribution per unit	
Product X = 30000 × ₹ 3 (i.e. ₹ 5 – 2)	= 90000
Product Y = 22500 × ₹ 6 (i.e. ₹ 8 – 2)	= 135000
Product Z = 12000 × ₹ 8 (i.e. ₹10 – 2)	= 96000
Revised contribution	= 321000
Fixed cost	= 110000
Budgeted profit	211000

From the above calculation it is observed that all suggestions would improve the budgeted profit. However, suggestion of Finance director is the best with the highest budgeted profit due to increase in sales more than the increase in variable cost.

Example 23

The following information is available from ABC Ltd. which produces and sells a single product:

	₹ Per unit
Material	16
Variable conversion cost	12
Agents' margin @ 10%	4

Fixed cost = ₹ 500000

Current sales = 90000 units

Capacity utilisation by the company = 60%

Suggestions have been made from various employees to increase sales, viz:

(i) Reduce sale price by 5%

(ii) Increase agents' margin by 25% over the current rates.

Evaluate both the suggestions and recommend if the company wants to maintain the current profit?

Solution:

Variable cost per unit= ₹ 16 +12 + 4 = ₹ 32

Contribution per unit = Selling price – Variable cost per unit
= ₹ 40 – 32 = ₹ 8.

Total contribution on current sales = 90000 × ₹ 8 = ₹ 720000.

Profit = Total contribution – Fixed cost
= ₹ 720000 – 500000 = ₹ 220000.

(i) Reducing sale price by 5%

Selling price = ₹ 40 – 5% of 40 = ₹ 38.

Agents' margin = 10% of 38 = 3.80

Variable cost per unit = ₹ 16 +12 + 3.80 = ₹ 31.80

Contribution per unit = ₹ 38 – 31.80 = ₹ 6.20.

Therefore, sales required to maintain the current profit of ₹ 220000

$$= \frac{\text{Fixed cost + Desired profit}}{\text{Contribution per unit}} = \frac{₹\ 500000 + 220000}{₹\ 6.20} = 116129 \text{ units.}$$

(ii) Increasing agents' margin by 25% over the current rates

Agents' margin = ₹ 4 + 25% of 4 = ₹ 5 or 12.5% of sales

Variable cost per unit = ₹ 16 +12 + 5 = ₹ 33

Contribution per unit = ₹ 40 – 33 = ₹ 7.

Therefore, sales required to maintain the current profit of ₹ 220000

$$= \frac{₹\ 500000 + 220000}{₹\ 7} = 102857 \text{ units}$$

Recommendation

The second proposal is recommended as contribution per unit is higher at ₹ 7 in comparison with ₹ 6.20 in the first proposal. Moreover, the number of units required to be sold to maintain the current level of profit is lower at 102857 units as against 116129 units in the first proposal. The company can increase its profit if it can increase the volume of sales beyond the level of 102857 units.

15.6 CONCLUSION

In the opening up of the economy and global competition the organizations can no longer dictate the market and the products manufactured by various companies are at present sold at competitive prices. The management of companies have now realized that if they are to survive and maintain their profitability and market share, they have to analyze, and control the cost of production which is in their domain, and offer the quality products at competitive price. This chapter examined the concept of marginal costing, cost-volume-profit analysis and demonstrated with examples how managerial decisions are taken by the organizations as a part of management control exercise by applying marginal costing techniques.

REVIEW QUESTIONS

15.1 Discuss with at least two examples how marginal costing technique can be applied by a company in taking management decisions?

15.2 A manufacturer with an overall capacity of 100000 machine hours has been so far producing a standard mix of 15000 units of product A, and 10000 units of product B, and 10000 units of product C. The total expenditure exclusive of fixed charges is found to be ₹ 209000.

The cost ratio among the products are: 1 : 1.5 : 1.75 for A, B, and C respectively per unit. The fixed charges come to ₹ 2.00 per unit. When the unit selling prices are ₹ 6.25 for A, ₹ 7.50 for B, and ₹ 10.50 for C, he incurs a loss.

He desires to change the product mix as under:

	Mix 1	Mix 2	Mix 3
A	18000	15000	22000
B	12000	6000	8000
C	7000	13000	8000

Advise the management, what mix would be the most beneficial to the firm.

15.3 XYZ Ltd. produces and sells two products A and B at 75% level of capacity. The cost sheets of these products are as under:

	Products	
	A	B
Total units produced and sold	600	400
Cost per unit	₹	₹
Direct material	2.00	4.00
Direct labour	4.00	4.00
Factory overhead (40% fixed)	5.00	3.00
Selling & Admn. overhead (60% fixed)	8.00	5.00
	19.00	16.00
Selling price per unit	23.00	19.00

Factory overheads are absorbed on the basis of machine hour which is a limiting factor. The machine hour rate is ₹ 2.00 per hour. The company receives an offer from Canada for the purchase of product A at a price of ₹ 17.50 per unit. Alternatively, the company has another offer from Middle-East for the purchase of product B at a price of ₹ 15.50 per unit. In both cases, a special packing charge of ₹ 0.50 per unit has to be borne by the company. The company can accept either of these two orders, but in any case, the company can supply such quantities as may be possible to produce by utilising the balance of 25% of its capacity.

Prepare:

(i) A statement showing feasibility of the two export proposals with your recommendations as to which proposal should be accepted.

(ii) A statement showing the overall profitability of the company after incorporating the export proposal recommended by you.

Part V

Auditing as a Tool of Management Control System

16 Auditing

16.1 INTRODUCTION

Adoption of a system of audit program by companies is recognition of the fact that the companies can no longer survive simply by producing and marketing a product. Audit constitutes an integral and on-going part of the business. It not only provides a way of clarifying the areas requiring information, but also suggests the most productive methods of eliciting, organizing, and presenting the information.

This chapter deals with meaning, nature and concepts of audit. It also explains the various types of auditing practices in an organization to show how auditing can be used by the management as a tool of management control system.

16.2 MEANING AND NATURE OF AUDIT

The origin of the word 'audit' lies in the Latin verb 'audire' which means 'to hear'. Audit is the examination and verification of records and evidences kept by an organization, by a professional or a group of professionals to confirm whether the records and evidences exhibit a true and fair view of the state of affairs of the organization.

Traditionally, audit has been used to monitor a company's financial performance by evaluating it against a set of standards imposed by the government regulators or by the professional standards groups. In companies 'financial audit' has been a well-established part of the management system for a long-time. Recently, most progressive companies have begun to apply the audit concept to a broader range of management processes. Presently, audit has become a tool for evaluating the performances of all key systems of the organization.

Audits fall into two main categories—Financial audit and non-financial audit.

16.3 DIFFERENCES AND SIMILARITIES OF FINANCIAL AUDIT (FA) AND NON-FINANCIAL AUDIT (NFA)

Differences

(i) FA relies primarily on standards set externally (by the government or professional standard institutions). NFA relies on standards set internally by the management based on customer and competitor information.
(ii) FA procedures are formalized and consistent from company to company. NFA procedures are fluid and should be adopted by each company.
(iii) FA standards are essentially the same from audit to audit. NFA standards change as performance of the organization improves.
(iv) FA's focus is on complying with standards set by the external groups. NFA focus is on exceeding standards set internally.
(v) In FA, audience is primarily external, with audit standards used for building credibility. In NFA, audience is generally internal, with date being used to improve performance.
(vi) FA is conducted yearly. NFA is conducted generally every 18 or 24 months.
(vii) FA focuses on measures that affect only financial performance. NFA focuses on a broad range of functions that contribute to the success or failure of a particular process.

Similarities

(i) Both FA and NFA measure compliance with a set of standards.
(ii) Both FA and NFA identify opportunities for performance improvement.
(iii) Both FA and NFA are systematic ways of generating performance data.
(iv) Both FA and NFA produce information that can be used to limit a company's liability.

16.4 MERITS AND DEMERITS OF AUDIT

Merits

Audit is a very powerful management tool and brings the following benefits:

(i) It identifies opportunities for improvement.
(ii) It gives a reality check.
(iii) It identifies backdated strategies.
(iv) It measures performance improvements of the organization.
(v) It increases management's ability to address concerns.
(vi) It improves teamwork within the organization.
(vii) It changes mind set of the employees for betterment.
(viii) It increases the employees' commitment to change.

Demerits

(i) Audit is not a panacea for solving all problems of the organization.
(ii) Audit cannot be used to prioritize improvement opportunities identified through the assessment process.
(iii) Audit cannot mobilize people to action.
(iv) Audit cannot help the management to bring about changes to solve problems.
(v) Audit cannot produce better information than the measures used to gather information.
(vi) Audit cannot improve performance by itself. The managers should therefore, approach audit with an open mind.

16.5 TIMING AND FREQUENCY OF AUDIT

Timing of audit depends on certain factors as follows:

(i) What are the seasonal or cyclical fluctuations in the business?
(ii) What is the best time for the personnel involved in the process to accommodate an audit?
(iii) When will an audit produce the most reliable results?
(iv) What is the effectiveness of the company's systems and processes as compared to its peers?
(v) What types of resources are needed to conduct audit? Does the company have adequate and qualified personnel to be engaged in the audit team for conducting audit?
(vi) Is the company serious enough to implement the recommendations of the previous audit reports?

One-time audit has a limited long-term value due to following reasons:

(i) Change in conditions makes one-time audit irrelevant. Regular audit helps to ensure that management priorities change with the circumstances.
(ii) Regular audit helps to monitor progress of the organizational activities.
(iii) Regular audit sets up a more realistic baseline for managers.

While financial audit is typically conducted once a year, the average frequency of non-financial audit is done for every 18 or 24 months.

16.6 AUDIT PROCESS

An audit process involves the following activities:

(i) Staff the audit team
(ii) Set up an audit plan
(iii) Lay the base work for audit
(iv) Analyze audit results
(v) Share audit results

(vi) Write audit report
(vii) Deal with reservations to audit recommendations carefully
(viii) Build an ongoing audit program

16.6.1 Staff the Audit Team

The audit team generally consists of 3 to 4 people, and reports to the CEO or Director (finance). An audit team should consist of people having substantial qualification, knowledge of systems and processes within the company, and in diverse areas. The team should consist of new incumbents as well as experienced personnel. Team members should possess strong analytical and interpersonal skills. They should be able to communicate well with their peers and establish strong working relationships. They should have an understanding of a company's overall strategy and its goals and objectives.

An audit team leader is selected from amongst the team members. He plays a very important role in the audit. The qualities required in a team leader are:

(a) Excellent interpersonal skills
(b) Good relationship with the CEO and other senior executives
(c) Strong analytical skills
(d) Ability to assimilate and process large complex data quickly
(e) Some knowledge of the functions to be audited and extensive knowledge of the type of process to be audited

16.6.2 Set Up an Audit Plan

Before the actual audit is conducted, it is necessary to prepare an audit plan which states how an audit should be done chronologically. It also spells out the allocation of responsibility of each member of the audit team and the completion time of conducting audit.

16.6.3 Lay the Base Work for Audit

This step requires garnering of support from all executives and employees of the organization before starting the audit works. The audit team leader or audit manager should hold discussions with the employees and the operation managers regarding the time of audit, the method of collection of data, and the process of audit. A checklist may be prepared for this purpose for ensuring performance of audit works systematically.

16.6.4 Analyze Audit Results

Audit results help the management to find out the opportunities for improvement as they identify the gaps between the company's targets and the actual performance.

16.6.5 Share Audit Results

Audit findings should be shared to the managers and executives of the department under audit in a clear manner so as to get their reactions against audit findings.

16.6.6 Write Audit Report

After the audit is over, the audit findings, results and recommendations are written in a formal report called an audit report which is sent to the higher authorities with a copy to the manager of the department under audit. An audit report serves as a base document to measure work performance of the department in future audits.

16.6.7 Deal with Reservations to Audit Recommendations

Generally, the reservations to audit recommendations arise from the management directly in the form of doubts about implementation of audit recommendations as well as from the other employees indirectly in the form of asking unnecessary details, etc. These resistances can be removed by way of free and fair dialogue with the managers in order to deal with difference of opinion, and encouraging employees to come out with the frank opinions.

16.6.8 Build an Ongoing Audit Programme

To make the audit works effective, the company should build an ongoing audit programme as it helps in monitoring improvement in work performance of the organization over a period of time.

16.7 AUDIT TOOLS AND TECHNIQUES

The collection of accurate and comprehensive data is one of the key factors for an effective audit. Data for audit can be collected through surveys, questionnaires, interviews, focus groups and direct observation. There are differences in the way these methods can be applied, depending on the type of audit, and the nature of the source data.

Several variables need to be taken into consideration in determining which method to use. These include the type of data being obtained, the number of people from whom responses must be obtained, and the resources available for completion of the research. Some other factors, viz., budget, timing, project ability, geography, etc., are also important in choosing a particular auditing method.

16.7.1 Surveys

Surveys help in collecting information on five variables. They are as follows:

(i) Background data (i.e., age, education, income, etc.)
(ii) Behavioral data (i.e., buying habits etc.)
(iii) Data on attitudes and beliefs
(iv) Data on opinions
(v) Data on knowledge of company programmes

Types of surveys

There are two types of surveys. They are:

(a) Written survey: It has lowest response rate. The data is unreliable.
(b) Telephone (oral) survey: It is the fast means of collecting data.

Limitations of surveys

There are plenty of limitations of surveys. They are mentioned hereunder:

(a) A survey imposes on the respondents, the structure and standards of relevance of the researcher.
(b) Surveys assume that all people use the same language and interpret survey questions in the same way.
(c) Surveys usually reveal only superficial information that is complete.
(d) A survey distorts the political reality of the organization implying that all opinions carry equal weight.
(e) The use of random samples in the survey approach assumes that the required information is distributed evenly throughout the organization and could lead the researcher to develop a distorted picture of the company.
(f) The survey process itself affects the responses depending on when and by whom the questions are asked.
(g) Surveys assume that people have opinions, but in reality, people may not disclose that they do not know or they do not have an opinion.
(h) Surveys assume a relationship between attitudes or opinion and behaviour.

Most survey instruments consist mainly of questions where the respondents have a clear defined set of responses to choose from. These are known as close-ended questions. The close-ended questions are easier to tabulate and aggregate. The open-ended questions are the questions where respondents provide their own answers. These serve as a rich source of data.

Audit teams may like to include a few open-ended questions at the end of the sections containing close-ended questions to provide respondents an opportunity to share information.

16.7.2 Questionnaires

Questionnaires may be used when the data needed is simple and concrete.

There are certain advantages by this method. They are as follows:

(i) They serve as a guide for interviewers.
(ii) They are easily distributed to the respondents.
(iii) They serve as a preparation tool for the audit team.
(iv) They supplement other data gathering techniques.

Structure of a questionnaire

The purpose of the questionnaire and the topic being covered govern the structure to be used in designing the questionnaire. Generally, the most broad questions are put in the beginning and the most specific ones at the end. Effective questionnaires should, therefore, use clear, easily understandable language, avoid ambiguous questions, avoid putting forth a point of view which is likely to be biased, and use short sentences.

16.7.3 Focus Groups

Focus group method serves another approach to data gathering. It allows the collection of more information and involvement of more people than is possible in one-on-one interviews. A focus group may have 5 to 10 personnel. The session may last for a couple of hours.

Successful and effective focus groups have a skilled facilitator, who is responsible for guiding the group and managing group dynamics, well-selected participants coming from a homogeneous group, and an effective moderator guide who targets the information required from the session. The facilitator manages the information flow between group members.

16.7.4 Interviews

It is another method of collecting data on sensitive subjects. Here the skilled interviewers can establish a relationship of trust with the respondent. Interviews are often used by the audit team. Interviews are more suitable as most respondents enjoy talking rather than writing. But interviews are among the most expensive research tools. Sometimes it is difficult to aggregate data gathered from interviews.

Types of interviews

Three types of interviews are in vogue:

(a) Structured interviews
(b) Semi structured interviews
(c) Unstructured interviews

16.7.5 Direct Observation

This method finds many applications in corporate environments, especially in the audit process. Various techniques are available under direct observation as follows:

(i) Participant observation
(ii) Field observation
(iii) Trace data
(iv) Archival data

16.8 AUDIT EVIDENCE

It is a kind of information used by the auditor to determine whether the financial statements being audited are in accordance with the established rules and regulations. It must possess four characteristics as follows:

(i) Persuasive
(ii) Relevant
(iii) Unbiased
(iv) Objective

16.9 MANAGEMENT AUDIT

Management audit is defined as an examination of the conditions and a diagnosis of deficiencies with recommendations for correcting them. The objectives of management audit can be enumerated as follows:

(i) To critically analyze and evaluate management performance
(ii) To detect and overcome existing managerial deficiencies and operational problems
(iii) To determine the effectiveness of management in planning, organizing, directing, and controlling the organization's activities

16.9.1 Types of Management Audit

Management audit can be categorized into six types. They are:

(i) Complete audit
(ii) Compliance audit
(iii) Programme audit
(iv) Functional audit
(v) Efficiency audit
(vi) Propriety audit

Complete management audit

It evaluates the company's current total activities and measures the gap between its existing policies and objectives, and its actual activities. Complete management audit is conducted from a positive point of view. When weaknesses in operations or people are uncovered, non-vindictive suggestions are given to improve operational performance and the productivity of the personnel concerned.

Compliance management audit

In this audit, the auditors are asked to identify the gaps between the company's existing policies and objectives, and its actual practice. The auditors do not make any recommendations for improvements. They simply present their observations to the top management.

Programme management audit

This audit focuses on a specific programme. It is designed to appraise performance within a specified programme.

Functional management audit

It measures the difference between actual performance of an organization and its objectives, with emphasis on a particular function.

Efficiency management audit

The objectives of efficiency audit are as follows:

(i) To invest the capital in areas that generate optimum returns
(ii) To plan and invest judiciously in various functions

Propriety management audit

The objective of this audit is to identify the loopholes in administrative rules and regulations, and to suggest methods for improving the execution of plans and projects.

16.9.2 Benefits of Management Audit

There are plenty of benefits of management audit. They are the following:

(i) It provides an early warning signal of managerial problems and related operational difficulties.
(ii) It can be used as a source of information in assisting the organization to accomplish the desired objectives.
(iii) It helps to objectively and impartially evaluate organizational plans, structure, and the directions that management gives in the form of strategies and management processes.

16.9.3 Steps for Organization of Management Audit

There are six steps to be followed for organizing the management audit:

(i) Devise the statement of policy
(ii) Set up a separate audit department
(iii) Allocate competent personnel
(iv) Conduct staff training programmes
(v) Fix up time and cost of audit
(vi) Fix up frequency of audit

Devise the statement of policy

The management's approval and support should be reflected clearly and categorically in the company's highest policy statement. The policy statement should lay down very clearly the scope of activities to be undertaken by the auditor. The statement must categorically state that the auditor is authorized to review administrative and management controls on any activity within the company.

Set up a separate audit department

Depending on the size and nature of the business, the company should set up a separate audit department. The head of this department should report to the top executive directly. The audit function should be totally independent and free from pressure of various groups in the company. The management auditor's goal, therefore, is to attain a level of operational independence without any compromise of his audit objectives.

Allocate competent personnel

The auditors should possess basic knowledge of the technology and commercial practice of the company, an analytical, pragmatic approach, and thorough understanding of the control system. They should have adequate qualifications, knowledge of law, taxation, accounting, economics, quantitative methods and EDP system.

Conduct staff training programmes

Continuous training programmes are necessary to be conducted to achieve quality in performing audit assignments.

Fix up time and cost of audit

The time and cost will vary for each audit assignment, depending on the nature of assignment, the number of auditors assigned to perform the work.

Fix up frequency of audit

It depends on the organization. Audit should be conducted often enough to provide protection against growing problems.

16.9.4 Essentials for Effective Management Audit

Following pre-requisites deserve mention for effective management audit:

(i) Selection of audit personnel
(ii) Competence of the auditors
(iii) Establishment of a pre-audit condition by the auditors
(iv) Willingness of the company's employees to accept change

Audits are meant to highlight the strengths and weaknesses of the company's operations. It is up to the management at all levels to reward employees or to take corrective action. Setting up of a general program for management audit requires the top management's approval and support. This support must be reflected clearly and categorically in the company's highest policy statement. Besides, management should allocate personnel, train them and decide on the timing and frequency of management audit.

16.10 INTERNAL AUDIT

Internal audit is an independent appraisal function established within an organization to examine and evaluate its activities as a service to the organization.
Following are the objectives of internal audit:

(i) To assist members of the organization in the effective discharge of their responsibilities
(ii) To avoid discrepancies from creeping into the systems, processes and operations of an organization
(iii) To monitor, track, and report discrepancies, inefficiencies of personnel in the organization

16.11 FINANCIAL AUDIT

It is defined as a critical statutory review by an independent auditor to examine the correctness of financial statements and to establish whether they present a true and fair view of the company's financial position on a particular date. It is a statutory audit conducted by an independent statutory auditor at the end of every financial year.

16.12 SPECIAL AUDIT

Section 233A of the Companies Act, 1956, empowers the Central Government to call for a 'special audit' where the Central Government has reason to believe:

(i) That the affairs of the company are not being managed on sound business principles or according to prudent commercial practices

(ii) That the company is being managed in a manner likely to cause serious injury or damage to the interests of trade, industry or business to which it pertains

(iii) That the financial position of the company is such as might endanger its solvency

This audit may be conducted either by the company's auditor or another independent auditor appointed by the Central Government. On receipt of the special auditor's report, the Central Government may take such action as circumstances might warrant as per provisions of the Act.

16.13 COST AUDIT

It is defined as a statutory audit conducted by an independent cost and works accountant as per provisions of Section 233B of the Companies Act, 1956, to verify the cost of production of a particular product on the basis of accounts as regards utilization of material or labour or other items of costs, maintained by the company. The cost auditor must report to the Central Government with a copy to the company, on the adequacy of cost accounting records maintained by the company as prescribed by the government and confirm that they give a true and fair view of the cost of production, processing, manufacturing, or mining activities, as the case may be.

16.14 SOCIAL AUDIT

Social audit is defined as a systematic attempt to identify, analyze, measure, evaluate and monitor the effect of an organization's operations on society.

Turnbull Committee (1995) defines social audit as 'the process whereby an enterprise measures and reports on its performance in meeting its declared social, community, or environmental objectives'.

16.14.1 Features of Social Audit

The features of social audit are as follows:

(i) Social audit adheres to the specified norms established by the organization or by outside agency.

(ii) Social audit influences the policies, objectives, and actions of the organization to improve its social performance.

(iii) Social audit is conducted by the knowledgeable professionals.

16.14.2 Approaches to Social Audit

There are four approaches to the social audit. They are as follows:

(i) Inventory approach
(ii) Programme management approach
(iii) Cost-benefit approach
(iv) Social indicator approach

16.14.3 Types of Social Audit

There are six types of social audit. They are as follows:

(i) Social balance sheet and income statement
(ii) Social performance audit
(iii) Macro-micro social indicator audit
(iv) Constituency group attitude audit
(v) Government mandated audit
(vi) Social process or programme audit

16.15 ENVIRONMENTAL AUDIT

Environmental audit is a management tool to objectively and systematically evaluate environment management systems in an organization. It provides an in-depth review of the company processes and progress in realizing long-term strategic goals. It is intended to measure the impact of an organization's operations on the environment against a predetermined set of criteria and to assess them in terms of costs. It is part of a continuing and cyclic process which may be used to assist in determining the environmental expenses incurred by companies. The environmental audit examines the company's performance as against its policy, and is undertaken with reference to performance of personnel, technology, system and documentation and how these are related to relevant standards of practice.

16.15.1 Objectives of Environmental Audit

The objectives of an environmental audit are as follows:

(i) Evaluation of efficiency of resource allocation, i.e., man, machine, materials
(ii) Identification of areas of risk, environmental liabilities, weakness in management systems, etc., in complying with regulatory requirement
(iii) Insuring the control on waste pollutant generation

16.15.2 Types of Environmental Audit

There are two types of environmental audit. They are: environmental compliance audit, and environmental management audit.

Environmental compliance audit

Environmental compliance audit checks the degree of conformance to laws and rule prescribed by the relevant regulatory authorities. It covers issues such as housekeeping, practices followed in storing dangerous chemicals, disposal of hazardous waste, method followed for releasing waste water, etc.

Environmental management audit

Environmental management audit is an appraisal of the company's internal capabilities to discharge its environment related responsibilities. It focuses on issues such as organizational structure, accountability, training of employees to respond to crisis situations and relationships between plant personnel and local regulatory authorities. It also examines the environmental policy statement of the company, the documentary procedures for preventing any damaging crisis situations, the type and frequency of review of the programmes.

16.15.3 Managing Environmental Issues

Generally, corporate environmental policy may serve one or more of the following environmental issues:

(i) Reducing costs through measures such as recycling or energy conservation
(ii) Reducing the possibility of industrial disasters
(iii) Establishing a good corporate reputation and earning the goodwill of the people
(iv) Providing employees a better work environment
(v) Maintaining a good relationship with the local community and regulatory authorities
(vi) Conforming to a code of ethics

16.15.4 Benefits of Environmental Audit

Environmental audit can generate various benefits for the organizations as follows:

(i) Environmental problems can be corrected before they are too large to control
(ii) Opportunities can be identified for cutting costs through measures such as waste minimization and recycling
(iii) Insurance costs can be reduced
(iv) Employees can be persuaded and motivated to take environmental issues seriously
(v) The corporate image can be improved

More number of companies are now realizing the need for a proactive approach to environmental issues instead of passive compliance with the laws. They are now getting these issues audited by a group of technically qualified external professionals as auditors. The right way to manage environmental issues is to integrate them with the company's corporate strategy. This implies collecting and storing information about environmental issues and dealing with the environmental risks like other business risks. Companies should have a clear idea of how investments in improving environmental performance will affect their competitive position.

16.16 CONCLUSION

Audit is the examination and verification of records and evidences kept by an organization, by a professional or a group of professionals to confirm whether the records and evidences exhibit a true and fair view of the state of affairs of the organization. Audits are of two types—financial audit and non-financial audit. Various purposes for conducting audit, audit processes, audit tools and techniques and audit evidence have been discussed in depth, in this chapter.

Management audit is an examination of the conditions and a diagnosis of deficiencies with recommendations for correcting them. The main objective of conducting a management audit is to critically analyze and evaluate management performance.

Internal audit is an independent appraisal function established within an organization to examine and evaluate its activities as a service to the organization.

Financial audit is a critical statutory review by an independent auditor to examine the correctness of financial statements and to establish whether they present a true and fair view of the company's financial position on a particular date.

Special audit is conducted by the Central Government when it has reason to believe that the affairs of the company are not being managed on sound business principles or according to prudent commercial practices, etc.

Cost audit is a statutory audit conducted by an independent cost and works accountant to verify the cost of production of a particular product on the basis of accounts as regards utilization of material or labour or other items of costs, maintained by the company.

Social audit is a process whereby an enterprise measures and reports on its performance in meeting its declared social, community, or environmental objectives.

Environmental audit is a management tool to objectively and systematically evaluate environment management systems in an organization. It is an appraisal of the company's internal capabilities to discharge its environment related responsibilities.

Various aspects of management audit, internal audit, financial audit, special audit, cost audit, social audit and environmental audit have been explained in this chapter.

REVIEW QUESTIONS

16.1 What do you mean by auditing? What are the similarities and dissimilarities of financial audit and non-financial audit?

16.2 What are the factors that determine the timing and frequency of audit?

16.3 Discuss the activities involved in an audit process?

16.4 Explain the various tools and techniques used in audit activities?

16.5 Define management audit? Discuss the various types of management audit?

16.6 How does management audit assist an organization in setting up a good management control system?

16.7 Write short notes on:

(a) Internal audit

(b) Financial audit

(c) Special audit

(d) Cost audit

(e) Audit evidence.

16.8 What is social audit? Explain the various aspects of social audit conducted by an organization?

16.9 Define environment audit? Discuss the various dimensions of environment audit?

17

Audit of Management Functions

17.1 INTRODUCTION

A business organization performs various activities. There are various departments to execute these functions. But the departments may not be able to perform their functions always efficiently and effectively. In order to survive in competition and prosper in business, it is necessary to make the departmental activities effective. That is why, there is a need for conducting regular audits of the functions of these departments. In this chapter, we discuss the functions of audit in various departments of an organization, viz., purchase department, human resources department, production or manufacturing department, sales department, research and development department, and marketing department.

17.2 PURCHASE DEPARTMENT

Purchase activities are one of the most crucial functions of the management. In a manufacturing organization, material costs constitute about 65% of the total cost of production. It is the responsibility of purchase department to place an order at the right time with right source to get the right quantity at the right price and right quality.

17.2.1 Functions of Purchase Department

The purchase department of an organization usually performs the following functions:

(i) To verify purchase requisitions coming from various departments

(ii) To invite tenders, quotations, etc.

(iii) To negotiate price with the vendors

(iv) To select the source of supply or to select the successful bidders

(v) To fix up delivery date, mode of dispatch, terms of payment, etc., and issue purchase order

(vi) To follow up delivery closely

(vii) To collect documents for receipt of materials

(viii) To ensure receipt of quality materials as specified in the purchase order

(ix) To check invoice

(x) To negotiate adjustments if any, with suppliers

(xi) To maintain the records e.g., vendor files, registers of suppliers, etc.

(xii) To serve as a source of information for user departments

17.2.2 Audit of Purchase Department

An audit of purchase department is conducted to control purchase costs and to identify loopholes, if any, in the purchase functions. While conducting an audit of purchase functions, an auditor should look into the following aspects:

(i) He should determine whether the organization has a system for collecting information relating to purchases.

(ii) He should analyze all the documents relating to purchase activity. He should look into the adequacy, format and correctness of the documents.

(iii) He should review critically the purchase procedure of the company.

(iv) He should ensure that there is no failure on the part of purchase department to get valid competitive questions.

(v) He should ensure that there is no loophole in the quality control measures adopted by the purchase department.

17.3 HUMAN RESOURCES DEPARTMENT (HRD)

HRD performs all important functions relating to HR of an organization. It establishes and controls HR systems and procedures.

17.3.1 Audit of Human Resources Department

The Human Resource (HR) audit is the process of examining policies, procedures, documentation, systems and practices with respect to an organization's HR functions. The purpose of an HR audit is to reveal the strengths and weaknesses of the HR system, and to identify the issues which need to be resolved.

The objectives of an HR audit are the following:

(i) To examine a company's compliance with established employment laws and regulations

(ii) To determine how to serve the relevant needs of shareholders and other stakeholders better

(iii) To streamline the company practices and procedures used in carrying out recruitment, wage and salary administration, leave of absence, benefits, training, discipline, termination, etc.

(iv) To establish an early warning system to identify problem issues before they actually arise.

17.3.2 Composition of HR Auditors

An HR audit is conducted by an audit team comprising executives from various levels of management. An HR auditor should take into consideration certain realities while conducting audit of HRD. It is not easy to measure the performance of the employees and their contributions to the success or failure of their companies. It is not easy to measure the impact of training programmes on the efficiency level of employees. It is also difficult for an auditor to have proper understanding of human behaviour and its influence in optimum utilization of resources for achieving the goals and objectives of the organization.

17.4 PRODUCTION OR MANUFACTURING DEPARTMENT

Every organization engaged in manufacturing and marketing of its products must have one or more manufacturing units at the same or different places. It has to provide all production facilities and processes to the production department for primary production activities, as well as various support activities, viz. repairs and maintenance, stores and other service functions.

An auditor conducting the audit of manufacturing department should preferably be a knowledgeable and technically qualified person who can understand the manufacturing processes and their inherent problems. The objective of the audit of manufacturing department is to ensure that actual procedures of production are in conformity with the standard procedures. It has also to ensure that there is a consistency of production process and process improvement taking place in the shop floor with minimum loss or wastage.

17.4.1 Audit of Production or Manufacturing Department

This audit is conducted to measure the effectiveness and efficiency of all production facilities and processes. A good manufacturing audit has the following characteristics:

(a) It helps people to do things more effectively through evaluation and feedback

(b) It uses rating schemes to classify problems discovered so that corrective action can be taken accordingly

17.5 SALES DEPARTMENT

Sales department of an organization discharges various activities relating to sales of products/services. The sales manager prepares the sales budget duly approved by the top management. He assesses the current sales position and compares with the budgeted sales and then takes appropriate actions for improvement of sales, if there is a shortfall. He also studies the sales environment, prepares and implements the sales strategies.

17.5.1 Audit of Sales Department

Sales audit is the process of examining and assessing the current state of sales, the sales environment, sales objectives, strategies and activities. There are two approaches to the sales audit, they are: (i) separate approach and (ii) collective approach.

A sales audit can be conducted in-house by the sales manager or by an outside professional consultant. Before conducting a sales audit, the company should ensure that it has a strong sales foundation and excellent sales relationship.

A sales auditor should ensure that all sales invoices have been received for the audit period. He should also interact with the depot manager and plan depot visits. During the sales audit, the data is usually collected from sales representatives through questionnaires pertaining to various aspects of sales like sales strategy, sales planning, territory allocation, motivating sales persons, sales analysis and control, etc.

17.6 RESEARCH AND DEVELOPMENT (R&D) DEPARTMENT

In the present era of tremendous competition at market place, and rapid technological advancement throughout the world, it has become imperative for any good organization to constantly innovate new concepts, products and procedures for its survival and retention of market share. In order to do so, the organization has to invest huge amount of money in R&D activities.

Generally, an R&D department is set up with qualified and experienced researchers. The responsibility of the R&D manager is to get R&D budget sanctioned every year for his department, select research projects to be undertaken and conduct a pilot project before its full scale commercialization.

17.6.1 Audit of Research and Development (R&D) Department

The organizations conduct R&D audits to ensure that their R&D efforts are fruitful and not simply a waste of money and resources. While conducting an R&D audit, the auditor should look into the following aspects:

(i) He should make sure that the company has allocated a specified amount as R&D budget based on Detailed Project Report (DPR) of each project.

(ii) He should ensure that the details of expenses of each project are maintained systematically.

(iii) He should make sure that there is control in material requisition and consumption.

(iv) He should ensure that R&D personnel are recruited based on merits and competence.

(v) He should see that the company does not incur unnecessary expenses on the unviable projects.

(vi) He should also see that the R&D activities are well-coordinated and within the overall objectives of the company.

17.7 MARKETING DEPARTMENT

This is one of the most important departments in an organization. The marketing department studies the company's marketing environment, sets marketing objectives and fixes up marketing strategies and activities.

17.7.1 Audit of Marketing Department

A marketing audit is conducted to cover all marketing activities of an organization. It is a systematic examination of marketing environment, and shows the areas in which marketing improvement can take place with the help of short-term and long-term plans. Generally, it is an independent audit conducted by an external agency appointed by the management to understand objectivity, and actual performance of the marketing department.

Marketing audit is conducted periodically. A checklist is prepared by the auditors to conduct internal marketing audits and is given to the employees to understand their opinions regarding the company's products, price, etc. The information collected provides help to the management to know the marketing efforts and strategies needed for further improvement of working of the marketing department.

Therefore, marketing audit is a comprehensive, systematic, independent and periodic examination of a company's marketing environment, objectives, strategies and activities. It is conducted to determine problem areas and opportunities, and recommend an action plan to improve the company's marketing performance.

17.8 ROLE OF AUDIT TOWARDS CONTRIBUTING COMPETITIVE ADVANTAGE OF A COMPANY

The competitive advantage of a company means its ability to outperform its competitors through innovations, efficiency, customer responsiveness, and quality. Audit can lead towards competitive advantage in several ways such as:

(i) Audit leads to a clearer sense of the company's identity, better understanding of the strengths, weaknesses, culture, preferences, and the competitive challenges of the company
(ii) Audit identifies opportunities to capitalize on a company's identity
(iii) Audit sounds a warning when a change in direction is required

17.9 CONCLUSION

Organizations conduct regular audit of functions of its various departments in order to survive in competition and grow in business. This chapter explained various aspects of the audits of functional departments, viz., purchase department, human resources department, production or manufacturing department, sales department, research and development department, and marketing department. Role of audit towards contributing competitive advantage of a company has also been explained here.

Review Questions

17.1 What is audit of management functions? Is it necessary to conduct audit of performance of the management in an organization?

17.2 Discuss the functions and audit of purchase department?

17.3 What are the objectives of conducting HR audit?

17.4 "An auditor conducting the audit of manufacturing department should be a knowledgeable and technically qualified person........". Justify the statement?

17.5 Discuss the audit of sales department of an organization?

17.6 Explain the various aspects to be considered by the auditor while conducting an R&D audit?

17.7 What is marketing audit? How is it conducted in an organization?

17.8 Discuss the role of audit towards contributing competitive advantage of a company?

Part VI

Management Control in Organizations

18

Management Control in Multinational Companies (MNCs)

18.1 INTRODUCTION

In the present era of global open economy, the companies have grown substantially in different countries. Therefore, the managers of today have to increase their awareness on various important global issues involving foreign investments, control of subsidiaries in other countries, cultural diversities in the countries where subsidiaries are situated, and global standards and practices. Multinational Companies (MNCs) have to adapt various control practices used in the home countries Head Quarters (HQs) to suit the requirements of the host countries (subsidiaries). They need to control their subsidiaries so that the subsidiaries can perform better and achieve higher profits. This chapter deals with various types of controls used by the MNCs on subsidiaries, and other important issues in control systems in MNCs.

18.2 TYPES OF CONTROLS EXERCISED BY MNCs

MNCs exercise different types of controls to monitor and improve the performance of their subsidiaries. These are:

(i) Personal controls through informal meetings between the officials of HQ and subsidiary for greater coordination and communication

(ii) Output controls through performance measurement to determine profitability, productivity, quality, and market share of the products of the subsidiary

(iii) Cultural controls directly or indirectly exercised to uphold, manage, and improve the work culture in the subsidiaries

(iv) Result controls for rewarding individuals or groups to generate good results of the subsidiaries

(v) Bureaucratic controls through imposition of rules, norms, and regulations on the subsidiaries

18.3 STRATEGIC CONTROL OF MNCs ON SUBSIDIARIES

As MNCs grow and as their operations become more complex, the MNC has to devise and implement strategies to control subsidiaries effectively.

The factors determining the influence of MNC on subsidiaries are as follows:

(i) Environment
(ii) Global competition
(iii) Demands of host-government
(iv) Joint ventures

18.3.1 Environment

With greater growth prospects in foreign markets, MNCs have started to invest and create a stronger asset base for their foreign subsidiaries.

18.3.2 Global Competition

In order to compete in the global market, an MNC has to constantly review and change its sourcing patterns, pricing strategies, product designs, etc.

18.3.3 Demands of Host-government

Host-government is the government of a country where the subsidiary of an MNC is situated. Often, the host-government intervenes in the operations of an MNC.

18.3.4 Joint Ventures

The MNCs cannot exercise excessive control because it fears that the joint venture may be called off, and it may be deprived of a prospective market.

18.4 ISSUES IN CONTROL SYSTEMS IN MNCs

Control systems of MNCs need modification or changes because they are influenced by a number of issues such as, cultural differences and differences in business environment.

18.4.1 Cultural Differences

Culture has a great influence on MCS as a number of behavioural problems arise in this regard. Basically there are four cultural dimensions such as, individualism, power distance, avoidance of uncertainty and masculinity.

Cultures are of two categories—individualistic, and collective. In individualistic culture, the employees give priority to their self-interest. In the collective culture, employees give more emphasis to group interest rather than individualistic interest. Power distance is the extent to which employees accept the unequal distribution of power. Generally, the employees who give more emphasis to power distance prefer centralization of authority. The employees giving less emphasis to power distance prefer decentralization and delegation of authority. Employees who prefer avoidance of uncertainty do feel uncomfortable in confronting difficult situations. Employees with the attribute of masculinity are assertive, and do not hesitate taking job responsibilities. However, they demand more independence at the workplace and prefer highly decentralized organization.

18.4.2 Differences in Business Environment

Certain elements of business environment that have an influence on control systems are as follows:

(i) Inflation
(ii) Business risks and uncertainty
(iii) Labour availability and quality

A MNC needs to evaluate the fluctuation in the rates of inflation critically and constantly as there is an element of financial risk involved. It is observed that the business risk and uncertainty is minimum in countries that are economically and politically stable rather than in countries which are vulnerable economically and politically. MNCs which operate through subsidiaries in the underdeveloped countries often face problem in appointing skilled labour and even good executives there.

18.5 ANALYSIS OF PROJECTS BY MNCs IN FOREIGN COUNTRIES

Apart from using various tools and techniques for appraisal of capital projects, viz. NPV, IRR, ARR Payback, etc., there are a number of other issues which should be considered by a MNC before deciding on projects in foreign countries. They are:

(i) Taxes on income from foreign investment projects
(ii) Political risks/expropriation risks
(iii) Economic risks–
  (a) Exchange rate risks
  (b) Inflation
(iv) Exchange rate exposure

18.5.1 Taxes on Income from Foreign Investment Projects

The rate of taxation differs from country to country. Taxes are levied not only on the income earned but also on the income (dividend) repatriated to the Head Quarters (HQs) of the MNC.

18.5.2 Political Risks/Expropriation Risks

This is the most vulnerable risk a MNC may face in overseas operations. Expropriation risks can take the shape of seizure of property or assets of a MNC.

18.5.3 Economic Risks

This risk can be divided into exchange rate risk, and inflation. Exchange rate risk arises out of the following:

(i) Interest rate differential
(ii) Relative inflation
(iii) Export competitiveness
(iv) Economic growth

Exchange rate fluctuations influence the cash flows of an MNC as they may be denominated in several currencies, and the value of each currency is different at different times. If a country's currency is depreciated, there has to be an increase in the prices of raw materials imported from other countries.

18.5.4 Exchange Rate Exposure

MNCs do face different types of exchange rate exposures. They are:

(i) Translation exposure
(ii) Transaction exposure
(iii) Economic exposure

The erosion or appreciation in the value of earnings, assets and liabilities is referred to as translation exposure. Transaction exposure indicates the exchange rate exposure that the MNC has in its cross-border transactions when the settlement of transactions is made at a future date. Economic exposure is the exchange rate exposure of MNCs cash flow to changes in the real exchange rate.

18.6 TRANSFER PRICING IN MNCs

Discussed in detail in Chapter 10.

18.7 BUDGETING AND BUDGETARY CONTROL FOR SUBSIDIARIES

It is an important tool that an MNC exercises to control expenditures of its subsidiaries. Budgetary data helps in comparing the actual performance against the budgeted figure. It helps the management to identify the areas in which greater control is to be exercised by the MNC. But the major problem while budgeting for subsidiaries pertains to exchange rate fluctuations, which may adversely affect the performance of foreign subsidiaries. It has been observed that the subsidiaries had used projected exchange rates for the purpose of budgeting, but they had reported to the HQ, the performance based on the actual rates. In order to establish better controllability, the MNC should ensure that the same exchange rates are used by the subsidiaries for the purpose of budgeting and reporting performance. Therefore, MNCs have to achieve goal congruence and ensure greater controllability.

18.8 CONCLUSION

Multinational companies (MNCs) have to adapt to various control practices used in the home countries head quarters to suit the requirements of the host countries (subsidiaries). They need to control their subsidiaries so that the subsidiaries can perform better and achieve higher profits. Various types of control exercised by the MNCs and the issues in control systems in MNCs have been discussed in this chapter. Apart from using various tools and techniques for appraisal of capital projects, viz. NPV, IRR, ARR, Pay-back, etc. a number of other issues, viz., taxes on income from foreign investment projects, political risks/expropriation risks, economic risks i.e., exchange rate risks, and inflation, and exchange rate exposure, which should be considered by a MNC before deciding on projects in foreign countries, have been explained here. MNCs have to achieve goal congruence and ensure greater controllability.

REVIEW QUESTIONS

18.1 What do you mean by a Multinational Company (MNC)? What are the different types of controls exercised by the MNCs?

18.2 Discuss the factors determining influence of MNCs on subsidiaries?

18.3 "Control systems of MNCs need modification or changes as they are influenced by a number of issues". Discuss the issues critically.

18.4 Explain what are the other issues to be considered by a MNC before deciding on projects in foreign countries?

18.5 Discuss how a MNC exercises budgetary control on its subsidiaries?

19

Management Control in Service Organizations

19.1 INTRODUCTION

Service organizations are the organizations that produce or sell services to their customers. These organizations, include professional organizations, viz. law firms, audit and accounting firms, management consultancy firms, etc., financial services organizations, viz., commercial banks, insurance companies, securities firms, etc., government organizations, health care organizations, hospitality organizations, etc. We discuss in this chapter, the characteristics of service organizations, the control systems in professional organizations, government organizations, and financial services organizations.

19.2 CHARACTERISTICS OF SERVICE ORGANIZATIONS

(i) Unlike manufacturing organizations which maintain inventories throughout the year, the services organizations cannot store their services. They have to match their current capacity with the demand by way of stimulating demand in the off-seasons through decrease in prices and reduction of manpower, etc.

(ii) Unlike manufacturing organizations in which the products can be inspected as to their quality before the products are marketed, the quality of services cannot be assessed before the services are rendered to the clients/customers.

(iii) Services organizations operate through small units set up in different places. These units are wholly-owned or franchised. They provide a basis for preparing budgets and exercising budgetary control.

19.3 MANAGEMENT CONTROL IN PROFESSIONAL ORGANIZATIONS

Professional organizations are those which provide specialized professional services. They may be law firms, audit and accountancy firms, or management consultancy firms.

These firms do possess following characteristics:

(i) Small size
(ii) Labour intensiveness
(iii) Different objectives and goals
(iv) Difficulty in measuring output
(v) Different marketing strategies

Generally, professional organizations are small in size and operate in a single location. Senior managers/partners personally monitor the performance of the subordinates. These firms prepare their own budget and exercise budgetary control. These organizations are labour intensive and employ qualified professionals. The goals of these organizations are to increase their sizes and network in terms of clientele, as well as to compensate to their employees satisfactorily. The nature of jobs handled by these organizations is such that it is difficult to set standards of performance as the jobs are non-repetitive. Unlike manufacturing organizations, the professional organizations do not market themselves openly. Marketing activities are done through personal and professional contacts, etc.

The most important aspects of management control systems in these organizations are as follows:

(i) Pricing
(ii) Strategic planning and budgeting
(iii) Control of operations
(iv) Performance measure and appraisal

Generally, the quoted price for services offered differs from profession to profession. It is based on time spent on the service. The strategic plan of a professional organization mainly concentrates on long-term staffing plan, and the budgeting and budgetary control can be exercised accordingly. The main area of exercising control of operations is to schedule the working hours of the staffs properly. Idle hours should be minimized. Prompt billing should be made to the clients using the appropriate rates. As stated earlier, it is difficult for a professional organization to assess the performance of its staffs. Generally, the performance appraisal of the employees is done based on human judgement which may be subjective at times.

19.4 MANAGEMENT CONTROL IN GOVERNMENT ORGANIZATIONS

Government organizations are also service organizations. They do also have certain special characteristics, as follows:

(i) Political influence
(ii) Public information
(iii) Attitude towards clients
(iv) Management compensation

Government organizations work under heavy political pressure. They work under the close vigil of print and electronic media. In order to avoid or reduce criticism of media, these organizations try to exercise greater control on their activities and limit the leakage of sensitive information. Though the main source of revenue for government organizations is the general public yet the quality of services offered to the public is awfully bad. The talented executives do not prefer working in a government organization as the salaries offered to them are much lower as compared to the salaries offered by the private organizations, although several pay revisions have taken place in government organizations.

The most important elements of management control system in these organizations are (a) strategic planning, and (b) performance measurement.

As part of the management control exercise, strategic planning is very important to a government organization. The main task under strategic planning is the prudent and judicious allocation of resources. Government organizations measure their performance in three ways as follows:

(i) Measurement of results or outcome
(ii) Measurement of process
(iii) Social indicators

A government organization measures the output or results that are related to the goals and objectives of the organization. It also measures the activity carried on by the organization to indicate the efficiency of performance. A social indicator is useful in the long-term analysis of strategic planning and progress. It reflects the overall achievement of the organization.

19.5 FINANCIAL SERVICES ORGANIZATIONS

Financial services organizations are involved in the business of managing money. They are commercial banks, insurance companies, securities firms, etc.

19.5.1 Commercial Banks and Their Characteristics

(i) As part of their normal business these banks accept cash deposits from the public and pay them interest on the amount deposited. They lend money in terms of loans and charge interest on the loans.
(ii) They also generate revenue through other financial products and services. Examples: credit cards/debit cards fee, payroll services, foreign exchanges, etc.
(iii) Reserve bank or the central bank regulates the money lending operations of commercial banks in various countries. For example, Reserve Bank of India is the regulatory body for all commercial banks operating in India.
(iv) These banks are exposed to three types of risks. They are as follows:
    (a) Credit risk i.e., risk of loaning money but not repaid;
    (b) Interest rate risk due to fluctuation between the rate of interest on deposits and the rate of interest on loans;
    (c) Transaction risk due to theft, embezzlement, etc.

Management control in commercial banks

Some of the management controls in commercial banks are as follows:

(i) Interest exposure
(ii) Loan losses
(iii) Transfer pricing
(iv) Expenditures
(v) Sharing of joint revenues, etc.

Commercial banks exercise control over interest exposure by way of communicating the existing rate of interest from time-to-time to the managers who are responsible for taking investment decisions. The managers adhere to these rates in exercising credit control. One of the many reasons for bank failure is non-repayment of loan by the customers. Control can be exercised by the auditors through a constant scrutiny on the bank loan transactions. The corporate office of the bank plays an important role in fixing up appropriate transfer price of money being transferred from one branch of the bank to the other. Budgeting is done for every branch of the bank and control on expenditures is exercised by the bank accordingly. By the recent implementation of core banking facilities, the sharing of revenues have been put in practice among different branches in order to help customers to carry out transactions in various branches depending on their convenience.

The Basel Committee, set up in 1975, laid down certain principles for better control and governance in banking transactions. The principles, framed from time-to-time, are related to banks' supervision, plans, procedures, policies, measurement of monetary system, internal control, management information, etc., for controlling authorities in banks.

19.5.2 Insurance Companies and Their Characteristics

Insurance companies are broadly classified into (i) life insurance, and (ii) non-life insurance.

Life insurance companies collect premiums from the policy holders, invest the premium money, earn revenues, and pay the specified amount to the beneficiaries on death of the policy holders or to the policy holders on maturity. Non-life insurance companies earn the same way and pay to the policy holders for specified losses, viz., loss of properties caused by fire, marine losses, theft and burglary, accidents, illness etc.

Management control in insurance companies

Control systems needed for managing insurance companies differ from those needed for managing commercial banks. Some of the important control systems implications for an insurance company pertain to product pricing, sales performance, expense control and investment control.

Generally, an established life insurance company offers a number of products (i.e. policies) to its prospective customers. The price (i.e., policy premium) of the product is fixed depending on age of the insured person, his/her life expectancy, health, habits, etc. Insurance companies focus mainly on the sales volume because it is not easy to assess the profitability of various policies. Expenditures are controlled through budgeting and budgetary control exercise by the top management. In the present era of liberalization, the insurance companies have also been allowed to invest money into commercial ventures, term loan and real estates.

19.5.3 Securities Firms and Their Characteristics

Firms that deal in shares or securities are called securities firms. They include investment bankers, securities traders, securities brokers and dealers, fund managers, and investment advisors.

Many securities firms set up their branches at different locations to offer services to various investors. Increased competition among securities firms have compelled them to live with thin profit margins. Due to opening up of global economy foreign investors have become an important source of funds. Therefore, the activities of securities firms have been increased considerably in the financial market.

Management control in securities firms

Some of the important management control issues in these types of firms are as follows:

(i) Customer relationships
(ii) Stars and team work
(iii) Fast information flow
(iv) Short-term performance
(v) Financial performance

It is difficult to measure the quality of products offered by the securities firms. Customer relationships play an important role in increasing the clientele of these firms. Quality of the products is largely dependent on the efficiency of the professionals. The senior professionals called 'stars' are the valuable assets of the firms. They have to exercise greater control in making decisions about buying and selling of securities. The results of these types of firms depend on the teamwork. The information system of these firms must be meaningful and should be communicated on immediate basis as soon as an important development takes place. These firms generally focus on short-term performance, say the current quarter. Financial performance of these firms is measured in terms of revenue.

19.6 CONCLUSION

Service organizations produce and market services to their customers. These organizations include professional organizations, viz., law firms, audit and accounting firms, management consultancy firms, etc., financial services organizations, viz., commercial banks, insurance companies, securities firms, etc., government organizations, health care organizations, hospitality organizations, etc. This chapter discussed in adequate details, the nature and characteristics of these firms and the various management control systems exercised by them in running their business effectively.

Review Questions

19.1 What do you mean by service organizations? Discuss the characteristics of service organizations?

19.2 Explain how management controls are exercised in:
   (a) Professional organizations
   (b) Government organizations.

19.3 What are meant by financial services organisations? Give some examples and explain their characteristics?

19.4 Explain how management controls are exercised in:
   (a) Commercial banks
   (b) Insurance companies
   (c) Securities firms.

20

Project Management Control

20.1 INTRODUCTION

A project is defined as a one-shot, time-tested, goal-directed, major undertaking, requiring the commitment of varied skills and resources. It is a package of time bound, scheduled and assembled activities dedicated to the attainment of a specific objective of successful completion of a work, on time and within the allotted budget.

A project first emerges as a **concept** and follows various stages, till it gets **commissioned**. A project is said to have started in an organization when management develops a project plan that specifies the work to be done and allocates resources for completion of the work. Management also determines the time frame within which the project must be completed. Managing people, money, time, and quality are of utmost importance for successful completion of a project. We examine in this chapter the various aspects of projects and their planning and control mechanisms to understand how these control systems help in improving the proper execution of projects.

20.2 PROJECTS CONTROL VIS-A-VIS CONTROL OF ONGOING ACTIVITIES

Projects control differs from control of ongoing activities. It is because of the fact that unlike other continuous or ongoing activities the projects control has many characteristics as follows:

(i) Single objective
(ii) Focus on projects
(iii) Balance between scope, cost and schedule

(iv) Performance standard
(v) Changes in project plan
(vi) Pace of project work
(vii) Influence of environment

Unlike continuous activities which have multiple objectives, the projects have a single objective. Most projects have a matrix structure that offers flexibility and effectiveness. The focus of management is mainly on accomplishment of the objective of projects, i.e. a satisfactory product within the time frame at a minimum cost. A tradeoff or balancing is necessary in projects between the scope, cost, and schedule of projects. Since the project design of each and every project is unique in itself, the performance standards for projects, are therefore, less reliable than performance standards for continuous activities. It is observed that project plans undergo a lot of changes due to unforeseen environmental problems which have great influence in projects. For example, the building and construction projects get adversely affected by the local climatic conditions. Generally, the projects commence slowly, but get momentum towards their completion.

20.3 PROJECT PLANNING AND SCHEDULING

20.3.1 Project Planning

Project planning is the process of developing the basis for managing the project, including the planning objectives, procedures, organization, routines, finance and other chain of activities. The nature of projects is different from the nature of ongoing activities. The plan of a project consists of three important parts. They are: (i) scope, (ii) schedule and (iii) cost.

The scope of the project indicates the specification of each activity involved in the project and fixes up responsibility of the personnel for completion of the project activities. The schedule does calculate the probable time required to complete the activities and indicates their interrelationships. Generally, networking techniques are used to estimate the schedules. Total costs of the project are the cost specific to the project and are incurred through the start up of a facility before its operation. While assessing the cost of a project, the project estimator estimates the quantity and price of the materials and labour, the technical scope and schedule of the project. When there is a cost overrun due to complexity or time overrun, the original plan for the project may have to be revised according to the time and situation.

20.3.2 Project Scheduling

Project scheduling is an important activity in project management. In the early age of scientific management, Henry L. Gantt introduced a system of scheduling, named as Gantt chart.

Gantt chart

The system consists of a graphical representation of various jobs, tasks or activities across time periods. Individual jobs, tasks or activities are described on the left hand of the graphical chart, and the scheduled times for accomplishing each job, task or activity are shown by open bars and plotted along a horizontal time (calendar) scale. A typical Gantt chart is shown in Figure 20.1.

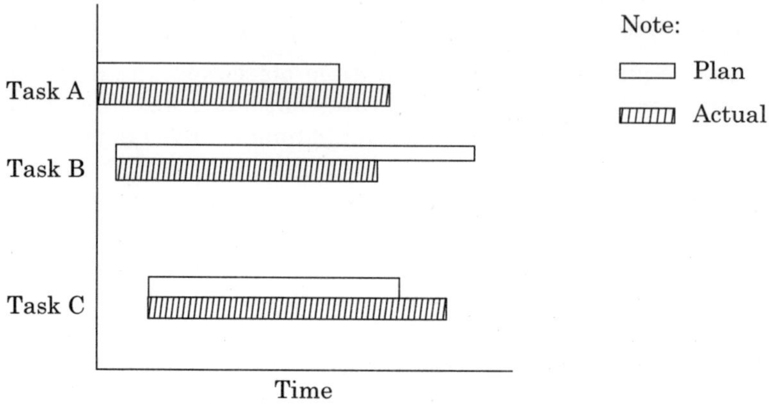

Figure 20.1 Gantt Chart.

Gantt chart is widely used for scheduling various tasks and activities in project management. The network information is also represented as Gantt chart.

Towards late 1950s, the network models were developed in USA for planning, scheduling and controlling large complex projects. The US Navy developed the program called Project Evaluation and Review Technique (PERT) for launching the Polaris Missile Program. DuPont, a chemical giant of USA developed the Critical Path Method (CPM) to manage its large developmental projects. Both these methods use network as a model which came to be known as Network Techniques in project management.

Network based scheduling

It involves network terminology as stated in Table 20.1.

Table 20.1 Network terminology

CPM	PERT
Arrow diagram	Network
Node	Event
Job	Activity
Duration	Expected time
Total float	Slack (primary)
Free float	Slack (secondary)

(a) Activity: It is a project work items having a specific beginning and endings.

(b) Network/arrow diagram: It is a diagram which shows the various activities by arrows and specifies the interrelationship between them.

(c) Critical activity: It is a project work item on the critical path having zero float time.

(d) Critical path: It is the longest continuous path of activities through a network diagram from beginning to end of a project. The total time required for critical path is the shortest duration of the project.

(e) Dummy arrow/activity: It is an arrow used in a network diagram to represent relationship between project items but not requiring any time or resources.

(f) Earliest finish time: It is the earliest possible time an activity can be completed without interfering with the completion of any of the preceding activities.

(g) Earliest start time: It is the earliest possible time an activity can begin without interfering with the completion of any of the preceding activities.

(h) Event: It is a point in time represented as a 'circle' at a junction of arrows in a network diagram.

(i) Expected time: It is a weighted average of the estimated optimistic, most likely and pessimistic time duration to complete an activity.

(j) Float: It is the amount of time by which an activity can be delayed without affecting the duration of the project.

(k) Free float: It is the amount of time by which an activity can be delayed without affecting the succeeding activities of the project.

(l) Latest finish time: It is the latest time in which an activity can be completed without delaying the end of the project.

(m) Latest start time: It is the latest time an activity can start without delaying the end of the project.

(n) Milestone: It is a major event in the project.

(o) Node: It represents an instantaneous point in time and occurs at the junction of arrows. It is shown graphically as a circle representing the beginning or end of an activity.

(p) Stimulation: It is a technique for evaluating alternative plans to determine the best schedule.

(q) Slack: It is used in a PERT network to show the difference between latest allowable finish time and the earliest possible starting time of a given event. It is analogous to 'float' in a CPM network.

(r) Total float: It is the amount of time a project item can be delayed without affecting the duration of the project.

(s) Work breakdown structure: It is an organization of project tasks shown by means of a hierarchical chart. The first level generally represents an overall summary of the project, while the last level provides a detailed set of day-to-day activities for completing the project.

Network objectives

(i) To foster orderliness and consistency in the planning and evaluating the project

(ii) To provide an automatic mechanism for identification of potential trouble spots in the areas of the project

(iii) To give operational flexibility to the project by allowing for experimentation in a stimulated sense

(iv) To allow for expeditious correction of recognized trouble areas

Some salient features of network models are as follows:

(a) Selection of specific identifiable events which are planned to occur. The events must be both meaningful and recognizable.

(b) Linking the planned events in order to graphically show the inter-dependencies among them.

(c) Estimation of the time necessary to move from event to event together with a measure of uncertainties involved.

(d) Analysis highlighting systematically relative criticality of events.

Critical Path Method (CPM)

It is a network planning technique that is activity-oriented, used for planning and scheduling a project. It is possible to complete a project in a very short duration by expanding a large amount of resources. In CPM, the main objective is to obtain a trade-off between the cost and completion date for a project. The use of additional resources to complete an activity earlier with consequent increase in resource input is called 'crashing' the activity.

Project Evaluation and Review Technique (PERT)

It is an event-oriented network diagramming technique used for planning and scheduling. PERT uses the concept of events which are points in time indicating the achievement of certain stages in the project. Since it was originally used for R&D projects which had an element of uncertainty about the duration of each activity, this had to be catered for in the monitoring model. Time durations for each activity are based on some form of weighted estimates.

Major differences between PERT and CPM are as follows:

(a) CPM uses single-time activity estimates, while PERT uses three-time activity estimates, e.g., optimistic time estimate, pessimistic time estimate, and most likely time estimate.

(b) In CPM time-cost trade-off procedures are used to expedite the project completion at minimum cost, whereas in PERT they are not used.

(c) In CPM the project activity duration times are deterministic. The use of three-time activity estimates in PERT allows the application of probability concept to assess the degree of certainty associated with project completion by a certain date.

(d) CPM is used for small and medium repetitive construction projects. PERT is used for managing one-time large complex projects.

In practice, the features of both PERT and CPM are combinedly used in managing the projects.

Network rules and their interpretation

Rule 1 Before an activity begins, all activities preceding it must be completed.

Rule 2 Arrows imply logical precedence only. Neither the length of the 'arrow' nor its 'compass' direction on the drawing has any significance.

Rule 3 Any two events may be directly connected by no more than one activity.

Rule 4 Event numbers must not be duplicated in a network.

Rule 5 Network may have only one initial event (with no predecessor) and only one terminal event (with no successor).

Network planning and scheduling

The level of detail in a network depends on the degree of accuracy and economy of presentation of the network. After deciding the level of detail, the activities to be included in the network are listed, indicating for each activity the predecessor activities. To establish precedence relationship the network planner should ask the following questions:

(i) What activity immediately precedes this activity?

(ii) What activity immediately follows this activity?

(iii) What activities can be carried out concurrently?

Example 1

A project consists of the following activities, and the immediate predecessors for each activity are also indicated below:

Activity	Immediate predecessor	Activity (Time in weeks)
A	—	2
B	A	5
C	A	3
D	B	3
E	A	4
F	B, E	6
G	C	8
H	D, F	7
I	G	2
J	H, I	4

Find out the critical path of the above activities?

Solution:

In Figure 20.2 we have,
Critical path = A(2) → E(4) → F(6) → H(7) → J(4) = 23 weeks
or
(Total project duration)

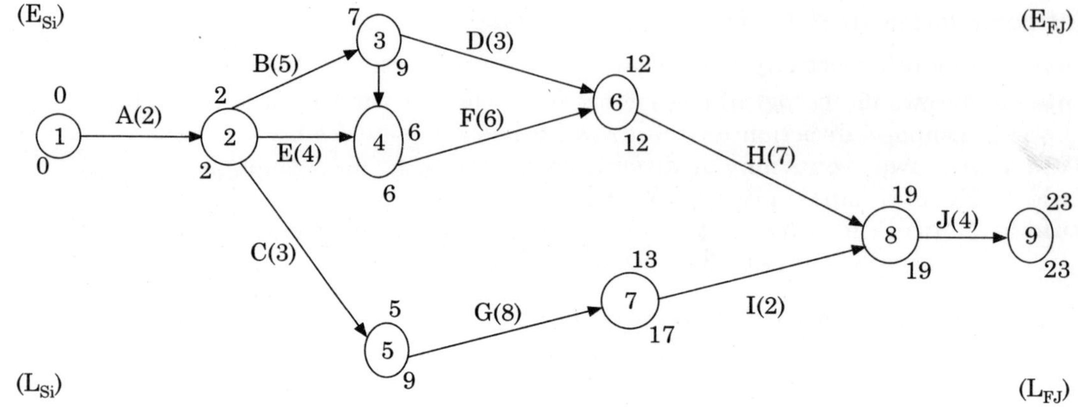

Figure 20.2 Network Diagram.

In CPM the activity time estimates are single-time estimates. But in PERT the activity time estimates are three-estimates. These are:

(i) Most optimistic completion time (t_o)

(ii) Most pessimistic completion time (t_p)

(iii) Most likely completion time (t_m)

Formula

$$\text{Time expected } (t_e) = \frac{(t_o + 4t_m + t_p)}{6}$$

$$\text{Variance } (\sigma^2) = \left(\frac{t_p - t_o}{6}\right)^2$$

or

$$\text{Standard deviation } (\sigma) = \sqrt{\frac{(t_p - t_o)}{6}}$$

The time estimates in CPM are deterministic and the time estimates are probabilistic in PERT.

Example 2

The following statistics regarding the project of a company are available:

Activity	Immediate predecessor	Estimated time duration (days)		
		t_o	t_m	t_p
A	—	1	1	7
B	—	1	4	7
C	—	2	2	8
D	A	1	1	1
E	B	2	5	14
F	C	2	5	8
G	D, E	3	6	15
H	F, G	1	2	3

You are required to:

(a) Draw the PERT network diagram.

(b) Identify the critical path.

(c) Find the expected duration and variance for each activity.

(d) What is the probability that the project should be completed within 17 days?

Solution:

Before drawing PERT network diagram and critical path let us find out:

(a) Time expected (t_e)

(b) Variance (σ^2) or standard deviation

Applying the formula of time expected (t_e) and variance we get the following result:

Activity	Time expected (t_e) [in days]	Variance (σ^2)
A	2	1
B	4	1
C	3	1
D	1	0
E	6	4
F	5	1
G	7	4
H	2	1/9

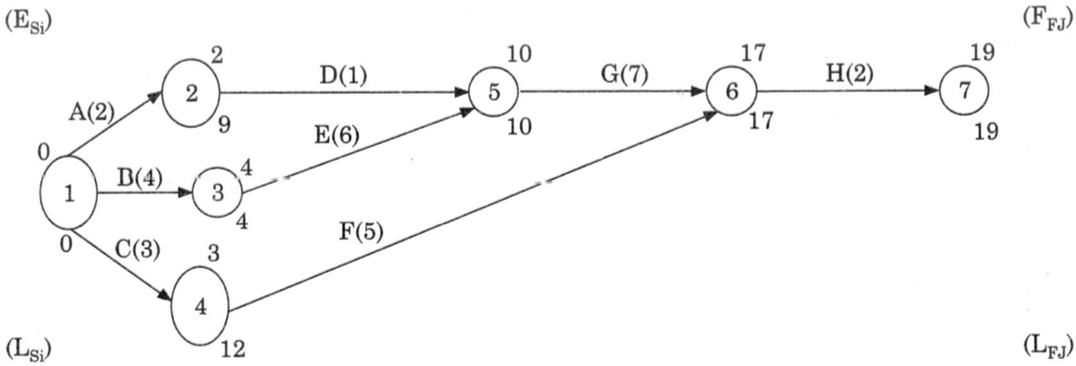

Figure 20.3 Network Diagram.

From Figure 20.3, we get

Critical path = B(4) → E(6) → G(7) → H(2) = 19

or,

Total project duration (t_e) = 19 days.

Variance of the critical path or Total variance (σ^2) =1 + 4 + 4 + 1/9 = 9.11

So, Standard deviation (σ) = $\sqrt{9.11} = 3.1$ days.

Therefore, probability that the project will be completed within 17 days (t_s) can be expressed as:

$$P(t_e \leq 17)$$

or $$P\left(Z \leq \frac{t_s - t_e}{\sigma}\right)$$

or $$P\left(Z \leq \frac{17 - 19}{3.1}\right)$$

or $$P\left(Z \leq \frac{(-)2}{3.1}\right)$$

or $$P(Z \leq (-)0.64)$$

or $$0.5 - P(0.64)$$

or $$0.5 - 0.2389$$

or $$0.2611$$

or $$26.11\%$$

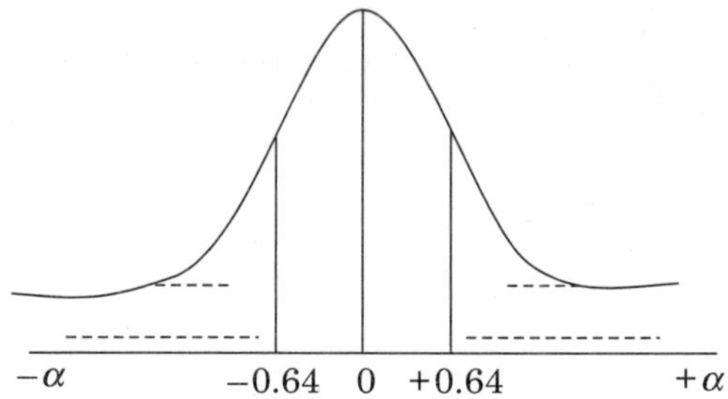

Figure 20.4 Area Distribution Curve.

There are other various activities that are required to be performed in the project planning stage, e.g.,

(i) Ordering of materials
(ii) Selecting personnel
(iii) Gathering information
(iv) Obtaining prior permission, etc.

All these activities must be controlled and integrated with other project activities to ensure smooth and successful completion of the project.

20.4 CONTROL OF PROJECTS

Once the project is planned, it has to be executed. During the execution stage, the project manager is concerned about controlling performance in terms of time and cost. He has to conserve the physical assets, human and financial resources of the organization.

The controls exercised by a project manager in a conservationist role are:

(i) Physical assets control
(ii) Human resource control
(iii) Financial control

In physical assets control, the project manager has to prepare a plant maintenance plan to ensure uninterrupted works for the project. He also exercises inventory control during the course of execution of the project. Human resource control involves training and development and placement of personnel in the project activities. A project manager has to ensure that the right man has been put in the right place. Financial control involves both regulatory as well as conservatory control of finance of an organization. It deals with regulation of capital flows for better ROI, capital investment decisions, project cost budgeting and budgetary control, etc.

20.5 PROCESS OF PROJECT CONTROL

Three types of control processes that are used by the management to control a project are as follows:

(i) Cybernetic controls
(ii) Go/no go controls
(iii) Post project controls

Cybernetic controls are used to monitor and control tasks on a continuous basis. The main control activity is performed by a sensor that measures one or more aspects of the output and transmits the results to a comparator. The comparator compares the results with the standards set. Thereafter, the output is sent to a decision maker to decide on the future action. If the deviation is large, the decision maker sends the output to an effecter for making changes necessary for the process or inputs in order to control the variation. Go/no go controls are used at periodical preset intervals in order to ensure completion of the project within time and cost estimated. Post project controls are used by the management after completion of the project to assess whether the objectives of the project have been accomplished in terms of time, quality and cost estimated.

20.6 PROJECT REPORTING

Project reporting is essential for controlling the projects. They are prepared on a continuous basis until the project is completed. There are five types of project reports. They are as follows:

(i) Current period project report
(ii) Project exception report
(iii) Cumulative project report
(iv) Project variance report
(v) Stoplight project report

Current period project report provides details of activities of the project in progress or recently completed. Project exception report provides details of deviations in regard to time and cost of the project. These reports prepared in tabular form, are very helpful to the managers in obtaining important information about the deviations. Cumulative project report provides details of all activities right from its inception up to the current status of the project. Project variance report indicates details of deviations between the actual output and planned output of the project. This report is also prepared in tabular form and represented graphically whenever needed for easy understanding of the senior management and taking corrective actions. In the stoplight project report colours are used to show the progress of the project at different stages. For example, a green sticker may be pasted on the top right hand corner of the report to show that the project is progressing well. A yellow sticker may be pasted on the report to indicate some minor problems in the execution of the project. A red sticker is pasted on the report to show that the project progress runs into rough weather in terms of major problems requiring urgent attention of the management.

20.7 PROJECT ORGANIZATION AND MANAGEMENT

There are six types of project organization structures, e.g.,

(i) Traditional organization structure
(ii) Task-force oriented organization structure
(iii) Organization structure with project management as staff function
(iv) Product type organization structure
(v) Matrix organization structure
(vi) Project-oriented organization structure

20.7.1 Traditional Organization Structure

It is a way of structuring the project organization similar to function-based production or manufacturing organization in which functional executives are directly under the chief executive of the organization. Each functional executive is responsible for a specific function in the organization.

This type of organization structure suffers from some disadvantages as follows:

(i) No strong control or authority of the project manager
(ii) No individual responsibility for the total project
(iii) Integration of activities difficult
(iv) Growing conflicts among the personnel

20.7.2 Task-force Oriented Organization Structure

In this structure, a taskforce is created by drawing personnel from various functional departments, and putting them under the project manager, who is delegated full authority to make decisions for the project, but within the functional organization's policies and procedures. This type of structure has some disadvantages as follows:

(i) It may not be possible always to create taskforce when there is shortage of specialists in the organization.
(ii) It is not suitable for large and complex projects.

20.7.3 Organization Structure with Project Management as Staff Function

In this structure the project management department provides special staff service function to all other functional departments, who will execute the project. The project manager has no control or authority as he cannot take decisions that are taken by the functional groups.

20.7.4 Product Type Organization Structure

Under this structure, the project manager maintains complete line authority over the entire project. This structure also has the following problems:

(i) Duplication of efforts, facilities and personnel, resulting in higher cost of project management
(ii) Technology suffers due to absence of strong functional groups

20.7.5 Matrix Organization Structure

It is the formal way of sharing authority between the project manager and the functional managers. In this structure an individual reports to two bosses, viz., the project manager and his functional manager. Here a mutually supportive relationship between two authorities must exist, otherwise project will suffer due to conflict of command.

20.7.6 Project-oriented Organization Structure

It is an arrangement in which the project manager has total authority including functional policies and procedures. This organization structure has some definite advantages, viz.

(i) It is a complete autonomous organization structure in which the project manager is the chief executive, and the ultimate responsibility rests with him.
(ii) Decision making and project execution is faster as several departments headed by the senior functional specialists can function independently with the project's own plans and policies.
(iii) It is ideally suitable for large, gigantic, complex, and geographically complex projects.

In most of the organization it is observed that a project team consists of personnel picked up from various line and service departments. This team is assembled for a specific project under the direction of a project manager. The team is temporary and is dissolved after completion of the project. The project manager steers the activities of the project. He has to exercise direct control and autonomy over the project team.

In order to discharge his functions effectively, a project manager is required to have lot of skills, some of which may be enumerated as follows:

(i) Team building skills
(ii) Leadership skills
(iii) Conflict resolution skills
(iv) Technical skills
(v) Planning skills
(vi) Organizational skills
(vii) Entrepreneurial skills
(viii) Administrative skills
(ix) Management support building skills
(x) Resource allocation skills

20.8 PROJECT COST OVERRUN AND WAYS TO OVERCOME

There may be cost overrun in a project due to incorrect cost estimation, which arises out of following reasons:

(i) Deliberate understatement of costs for obtaining sanction of the top management
(ii) Choice of untested designs/processes
(iii) Choice of collaborators
(iv) Choice of wrong equipments or incompetent suppliers/contractors
(v) Faulty engineering data/specifications
(vi) Escalation and adverse changes in foreign currency exchange rates
(vii) Incorrect collection and interpretation of past data and judgements

Cost overrun can occur at following stages of the project:

(i) Prefeasibility stage
(ii) Evaluation stage
(iii) Choice of technology stage
(iv) Contracting and procurement stage
(v) Construction stage
(vi) Communicating and start-up stage

20.8.1 Prefeasibility Stage

(i) Delay in acquiring land and bureaucratic delays in obtaining environmental clearance
(ii) Inadequate communication facilities, poor infrastructures such as bad road, absence of sufficient water sources, etc.

20.8.2 Evaluation Stage

(i) Hurried evaluation by an inadequate study, resulting in lack of clarity on the project scope, wrong estimation of cost and resources
(ii) Wrong selection of location
(iii) Incompetence of consultants and wrong economic studies, etc.

20.8.3 Choice of Technology Stage

(i) Choice of outdated technology
(ii) Delay in completing detail engineering, non-availability of design data, delay in freezing design and specifications, etc.

20.8.4 Contracting and Procurement Stage

(i) Casual approach to the preparation of tender documents, rate release of them, delay in evaluating bids

(ii) Wrong selection of venders, fabricators/contractors due to lowest cost syndrome
(iii) Delay in issuing import license, opening of Letter of Credit (L/C), late in issuing guarantees to overseas suppliers
(iv) Time consuming procedure relating to procurement of imported materials, poor logistics planning, etc.

20.8.5 Construction Stage

(i) Starting construction activities without ensuring availability of working drawings, sequential supply of equipments and materials
(ii) Low productivity of contractors/fabricators
(iii) Poor monitoring and lack of co-ordination, delay in progress payment to contractors and settlement of claims, etc.

20.8.6 Communicating and Start-up Stage

(i) Delay in availability of manuals
(ii) Failure of certain equipments, parts, design changes
(iii) Delay on the part of equipment suppliers
(iv) Defects in erection and installation

Project management is an integrated multi-disciplinary function aimed at completing the project successfully through systematic planning, organizing, execution and control. In order to make the project a complete success the project management has to ensure the following:

- The selection and choice of the project is made after an in-depth feasibility study from all angles such as technical, operational, and economic
- The project is undertaken after satisfying all statutory regulations and completing all arrangements for raising funds
- The various phases of the project are thoroughly analyzed and planned with utmost cohesion and integration, and execute it with highest possible efficiency
- The progress of the project is reviewed with a view to exercising adequate control

20.9 PROJECT AUDIT

Project audit is a planned and documented activity performed by qualified personnel to determine by investigation, examination and evaluation of objective evidence, the adequacy and compliance with established procedures or applicable documents, and effectiveness of implementation. The project audit is conducted to identify problems in the project and to prevent minor discrepancies from becoming major problems. There are three levels of project audit as follows:

(i) General audit
(ii) Detailed audit
(iii) Technical audit

A general audit covers all dimensions of auditing. It is a comprehensive audit conducted by the management within a short period of time. When the general audit reveals serious problems or risks in the project, a detailed audit is conducted immediately to examine the project in minutest details. A technical audit is conducted when the project manager is not able to identify the technical defects/problems in a project due to whatsoever reasons.

20.10 PROJECT EVALUATION

Project evaluation is the process of evaluating the performance and progress of a project in comparison to what was planned. The evaluation of a project involves evaluation of project performance, and evaluation of project results.

The purpose of the project performance evaluation is to provide assistance to the project manager to take decisions regarding rewards, promotion, relocation, etc. While evaluating the project performance, two more aspects like budget overrun and hindsight are needed to be considered. The evaluation of results depends on the type of projects being evaluated. However, it involves comparison of actual results with those of anticipated results.

20.11 CONCLUSION

Project is a package of time bound, scheduled and assembled activities dedicated to the attainment of a specific objective of successful completion of a work, on time and within the allotted budget. It first emerges as a concept and follows various stages, till it gets commissioned. The plan of a project consists of three important parts, viz., scope, schedule and cost. For scheduling a project, three techniques viz. Gantt chart, Critical Path Method (CPM) and Project Evaluation and Review Technique (PERT) are generally used. This chapter showed with examples how network based planning and scheduling is conducted by the project management by applying CPM and PERT methods. It has also explained various types of controls exercised by a project manager, control processes, project reports, project organizations and management, causes of project cost overrun and control, project audits and evaluation.

REVIEW QUESTIONS

20.1 Define a project? Enumerate the characteristics of project control?

20.2 Write short notes on:

(a) Project planning
(b) Project scheduling
(c) Gantt chart
(d) Project audit
(e) Project evaluation.

20.3 What is PERT and CPM? How does PERT differ from CPM?

20.4 Explain the network rules and interpret them?

20.5 How a project manager controls his projects? What are the various processes of project control?

20.6 Explain the various types of project organization structures?

20.7 Enumerate the various skills required by a project manager in discharging his functions effectively?

20.8 What is project cost overrun? What are the reasons for cost overrun at various stages? How can it be minimized?

20.9 The following statistics regarding the project of a company are available:

Activity	Immediate predecessor	Estimated time duration (days)		
		t_o	t_m	t_p
A	–	1	1	7
B	–	1	4	7
C	–	2	2	8
D	A	1	1	1
E	B	2	5	14
F	C	2	5	8
G	D, E	3	6	15
H	F, G	1	2	3

where,

most optimistic completion time is t_o

most pessimistic completion time t_p

most likely completion time t_m

(a) Draw the PERT network diagram.

(b) Identify the critical path.

(c) Find the expected duration and variance for each activity.

(d) What is the probability that the project should be completed within 17 days?

21

Management Control in Non-profit Organization

21.1 INTRODUCTION

A non-profit organization is an organization which does not work for profit. It operates in the interests of society. The sources of funds for non-profit organizations are contributions, grants, and operating surplus. Most non-profit organizations provide services. This chapter deals with the goals and objectives, characteristics, and various aspects of management control system of the non-profit organizations.

21.2 GOALS AND OBJECTIVES OF NON-PROFIT ORGANIZATIONS

Non-profit organizations face difficulty in measuring the success of their goals and objectives. They usually determine the achievement of their goals in three ways. First, these organizations define their goals in narrow sense so that they can measure the progress easily. Second, they invest in research to assess how their performances help in achieving the goals and objectives. Third, they develop micro-level goals to measure their achievement and also to facilitate these goals to be implemented in a broader scale.

21.3 CHARACTERISTICS OF NON-PROFIT ORGANIZATIONS

Certain characteristics are observed in functioning non-profit organizations. They are:

(i) Lack of resources

(ii) Informal organization structure

(iii) Mission vs. financial results
(iv) Difficulty in assessing cost-effectiveness and quality of service
(v) Board of governors with dual responsibility
(vi) Staff level
(vii) Volunteers' participation in service

It is a fact that most non-profit organizations are severely handicapped in their functions due to lack of adequate infrastructure and resources. The hierarchical structures of non-profit organizations are informal. These organizations run in style of total participation and consensus. There is always a tension between mission and financial results of the non-profit organizations. The missions or goals are given more emphasis than the financial outcomes. Most non-profit organizations do not have adequate system for evaluation of their performance as they do not get clear feedback from the market to know about the quality of service provided to their clients. It is difficult to assess cost-effectiveness of the service as well.

The board of governors of a non-profit organization has dual responsibilities. On the one hand, the board has to ensure that the public interests are served by the organization, and on the other, the board is expected to help the organization in various ways to make it effective. Unfortunately, most of the board members are not professionals in these areas of activities. That is why they have to depend much on the staffs of the organization. The efficiency level of staffs is not satisfactory because these organizations do not have much means to afford training and development programmes for their staffs. Generally, the non-profit organizations have to depend on the active participation of their volunteers whose contribution to the society is remarkable.

21.4 MANAGEMENT CONTROL IN NON-PROFIT ORGANIZATIONS

Traditionally, non-profit organizations have poor management control systems. The management consisting of professionals like teachers, doctors, social workers, etc., do not attach importance to managerial skills and give priority to the fulfillment of professional goals. The effectiveness of management control systems of these organizations depend largely on the effectiveness of the board's functioning.

However, a positive aspect for control, seen in non-profitable organizations, is employee commitment. Non-profit organizations dominated by professionals do have little regard for management control systems. The employees feel rewarded when they achieve the goals mentioned in the mission statement as the financial rewards are non-existent or negligible.

Performance of non-profit organizations is extremely difficult to measure in terms of quantity as these organizations provide services in terms of quality. It is observed that many non-profit organizations design three types of performance indicators. They are:

(i) Success in mobilizing resources
(ii) Effectiveness of staff on the job
(iii) Progress in meeting goals and objectives

21.5 BUDGETING AND BUDGETARY CONTROL IN NON-PROFIT ORGANIZATIONS

The non-profit organizations spend money from three sources to operate their activities. The sources are:

(i) General funds for day-to-day operations
(ii) Plan funds for planned expenditures
(iii) Other funds for meeting contingencies

Programming is an important and time consuming process in non-profit organizations. They have to work within their budgets and cannot exceed the set monetary limits.

21.6 CONCLUSION

A non-profit organization is an organization which does not work for profit. It operates in the interests of society. There are certain characteristics in functioning non-profit organizations. Most non-profit organizations are severely handicapped in their functions due to lack of adequate infrastructure and resources. The board of governors of non-profit organizations has dual responsibilities. The organizations dominated by professionals have little regard for management control systems. They have to work within the limits of budgeted funds.

REVIEW QUESTIONS

21.1 What do you mean by a non-profit organization?

21.2 Discuss the characteristics of non-profit organizations?

21.3 State how management control system is exercised in non-profit organizations?

21.4 Explain budgeting and budgetary control are exercised in non-profit organizations?

Part VII

Current Issues and Management Control

22

Ethics and Management Control

22.1 INTRODUCTION

The word 'ethics' owes its origin to Greek word 'ethos' which means a system of moral principles, the basis for deciding right and wrong actions, and implies customs, habits, noble traits in character, discipline, culture and disposition. Ethical principles are the rules of conduct that are derived from ethical values, known as six pillars, viz., trustworthiness, respect, responsibility, fairness, caring and citizenship. These values are inseparable from one another and are closely interwoven and interlinked with each other. In this chapter we discuss the importance of ethics in management, factors influencing ethical environment in an organization, control-related ethical issues, and various other important aspects of ethics related to management control.

22.2 IMPORTANCE OF ETHICS IN MANAGEMENT

Ethical values now-a-days, are not looked upon any longer, as costs imposed on the industry or a check on efficiency and profit maximization, but are regarded as imperatives for sustainable corporate growth and competitive edge. The ethical values in relation with 'competitors' explore the issue of how far a business should go in trying to beat a competitor. The ethical values in relation to 'employment' raise question on whether an employer owes any special duties to employees beyond legal ones. Ethical values in relation to customers explore the extent to which ethical considerations restrict the traditional attitude of caveat emptor in this area. Ethical values in relation to society consider whether business owes any duty to society other than profit making.

22.3 FACTORS INFLUENCING ETHICAL ENVIRONMENT IN AN ORGANIZATION

The following factors, by and large, influence the ethical environment in an organization:

(i) Ethical vision of management which may need a review
(ii) Holistic human values the organization has developed
(iii) Ethical code acquired within the organization
(iv) Source of individual inspiration
(v) Managerial character and ethical dedication
(vi) Work place environment and compulsion to follow the ethical norms

A company is characterized by its ethical culture, which remains paramount in its daily operations. When a company's board of directors adopts ethics and declares it as its credo to its management group, executives and employees, ethics would automatically pervade the organization and build a fair amount of goodwill for the business. Many good organizations, in order to upheld and ensure ethical practices within the organization and outside have developed a 'code of conduct' for their employees. There also exists another form of document called a 'code of ethics'. These codes do help to make the employees and executives sensitive to their own behaviour and ethical implications.

22.4 CORPORATE SCAMS AND UNETHICAL PRACTICES

In the present complex and competitive corporate world, it is regrettably observed that quite a number of promoters and executives in the helm of affairs in corporate management do not attach much importance to ethical values and principles. Corporate scandals and frauds of various dimensions are occurring every day across the world, primarily due to unlimited greed of these managers holding the reign of power to accumulate personal wealth by dubious means, thereby misusing their corporate power, position, authority, making mockery of fiduciary responsibility and accountability and harming and hurting the interests of various stakeholders.

There are a number of scandals rocking the corporate world including the USA, the UK, France, Germany, Japan, South Korea and India involving various types of corporate frauds and malpractices, which are as follows:

(i) Falsification of accounts by showing inflated profits
(ii) Embezzlement of company funds by dubious means
(iii) Siphoning of company's funds through fictitious transactions
(iv) Making fraudulent investments
(v) Financial irregularities
(vi) Breach of fiduciary duties
(vii) Breach of trust
(viii) Breach of confidential information
(ix) Dishonesty
(x) Non-disclosure of material facts
(xi) Insider trading

(xii) Misfeasance, misappropriation, maladministration

(xiii) Corruption and bribery

(xiv) Milking the company by fabulous salaries, perks, amenities, and facilities, generous stock options

(xv) Hefty compensation and severance benefits to the board members, CEOs, and other key executives

Besides, there are a number of misdemeanors in the corporate working such as, sexual harassment of women by the senior employees, employment and exploitation of child labour, discrimination in employment and pay based on sex, colour, race, etc., and reckless destruction of precious natural resources, thereby hampering ecological balance and biodiversity of the universe.

22.5 CONTROL-RELATED ETHICAL ISSUES

There are a number of ethical issues that have strong implications for control systems within an organization. These issues are:

(i) Budgetary slack

(ii) Defective guidelines/flawed control indicators

(iii) Manipulation of financial accounts

(iv) Excessive tight control measures

Budgetary slack is the difference between the proposed budget expectations of the management and the previously established expectations. Creating budgetary slack is unethical, especially in an organization that pays performance-linked bonuses/ incentives. Therefore, the budgetary slack leads to show dysfunctional behaviour and indulgence in management dishonesty. It also results in loss of profitable opportunities and increased overall costs of the organization. Management guidelines to the employees are supposed to act as control measures to monitor and control the behaviour and activities of the employees. Unfortunately, in many organizations these guidelines are defective, unclear, and sometimes absent. The flawed guidelines indulge employees to act in a way that may be disastrous for the organization. Again manipulation of financial accounts to inflate earnings of the management is one of the most important ethical issues the financial accountants face in their daily practices. The managers indulging in inflating earnings mislead all stakeholders regarding the actual profitability and stability of their organizations. Another important ethical issue is the practice of excessive tight control measures by the management. Unnecessary tight supervision may reduce employees' freedom of work and morale of employees.

22.6 REGULATION OF ETHICAL CONDUCT THROUGH MANAGEMENT CONTROL

An organization should conduct ethics programmes in order to prevent employees from resorting to unethical practices. Organizations can adopt a cybernetic approach to develop an ethics programme by following six steps:

Step I: Comply with all laws, ethical codes and policies of the organization.

Step II: Sensitize all managers and employees as to what kind of behaviour is improper.

Step III: Audit the behaviour of employees regarding their interaction with all stakeholders.

Step IV: Report significant deviations from the desired ethical conduct.

Step V: Investigate violations of the prescribed ethical conduct.

Step VI: Implement regulations to correct improper behaviour.

The focus of ethics programmes rest on developing a corporate code of conduct, which should be followed by all employees.

22.7 MANAGEMENT CONTROL SYSTEM FOR ETHICS PROGRAMME

We have seen from discussions in the previous chapters that a management control system is made up of the following:

(i) Management style and culture
(ii) Infrastructure
(iii) Rewards and punishment
(iv) Coordination and integration
(v) Environment

A good work culture and management style of functioning in an organization imbibes the ethical conduct of employees. The board of directors of a company should set up an ethics committee to monitor implementation of ethics programmes in the organization. Rewards and punishment can also enforce ethical behaviour and conduct of employees. There should be a formal channel of communication to report violation of ethical norms. In order to make the control system to be ethical, an organization should create an environment that are fair to all employees and conducive to ethical conduct of employees.

22.8 CONCLUSION

Ethics means a system of moral principles, the basis for deciding right and wrong actions, and implies customs, habits, and noble traits in character, discipline, culture and disposition. Ethical values now-a-days are regarded as imperatives for sustainable corporate growth and competitive edge. This chapter examined various aspects of control-related ethical issues, regulation of ethical conduct, etc., of employees in an organization.

REVIEW QUESTIONS

22.1 Define the term ethics? What is the importance of ethics in management?

22.2 Discuss the factors influencing ethical environment in an organization?

22.3 "There are a number of scandals rocking the corporate world involving various types of corporate frauds and malpractices". Discuss the statement critically.

22.4 What are the control related ethical issues and regulation of ethical conduct through management control?

22.5 Discuss the management control system for ethical programme?

23

Corporate Governance and Management Control

23.1 INTRODUCTION

Corporate governance is the system by which business companies are directed and controlled. It is a system of structuring, operating, and controlling a company with a view to achieving long-term strategic goals to satisfy the stakeholders, viz., shareholders, creditors, employees, customers, suppliers, etc., and complying with the legal and regulatory requirements, besides meeting environmental and local community needs. It includes the policies and procedures adopted by a company to achieve its objectives in relation to shareholders, employees, customers and suppliers, regulatory authorities and the community at large. It prescribes a Code of Corporate Conduct in relation to all the stakeholders. Therefore, a framework of effective accountability to the stakeholders is the essence of corporate governance. This chapter deals with various aspects of corporate governance in a company and its influence in controlling management operations at all levels of business.

23.2 GOVERNANCE VS. MANAGEMENT

Corporate governance and corporate management are defined in the context of legal doctrines and regulatory activities which elaborate the rights and responsibilities in the two-dimensional relationship between the boards (acting as the agents of shareholders) and the senior management. The fundamental distinctions between governance and management are:

(i) Managers operate within the hierarchy of the delegated responsibility and authority. But all board members are jointly and individually responsible, and they have equal rights and duties.

(ii) The responsibility of the board is to govern the company while the managers' task is to run its business.
(iii) Governance has an external focus, whereas management has an internal focus.
(iv) Governance assumes an open system while management assumes a closed system.
(v) Governance is strategy-oriented, whereas management is task-oriented.
(vi) Governance is concerned with 'where the company is going' and management is concerned with 'getting the company there'.

23.3 PRINCIPLES OF CORPORATE GOVERNANCE AND MANAGEMENT CONTROL

Despite the differences mentioned in Section 23.2, both corporate governance and management control are interlinked in approach and complimentary to each other, as corporate governance principles and the principles of management control revolve around the basic interrelated segments. These are: (i) integrity and fairness, (ii) transparency and disclosures, and (iii) accountability and responsibility.

23.3.1 Integrity and Fairness

Integrity and fairness occupy a central position in the studies and research in corporate governance and management control. The understanding and practice of ethics and the related value system lie at the heart of this element. The top management has to inculcate a culture of ethical practices which will be demonstrated and percolated to the other levels within the organization to create a culture which would reflect ethics, fair play and integrity par excellence. In this context, there is a need for a 'code of conduct' for Board of Directors (BODs) and senior management. The code should be so designed to reflect the intention of highest standards of integrity to be followed in practice. The BODs are required to discharge fiduciary responsibilities as they act as trustees of shareholders and other stakeholders. The foundation of trusteeship concept is integrity, fairness and ethical standards of the highest order.

23.3.2 Transparency and Disclosures

The element of transparency and disclosures in corporate governance is equally important. The Board of directors (BODs) and its committees are expected to work in a harmonious manner to review all the activities and results on a periodic basis. The effectiveness, however, would depend on strong MIS, active role of audit committee, proper internal control, systems and procedures and the vigilant monitoring and supervisory role of the BODs. An important requisite in this regard would be to step up a well-developed and interactive websites by the companies for transmission of all information relating to business and its performance on a real time basis.

23.3.3 Accountability and Responsibility

Accountability and responsibility is the third pillar in the principles of good corporate governance and good management control. A company which follows high ethical standards and discloses more than what is required would always have the courage to be accountable to all stakeholders for any act of omission and commission. A company of high standards of integrity and with good performance record would generally have concerns for the society, which would be visible from the discharge of duties on social responsibility.

23.4 IMPORTANCE OF CORPORATE GOVERNANCE AND MANAGEMENT CONTROL

In the past the government was expected to ensure good corporate conduct and performance. Most shareholders believed that stringent government controls would prevent malpractices of the company management. Gradually, the shareholders started to believe that there is a need for market driven corporate governance that would be more realistic and flexible for corporate management and control. This led to the birth of 'self-imposed' or 'self-regulated' corporate governance.

Many factors have contributed importance of corporate governance:

(i) The responsibility for ensuring good corporate conduct, management and control
(ii) Active participation of individual and institutional investors
(iii) Increasing competition in global economy

With the relaxation of direct and indirect administrative controls by the government, an alternative mechanism became necessary to monitor performance of companies in free markets. Shareholders believed that market forces could ensure good corporate conduct, management and control by way of rewarding success and punishing failures of the companies.

In the growth of global fund management business, the competition has forced the FIs, FIIs to take an active role in governance in order to safeguard their investments in the companies. Sometimes, they compel the company management to induct their representative into the BODs of the companies. Besides, many institutional investors express their views strongly in regard to various corporate matters, such as, financial and operational performance, internal control system in companies, business strategy, remuneration of top management, and monitor and control the performance of companies closely.

The enhanced competition in the global economy has compelled companies to perform better by implementing various management control exercises such as, cost control and cost reduction, quality control, corporate restructuring, strategic cost management, mergers and acquisitions, transfer pricing, etc. All these activities can be carried out successfully only if there is proper corporate governance.

23.5 STAKEHOLDERS' EXPECTATIONS, VALUE CREATION AND MANAGEMENT CONTROL

The need for setting up of a foundation of value creation drive has been felt as a prime point on top of the corporate agenda. Governing companies in an effective manner should ultimately result in transparency and best practices on the one hand, and a healthy bottom line on consistent basis for all the stakeholders on the other. The global debate now is increasing in favour of not only ethics, but also on creation of value in a transparent manner. Therefore, higher volume of long-term value creation for all stakeholders should be the prime concern for the board. To adopt transparent practices in managing the companies and to ensure a better value management we have to know the stakeholders expectations, as also the ability of the companies to satisfy expectations.

Expectations of various stakeholders (including shareholders) from the companies can be listed as follows:

Stakeholders	Expectations
(i) Shareholders	(a) Increase in the future earning of the company (b) Increase in the market capitalization of investment (c) A fair and steady rate of return (i.e., dividend) on investment
(ii) Employees	(a) Stability of employment (b) Recognition of service by providing fair remuneration as also incentives (c) Help improve standard of living
(iii) Customers	(a) Provide quality goods or services at a fair price and on fair terms (b) Restraint from restrictive practices or unfair practices
(iv) Competitors	(a) Restraint from adopting any strategy to elbow competitors out with unfair or restrictive practices or through violation of competition law norms
(v) Creditors	(a) Ability to pay the principal and interest as per contractual obligations
(vi) Government	(a) Behave as a responsible and good corporate citizen (b) Non-evasion of taxes and dues to the government (c) Involvement in social cause, e.g., charities, donations, etc.
(vii) Community	(a) Growth in employment generation to secure good local employment (b) Protection of environment
(viii) Public at large	(a) To hold the board accountable for • Limiting senior executives' compensation • Full environmental protection • Avoidance of fraud within the company • Caring for employees

From the above list of expectations of various stakeholders it is quite evident to say that it is essential to adopt transparent practices in managing and controlling the companies to ensure a better value management for the stakeholders.

In an open economy, it is extremely important how strategies are made by a corporation. The main strategies adopted by a company may be: business portfolio strategy, vertical integration, horizontal integration, and financial holding strategy.

The core of all strategies is to deliver the best value for the stakeholders. The ultimate test is to see whether the company has generated wealth in reality or has earned future earning capabilities as to ensure increased market capitalization in the scrip. However, the fact remains that the company is responsible to the stakeholders for value creation on a continuous basis, and hence, the focus should be to find out the gap and the cause of the gap between the stakeholders expectations and corporate value creation.

23.6 BOARD OF DIRECTORS (BODs) AND THEIR ROLES AND RESPONSIBILITIES

The main responsibility of governing a company is on the Board of Directors (BODs). Directors are appointed by the shareholders of the company and the board appoints one or more of them as managing director/whole time directors/executive directors to be approved by the shareholders. The roles of the BODs and the shareholders are interactive and therefore, the quality of governance depends on the level of interface set up by them. Ideally, the BODs should be the heart and soul of a corporate. Whether the company grows or declines depends mostly on the sense of purpose and direction, the values, the will to generate stakeholders' satisfaction and the drive to achieve. BODs are accountable in many ways to the shareholders and stakeholders in a company. The directors are required to achieve a balance between competing interests of shareholders, customers, lenders, promoters and directors.

The board structure distinguishes between those directors who hold management positions in the company and those who do not. Those who occupy management positions are referred to as 'executive directors' and those who do not are called 'non-executive directors'. Two variants of the non-executive directors do exist – one, who are genuinely 'independent' of the company's affairs, other than holding their board appointment and receiving sitting fees only. On the other hand, there are non-executive directors in the board, whose positions might bring their objectivity and independence into questions. For example, a retired executive of the company (who is receiving company's retirement benefits) now sitting on the board, a director being the representative of a major block of shares, a significant supplier, customer, etc. These directors are not independent from the point of view of accountability because of their sectional interests. However, each member of the board bears the same duties and responsibilities in law irrespective of their positions.

While governing the activities of a company, the directors assume the following two roles:

(i) The performance role
(ii) The conformance role

23.6.1 The Performance Role

In this role the directors perform various activities that aimed at improving the overall managerial performance of the company. They act as a source of knowledge, expertise, and external information. They cater to the needs of the company for networking, representing and adding status. The non-executive/independent directors, being specialists have the following roles:

(i) To direct the company and to bring wider experience, technical expertise, independent judgement, new ideas, information related to international markets, financial/technical environment, etc., which are not readily accessible to the company
(ii) To monitor, challenge and control the performance of executive directors and managers
(iii) To ensure installation of adequate control systems in place, in order to protect the interests of the company as also the interests of the stakeholders.

23.6.2 The Conformance Role

In this role the directors are concerned with ensuring that the company follows the rules, policies and procedures laid down by the various acts as also by the board. This is a very complex role as it involves monitoring, and evaluating the performance of the board members.

Directors stand in a fiduciary position towards the company. The courts have determined the broad areas of directors' duties as:

(i) The fiduciary duty of loyalty and good faith
(ii) The duties of care and skill

They are liable for negligence, breach of trust, and misfeasance of their capacities as agents or trustees or as both.

23.7 COMMITTEES' RECOMMENDATIONS ON CORPORATE GOVERNANCE

Consequent to the several incidents of corporate failures during the late 1980s and the early 1990s, many countries in the world had felt the need for corporate governance code. Accordingly, the codes or principles had been developed by the renowned International Committees on various aspects of corporate governance such as, selection, duties, responsibilities of directors, board's performance evaluation, remuneration of directors, formation and functioning of audit committee, remuneration committee, nomination committee to monitor performance of companies, auditors and their responsibilities, accounting standards, financial reporting, internal control, disclosure and transparency, etc.

Some of these International Committees are:

(i) Cadbury Committee (1992)
(ii) Greenbury Committee (1995)
(iii) Hampel Committee (1998)
(iv) LSE Combined Code (1998)
(v) OECD Principles for Corporate Governance (1999)
(vi) Blue Ribbon Committee (1999)
(vii) Turnbull Committee (1999)

Out of the recommendations of these Committees, we select recommendations of Turnbull Committee for our deliberation as these recommendations directly look into the aspects of internal management control requirements of companies and provide guidance in this regard.

23.7.1 The Turnbull Committee Report (1999)

When the Combined Code of the Committee on Corporate Governance was published, the Institute of Chartered Accounts in England and Wales agreed with the London Stock Exchange that it would provide guidance to assist listed companies to implement the requirements in the code relating to internal control. Accordingly, the Institute set up an Internal Control Working Party headed by Nigel Turnbull to look into the aspects of internal control requirements of the combined code and provide guidance in this regard. The Committee submitted their report to the Institute which published the same in September 1999.

The contents of the report is segregated into six sections as follows:

(i) Introduction—detailing internal control requirements of the Combined Code, objectives of the guidance, the importance of internal control and risk management, group of companies

(ii) Maintaining a sound system of internal control—detailing responsibilities, elements of a sound system of internal control

(iii) Reviewing the effectiveness of internal control—detailing responsibilities, the process for reviewing effectiveness

(iv) The board's statement on internal control

(v) Internal audit

(vi) Appendix—showing assessment of the effectiveness of the company's risk and control processes.

Some essential items of guidance given by the Committee on internal control are mentioned hereunder:

(i) The guidance should be followed by the boards of listed companies in

  (a) Assessing how the companies have applied combined principles,

  (b) Implementing the requirements of the combined code provisions, and

  (c) Reporting on these matters to shareholders in the annual report and accounts.

(ii) The guidance is intended to reflect sound business practice whereby internal control is embedded in the business process, remain relevant over time in the continually business environment, and enable each company to apply it after taking into account of its particular circumstance.

  The guidance requires directors to exercise judgement in reviewing how the company has implemented the requirements of the code relating to internal control and reporting to shareholders thereon.

(iii) The guidance is based on the adoption by a company's board of a risk-based approach to establishing a sound system of internal control and reviewing its effectiveness. This should be incorporated by the company within its normal management and governance process.

(iv) Internal control should ensure reliability of internal and external reporting and compliance with laws and regulations.

(v) Effective financial controls including the maintenance of proper accounting records are an important element of internal control. They should ensure that the company is not unnecessarily exposed to avoidable financial risks. They also should contribute in safeguarding of assets, including prevention and detection of fraud.

(vi) The board is responsible for the company's system of internal control. It should set appropriate policies on internal control and seek regular assurance which would enable it to satisfy itself that the system is functioning effectively. The board must further ensure that the system of internal control is effective in managing risks.

(vii) The board's deliberation should include consideration of the factors, e.g., (a) the nature and extent of the risks facing the company, (b) the extent and categories of risk which is acceptable for the company to bear, (c) the likelihood of the risks materializing, (d) the company's ability to reduce the incidence and impacts on the business of risks, and (e) the costs of operating particular controls relative to the benefit obtained in managing the related risks.

(viii) It is the responsibility of the management to implement the board policies on risk and control. Management should identify and evaluate the risks for consideration by the board and design, operate and monitor a suitable system of internal control to implement the board adopted policy.

(ix) All employees have some responsibility for internal control as part of their accountability for achieving objectives. They should have requisite knowledge, skills, information and authority to establish, operate and monitor the system of internal control.

(x) An effective internal control system should facilitate efficient operation; help ensure the quality of internal and external reporting and compliance with applicable laws and regulations.

(xi) The internal control system should reflect its control environment which includes control activities, information and communication process, and processes for monitoring the continuing effectiveness of the system.

(xii) The system should be embedded in the operations of the company, be capable of responding quickly to evolving risks to the business, and include procedure for reporting immediately to the appropriate levels of management about any significant failure or weakness in the system for corrective action.

(xiii) A sound internal control system should provide reasonable assurance that a company would not be hindered in achieving its business objectives or in the orderly and legitimate conduct of its business.

(xiv) Reviewing the effectiveness of internal control is an essential part of the board's responsibilities. Management should be accountable to the board for monitoring the system of internal control and assuring compliance to the board.

(xv) The role of the board committee in the review process would be decided by the board. It should take the responsibility for disclosures on internal control in the annual report and accounts.

(xvi) The board should regularly receive and review reports on internal control. It should undertake an annual assessment for the purpose of making its public statement on internal control to ensure that it has considered all significant aspects of internal control for the company.

(xvii) Internal control considered by the board should include all types of controls including those of an operational and compliance nature, as well as internal financial controls.

(xviii) The board should define the process to be adopted for its review of the effectiveness of internal control. This should encompass both the scope and frequency of the reports received and reviews during the year, and also the process for its annual assessment.

(xix) The reports from management to the board should provide a balanced assessment of the significant risks and the effectiveness of the system of internal control in managing those risks. Any significant control failures or weaknesses identified should be discussed in the reports, including the impact that they have had on the company and the action being taken to rectify them. There should be openness of communication by management with the board on matters relating to risk and control.

(xx) While reviewing reports during the year, the board should:

- (a) Consider what are the significant risks and assess how they have been identified, evaluated and managed;
- (b) Assess the effectiveness of the related system of internal control in managing the significant risks;
- (c) Consider whether necessary actions are being taken promptly to remedy any significant failures or weaknesses; and
- (d) Consider whether the findings indicate a need for more extensive monitoring of internal control system.

(xxi) The board's annual assessment should consider:

- (a) The changes since the last annual assessment in the nature and extent of significant risks, and the company's ability to respond to changes in its business and the external environment,
- (b) The scope and quality of management's ongoing monitoring of risks and of the system of internal control, and the work of its internal audit functions;
- (c) The extent and frequency of the communication of the results of the monitoring to the board;
- (d) The incidence of significant control failures or weaknesses and the extent to which they have resulted in unforeseen outcomes or contingencies, and a material impact on the company's financial performance; and
- (e) The effectiveness of the company's public reporting processes.

(xxii) Should the board become aware at any time of a significant failure or weakness in internal control, the board should determine how this failure arose and reassess the effectiveness of the management's ongoing process for designing, operating and monitoring the system of internal control.

(xxiii) In its narrative statement of how the company has applied combined code principle, the board should disclose that:

(a) There is an ongoing process for identifying, evaluating and managing the significant risks faced by the company;

(b) It has been in place for the year under review and up to the date of approval of the annual report and accounts;

(c) It is regularly reviewed by the board and accords with the guidance in this document. This disclosure should also include an acknowledgement by the board about its responsibility for setting up and reviewing the system of internal control.

(xxiv) The board should summarize the process it has applied in reviewing the effectiveness of the system and also disclose the process of application of the internal control aspects in the annual report and accounts.

(xxv) The board should ensure that disclosures provide meaningful and high level information.

(xxvi) The board of a company that does not have an internal audit function should assess the need for such a function annually. Where there is an internal audit function, the board should annually review its scope of work, authority and resources.

(xxvii) If the company does not have an internal audit function and the board has not reviewed the need for one, the listing rules require the board to disclose these facts.

Besides the above guidance, the Committee, for assessing the effectiveness of the company's risk and control processes, prescribed certain questionnaire for the board to consider and discuss with management when regularly reviewing the reports on internal control and carrying out its annual assessments.

In order to understand the standards of governance desired for implementation in Indian corporate houses, various recommendations have been submitted by several National Committees on principles of corporate governance and code of best practice. These Committees are:

(i) CII Code of desirable Corporate Governance (1998)

(ii) Kumar Mangalam Birla Committee (2000)

(iii) Naresh Chandra Committee (2002)

(iv) N R Narayana Murthy Committee (2003)

(v) J J Irani Committee (2005)

All the above Committees recommended the codes of best practices more or less in the same lines as the recommendations of the International Committees.

23.8 LEGAL AND REGULATORY FRAMEWORK OF CORPORATE GOVERNANCE FOR MANAGEMENT CONTROL

The issue of accountability of management is fundamental to the concept of the company and that the mechanism through which it should work must be prescribed by law. The legal framework of the countries all over the world has always intended that the management should be accountable to the directors who in turn, should be accountable to the stakeholders. A need was felt by the industrialized countries viz. the USA, the UK, Germany, Japan, France, etc., for legislation of corporate governance, particularly in regard to the financial system due to the lack of accountability of the corporate management consequent to the several scams and lack of management control which had shaken the governance systems in the companies of these countries.

In India, the regulatory and legal framework of corporate governance has been implemented through:

(i) Securities and Exchange Board of India (SEBI) as the government appointed regulator and monitoring agency; and
(ii) Amendments to the Companies Act, 1956.

23.8.1 Clause 49 of the Listing Agreement

SEBI introduced a Clause 49 of the Listing Agreement of the stock exchanges on 21st February, 2000, specifying the principles of corporate governance. Thereafter, six circulars were issued during the period 2000 – 2003, detailing the provisions of corporate governance, its applicability, reporting requirements, and amendments to Clause 49. These circulars were superseded and replaced by a new circular dated 29th October, 2004 which made the overhaul of Clause 49 of the Listing Agreement.

The latest revised Clause 49 contains the regulations regarding various aspects of corporate governance. It has 7 (seven) sub-clauses and 4 (four) Annexure. The items included in sub-clauses are: board of directors, audit committee, subsidiary companies, disclosures, CEO and CFO certification, Report on corporate governance, and Compliance. The items included in the Annexure are: (IA) Information to be placed before board of directors, (IB) Format of quarterly compliance report on corporate governance, (IC) Suggested list of items to be included in the report on corporate governance in the annual report of companies, (ID) Non-mandatory requirements.

With all the revisions, modifications, and new requirements included in the revised Clause 49 of the Listing Agreement, SEBI has played a significant role in uplifting the standards of corporate governance in this country.

23.8.2 Amendments to the Companies Act, 1956

Some of the important amendments to the Companies Act, which have a direct bearing on improvement in the standards of corporate governance, are as follows:

The Companies (Amendment) Act, 1999

(i) Buy back of shares (Section 77A)
(ii) Issue of sweat equity shares (Section 79A)

(iii) Establishment of Investor Education and Protection Fund [Section 205(c)]
(iv) Liberalization of Inter-corporate loans and investment norms

The Companies (Amendment) Act, 2000

(i) Penalties increased by almost ten times for non-compliance in various Sections of the Act
(ii) Issue of shares with differential rights (Section 86)
(iii) Passing of resolutions by postal ballot (Section 192A)
(iv) Directors' Responsibility Statement [Section 217(2AA)]
(v) Additional powers and duties of auditors (Section 227)
(vi) Minimum number of directors including election of small shareholders' director (Section 252)
(vii) Maximum number of directorships in companies reduced from 20 to 15 (Section 275)
(viii) Audit Committee (Section 292A):

The Companies (Amendment) Act, 2001

(i) Liberalization of buy back norms

All the above amendments to the Companies Act have increased manifold the duties and responsibilities of directors in the companies in order to improve the standards of corporate governance.

We now discuss hereunder, three most important provisions and enactments included in the Clause 49 of the Listing Agreement (SEBI) as well as The Companies (Amendment) Act, 2000 as they have a direct bearing on management control system of a listed corporate.

CEO and CFO certification [*Clause 49 of the Listing Agreement* (*SEBI*)]

The CEO, i.e. the managing director or manager appointed in terms of the Companies Act, 1956 and the CFO, i.e. the whole time finance director or any other person heading the finance function discharging that function shall certify to the board that:

(a) They have reviewed financial statements and the cash flow statement for the year and that to the best of their knowledge and belief:
   (i) these statements do not contain any materially untrue statement or omit any material fact or contain statements that might be misleading;
   (ii) these statements together present a true and fair view of the company's affairs and are in compliance with existing accounting standards, applicable laws and regulations.

(b) There are, to the best of their knowledge and belief, no transactions entered into by the company during the year which are fraudulent, illegal or violative of the company's code of conduct.

(c) They accept responsibility for establishing and maintaining internal controls and that they have evaluated the effectiveness of the internal control systems of the company and they have disclosed to the auditors and the audit committee, deficiencies in the design or operation of internal controls, if any, of which they are aware and the steps they have taken or propose to take to rectify these deficiencies.

(d) They have indicated to the auditors and the audit committee:

(i) significant changes in internal control during the year;

(ii) significant changes in accounting policies during the year and that the same have been disclosed in the notes to the financial statements; and

(iii) instances of significant fraud of which they have become aware and the involvement therein, if any, of the management or an employee having a significant role in the company's internal control system.

Directors' responsibility statement [Section 217(2AA) of the Companies (Amendment) Act, 2000]

Under this Section the board's report shall include a 'directors' Responsibility Statement' indicating therein:

(a) That in the preparation of annual accounts, the applicable accounting standards had been followed along with proper explanation relating to material departures;

(b) That the directors had selected such accounting policies and applied them consistently and made judgements and estimates that are reasonable and prudent so as to give a true and fair view of the state of affairs of the company at the end of the financial year and of the profit or loss of the company for that period;

(c) That the directors had taken proper and sufficient care for the maintenance of adequate accounting records in accordance with the provisions of the Act for safeguarding the assets of the company and for preventing and detecting fraud and other irregularities;

(d) That the directors had prepared the annual accounts on a going concern basis.

Audit committee [Section 292A of the Companies (Amendment) Act, 2000]

1. Every public company having paid up capital of not less than ₹ 50 million shall constitute a committee of the board known as 'audit committee' which shall consist of not less than three directors and such number of other directors as the board may determine of which two-thirds of the total number of members shall be directors, other than managing or whole time directors.
2. Every audit committee constituted under sub-section (1) shall act in accordance with terms of reference to be specified in writing by the board.
3. The members of the audit committee shall elect a chairman from amongst themselves.
4. The annual report of the company shall disclose the composition of the audit committee.
5. The auditors, the internal auditor, if any, and the director in-charge of finance shall attend and participate at meetings of the audit committee but shall not have the right to vote.

6. The audit committee should have discussions with the auditors periodically about internal control systems, the scope of audit including the observations of the auditors and review the half-yearly and annual financial statements before submission to the board and also ensure compliance of internal control systems.
7. The audit committee shall have authority to investigate into any matters in relation to the items specified in this section or referred to it by the board and for this purpose, shall have full access to information contained in the records of the company and external professional advice, if necessary.
8. The recommendations of the audit committee on any matter relating to financial management including the audit report, shall be binding on the board.
9. If the board does not accept the recommendations of the audit committee, it shall record the reasons there for and communicate such reasons to the shareholders.
10. The chairman of the audit committee shall attend the annual general meetings of the company to provide any clarification on matters relating to audit.
11. If a default is made in complying with the provisions of this section, the company, and every officer who is in default, shall be punishable with imprisonment for a term which may extend to one year, or with fine which may extend to ₹ 50000, or with both.

23.9 CONCLUSION

Corporate governance is a system of structuring, operating, and controlling a company with a view to achieving long-term strategic goals to satisfy the stakeholders, viz., shareholders, creditors, employees, customers, suppliers, etc., and complying with the legal and regulatory requirements, besides meeting environmental and local community needs. Although there are some fundamental differences between the governance and management, both corporate governance and management control are interlinked in approach and complimentary to each other. Both corporate governance principles and the principles of management control revolve around the basic inter-related segments. These are: integrity and fairness, transparency and disclosures, and accountability and responsibility. This chapter discussed the importance of corporate governance, stakeholders' expectations, value creation and their impact on management control. In this context, the roles and responsibilities of the directors, Turnbull Committee's recommendations on the code of governance, legal and regulatory framework of corporate governance pertaining to management control system have also been dealt with in this chapter.

REVIEW QUESTIONS

23.1 Define corporate governance? What are the fundamental distinctions between governance and management?

23.2 Discuss the principles of corporate governance as an aid to management control?

23.3 Who are the stakeholders of a company? What are their expectations towards the company?

23.4 Explain the roles and responsibilities of directors of a company?

23.5 Name some of the international and national committees that recommended the principles of corporate governance and code of best practices in the organizations?

23.6 Discuss the Turnbull Committee Report (1999) recommending various aspects of internal control systems and procedures to be followed by an organisation towards effective management control system?

23.7 Discuss the legal and regulatory framework of corporate governance for management control in India?

23.8 Write short notes on:

(a) Clause 49 of the Listing Agreement

(b) Amendments to the Companies Act, 1956.

Appendix I

Total Quality Management Systems

Organizational Infrastructure

- Strategic business units
- Personnel support for quality assurance
- Responsibility distribution for quality assurance
- Dedicated team for quality management

Management Style and Work culture

- Management style of functioning
- Work culture to work as a team
- Recognition of value system
- Vigorous customer attention
- Confidence of stakeholders
- Continuous improvement process

Control Processes

- Bench marking
- Bench trending
- Target costing
- Activity based costing
- Quality costing
- Life cycle costing
- Process quality teaming
- Budgeting and budgetary control
- Standard costing and variance analysis
- Marginal costing
- Auditing
- Project management and control

Rewards and Recognition

- Consistency and quality performance
- Various methods of recognition for quality assurance

Communication and Coordination

- Free and fair communication
- Involvement of all employees for quality assurance
- Training in TQM

Appendix II

Product Matrix Organization

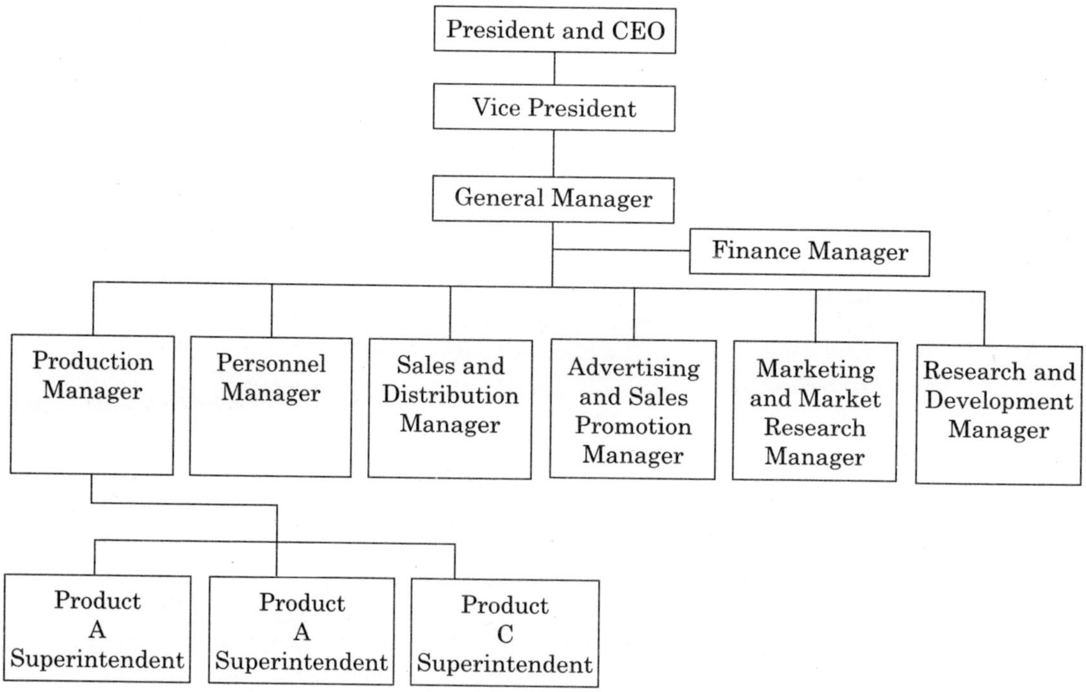

Appendix III

Formal Control System for Adaptive Organization

Organizational Infrastructure

- To be formed and dissolved whenever required

Management Style and Work Culture

- To provide opportunities to employees to receive:
  - (a) Global awareness
  - (b) Continuous learning and training
  - (c) Flexibility towards adjustment, and
  - (d) Acceptance of new assignments and responsibilities

Formal Control Processes

- To concentrate on:
  - (a) Organization's vision
  - (b) Business strategy
  - (c) Proper information system

Rewards and Recognition

- To motivate employees to achieve the goals and objectives of the organization

Integration and Coordination

- To achieve high level of awareness, skill, commitment and integrity within employees for attaining goals and objectives of the organization

Appendix IV

Informal Control System for Adaptive Organization

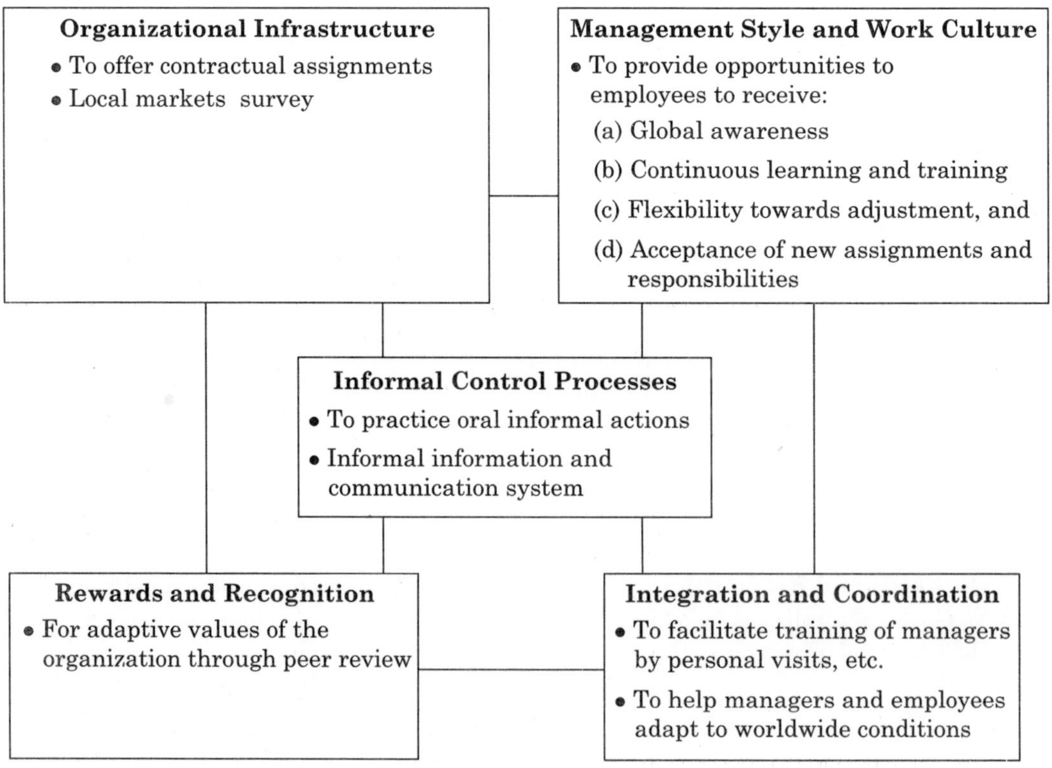

Appendix V

General Benchmarking Process

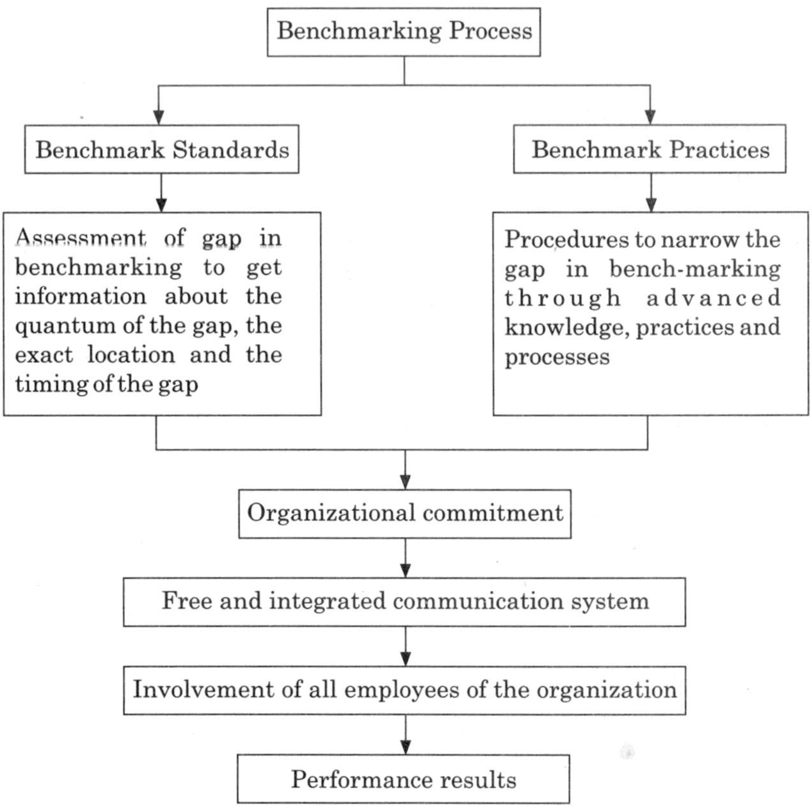

Appendix VI

Quality Process Teaming Structure

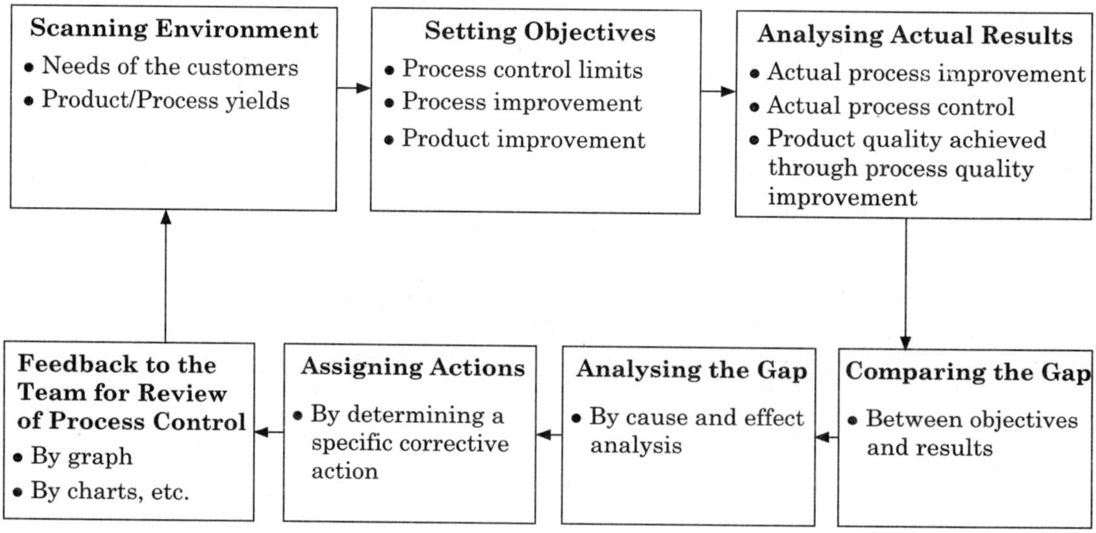

Glossary

Accounting Rate of Return (ARR) or Return On Investment (ROI) method: This method uses accounting information as revealed by the financial statements, to measure the profitability of an investment project. The ARR is found out by dividing the average post-tax profit by the average investment.

Activity Based Costing: Activity based costing (ABC) is a system that focuses on activities as the fundamental cost objects and uses the cost of these activities for compiling the costs of products and other cost objects. The product cost is built up from the cost of the specific activities undertaken to manufacture it.

Angle of Incidence: It is the angle between sales and total cost line. This angle is an indicator of profit-earning capacity of the firm over the break even point sales.

Audit: Audit is the examination and verification of records and evidences kept by an organization, by a professional or a group of professionals to confirm whether the records and evidences exhibit a true and fair view of the state of affairs of the organization.

Audit Evidence: It is a kind of information used by the auditor to determine whether the financial statements being audited are in accordance with the established rules and regulations.

Balanced Score Card: It takes into account financial and non-financial measures, short-term and long-term goals, external goals, internal improvements, past outputs, and on going requirements, as the indicators of future performance. It plays an important role in strategy implementation and performance measurement.

Basic Standard: It is the standard established for use over a long period from which a current standard can be developed.

Bench Trending: Bench trending includes a projection of the critical market conditions and the consumer preference variables. It identifies consumer preference, new entrants, innovation threats and other market critical variables for long-term success of the organization.

Benchmarking: Benchmarking is a continuous process of comparing products and operations against the best practices in the industry.

Break Even Chart: It is the chart which shows the profitability or otherwise of a firm at various levels of activity. It indicates the point at which neither profit nor loss is made.

Budget: The Terminology (CIMA-London) defines a budget as "a plan quantified in monetary terms, prepared and approved prior to a defined period of time, usually showing planned income to be generated and/or expenditure to be incurred during that period and the capital to be employed to attain a given objective".

Budget Centre: A budget centre is a section of an organization developed for the purpose of budgetary control, and is intended to facilitate formulation of various budgets with the help of head of the department.

Budget Manual: It is a written document which contains standing instructions regarding the procedures to be followed at the time of budget preparation.

Budget Period: It is the period for which a budget is prepared and used. The budget period usually covers one year.

Budgetary Control: As per CIMA-London Terminology, "Budgetary Control is the establishment of budgets, relating the responsibilities of executives to the requirements of a policy, and the continuous comparison of actual with budgeted results, either to secure by individual action the objective of that policy or to provide a basis for its revision."

Carryovers: It refers to an annual carryover of a part of the amount determined by the bonus formula to the bonus pool. The board of directors decides the percentage to be carried every year.

Continuous Process Improvement (CPI): It is the philosophy of doing business in such a way that every member of the organization is encouraged to strive and serve the customers efficiently.

Contribution: Contribution or gross margin is the difference between sales value and the variable costs.

Corporate Governance: Corporate governance is a system of structuring, operating, and controlling a company with a view to achieving long-term strategic goals to satisfy the stakeholders, viz., shareholders, creditors, employees, customers, suppliers, etc., and complying with the legal and regulatory requirements, besides meeting environmental and local community needs.

Cost Audit: It is defined as a statutory audit conducted by an independent cost and works accountant as per provisions of Section 233B of the Companies Act, 1956, to verify the cost of production of a particular product on the basis of accounts as regards utilization of material or labour or other items of costs, maintained by the company.

Cost Centre: A cost centre is a location, function or items of equipment in respect of which costs may be ascertained and related to cost units for control purposes.

Cost Driver: A cost driver is an allocation base which is selected keeping in view the major activities of the firm, and how each item of cost is linked up with these activities at different levels.

Cost Driver Analysis: It is a useful technique which integrates the problem-solving and analytical tools for quality and process improvement. It generates information needed to reduce costs and improve the overall financial performance of the organization.

Critical Path: It is the longest continuous path of activities through a network diagram from beginning to end of a project. The total time required for critical path is the shortest duration of the project.

Critical Path Method (CPM): It is a network planning technique that is activity-oriented, used for planning and scheduling a project. It is possible to complete a project in a very short duration by expanding a large amount of resources. In CPM, the main objective is to obtain a trade-off between the cost and completion date for a project.

Current Standard: It is a standard which is established for use over a short period of time and is related to current conditions.

Deferred Payments: Under this system, the bonus is calculated annually, but the employees receive the payments over a period of years.

Depreciation: It is the nature of a recovery of sunk cost of an asset due to the past decision.

Differential Cost: Differential cost is the additional cost incurred or to be incurred arising out of a decision taken by the management. It is also called incremental cost which is the result of a management decision as compared to not taking such decision.

Discounted Payback (DPB): It is defined as the number of years required in recovering the cash outlay of the project on the present value basis.

Economic Exposure: Economic exposure is the exchange rate exposure of a multinational company's cash flow to changes in the real exchange rate.

Environment Audit: Environmental audit is a management tool to objectively and systematically evaluate environment management systems in an organization. It examines the company's performance as against its policy, and is undertaken with reference to performance of personnel, technology, system and documentation and how these are related to relevant standards of practice.

Ethics: Ethics means a system of moral principles, the basis for deciding right and wrong actions, and implies customs, habits, and noble traits in character, discipline, culture and disposition.

Expected Standard: Expected standard is that standard which is anticipated to be attained during a future specified budget period.

Financial Audit: It is defined as a critical statutory review by an independent auditor to examine the correctness of financial statements and to establish whether they present a true and fair view of the company's financial position on a particular date. It is a statutory audit conducted by an independent statutory auditor at the end of every financial year.

Fixed Budget: A fixed budget is a budget which is designed to remain unchanged irrespective of the volume of output.

Fixed Costs: Fixed costs are the costs that remain fixed or constant irrespective of the volume of output or activity. Fixed costs are considered as period costs.

Flexible Budget: A flexible budget is a budget which, by recognizing the difference in behaviour between fixed and variable costs in relation to fluctuations in output, turnover, or other variable factors, is designed to change appropriately with such fluctuations.

Gantt Chart: It is a graphical representation of various jobs, tasks or activities across time periods. Individual jobs, tasks or activities are described on the left hand of the graphical chart, and the scheduled times for accomplishing each job, task or activity are shown by open bars and plotted along a horizontal time (calendar) scale.

Ideal Standard: An ideal standard is that standard which can be attained under the most favourable conditions. This standard is fixed with very high degree of efficiency which is almost impossible to attain.

Incremental Profit: It represents the contribution to the total profit of the firm which is specifically traceable to the alternative. Incremental profit = Incremental revenues – Incremental costs.

Information Asymmetry: When the principal (manager) has inadequate information about the activities of the agents (subordinates), he cannot ascertain the agent's contribution to the company's results. This situation is called 'information asymmetry'.

Internal Audit: Internal audit is an independent appraisal function established within an organization to examine and evaluate its activities as a service to the organization.

Internal Rate of Return (IRR) Method: It is a discounted cash flow technique which takes account of the magnitude and timing of cash flows. The IRR is that discount rate which equates investment outlay with the present value of inflows received after a period of time.

Just-In-Time (JIT): It is a Japanese philosophy which is used for managing all types of inventory, purchase, and production functions in an organization. The main purpose of this philosophy is to reduce inefficiency and unproductive time and cost in the production process.

Life Cycle Costing: It is defined as the accumulation of costs for activities that occur over the entire life cycle of a product from inception to abandonment by the manufacturing organization and the customers. It provides a framework for managing the cost and performance of a product over duration of its life.

Limiting Factor or Key Factor or Principal Budget Factor: CIMA-London Terminology defines a key factor or limiting factor or principal budget factor as "a factor which at a particular time or over a period will limit the activities of an organization and which is therefore, taken into account in preparing budgets".

Management Audit: Management audit is defined as an examination of the conditions and a diagnosis of deficiencies with recommendations for correcting them.

Management By Objectives (MBO): MBO is a process of joint setting of goals/ objectives by the superior and the subordinate, and clarifying on the objectives itself. It involves both economic performance and human performance.

Management Control System: Management control system is a set of interrelated communication structure that facilitates the processing of information to assist managers in coordinating the parts and attaining the purpose of an organization on a continuous basis. It is imperative for the successful attainment of corporate goals and objectives.

Margin of Safety: It is represented by excess sales over and above the break-even point sales.

Master Budget: It is defined as a budget which is prepared from the functional budgets in summary form. When all functional budgets are prepared, they are summarized to produce budgeted profit and loss account, and budgeted balance sheet.

Moral Hazard: A situation in which the agent misinterprets private information to his principal due to divergence in preference is termed as 'moral hazard'.

Multi-product Break-even Chart: In this chart it is possible to draw a break even chart for the company as a whole considering all products in one chart. In such case the BEP is where the average contribution line cuts the fixed cost line, assuming proportions of sales mix remaining unchanged.

Net Present Value (NPV) Method: It is a process of calculating the present value of a project's cash flows, using the opportunity cost of capital as the discount rate, and finding out the net present value by subtracting the initial investment from the present value of cash flows.

Normal Standard: It is the average standard which is anticipated, can be attained over a future period of time, preferably long enough to cover a trade cycle.

Opportunity Costs: These are the costs that represent the benefit foregone in sacrificing the best alternative.

Payback (PB) Period: It is defined as the number of years required to recover the original cash outlay invested in a project.

Performance Shares: Under this incentive plan employees are awarded a specified number of shares when they meet specific long-term goals. They are given based on performance and are not affected by increase or decrease in stock price.

Phantom Stock Plan: This plan provides incentives to the executives either in the form of cash or shares. After a specified date, the manager is entitled to receive the amount of fair market value of phantom shares credited to his account.

Process Quality Teaming: It is a popular concept which combines several successful total quality techniques into a cybernetic control system with features like, feedback loops, action plans, and environmental scanning.

Profitability Index (PI) or Benefit-Cost (B/C) Ratio: It is the ratio of the present value of cash inflows, at the required rate of return, to the initial cash outflow of the investment.

Profit-Volume Graph (P/V Graph)/Profit Chart: It is the chart that shows the relationship between profit and volume

Profit-Volume Ratio: This ratio expresses the relation of contribution to sales.

Project: A project is a package of time bound, scheduled and assembled activities dedicated to the attainment of a specific objective of successful completion of a work, on time and within the allotted budget. It first emerges as a concept and follows various stages, till it gets commissioned.

Project Audit: Project audit is a planned and documented activity performed by qualified personnel to determine by investigation, examination and evaluation of objective evidence, the adequacy and compliance with established procedures or applicable documents, and effectiveness of implementation. It is conducted to identify problems in the project and to prevent minor discrepancies from becoming major problems.

Project Evaluation and Review Technique (PERT): It is an event-oriented network diagramming technique used for planning and scheduling a project. PERT uses the concept of events which are points in time indicating the achievement of certain stages in the project.

Quality Costing: It is a system which monitors and accumulates the costs incurred by a firm in maintaining or improving product quality.

Relevant Costs: These are the future costs which have not been incurred. For a cost to be relevant, it must be a future cost, and must be affected by the decision being taken or not taken by the management.

Replacement Cost: The current value of the asset is called replacement cost.

Reward System: It is an important mechanism that encourages and motivates managers to achieve objectives. It is meant to induce a high level of individual, group or organizational performance to achieve the overall goals and objectives of the company.

Slack: The difference between the budget amount and the best estimate is known as 'slack'.

Social Audit: Social audit is defined as a systematic attempt to identify, analyze, measure, evaluate and monitor the effect of an organization's operations on society. Turnbull Committee (1995) defines social audit as 'the process whereby an enterprise measures and reports on its performance in meeting its declared social, community, or environmental objectives'.

Special Audit: Section 233A of the Companies Act, 1956 empowers the Central Government to call for a 'special audit' where the Central Government has reason to believe that the (a) affairs of the company are not being managed on sound business principles or according to prudent commercial practices; or (b) the company is being managed in a manner likely to cause serious injury or damage to the interests of trade, industry or business to which it pertains; or (c) the financial position of the company is such as might endanger its solvency.

Standard Cost: Standard cost is a predetermined amount of what cost ought to be incurred for a given level of activity under specified condition.

Standard Costing: Standard costing is a technique which uses standards for costs and revenues for the purpose of control through variance analysis.

Stock Appreciation Rights: This incentive plan gives the executives the right to receive cash payments based on the increase in value of stock from the time of the award until a specified future date depending on market price.

Stock Option: A stock option gives an executive the right to buy a certain number of shares in the company at a fixed price for a certain number of years.

Strategic Cost Management (SCM): Strategic cost management is defined as the application of costing information to the development and implementation of a company's strategy.

Strategic Positioning Analysis: It refers to the way in which an organization positions itself against the competitors in the market. A company can choose to compete in the market either on the basis of cost leadership or differentiation. It means that in order to remain competitive, a company has to offer its products either at a lower cost or with a greater number of features.

Sunk Cost: It is the cost incurred in purchasing a capital asset. Depreciation is in the nature of a recovery of sunk cost due to the past management decision.

Target Costing: Target cost is the maximum manufacturing cost of a product. Target costing is done to encourage various design and production departments to find less expensive ways of achieving similar or better features and quality of product.

Total Bonus Pool: It refers to a system wherein shareholders approve on the formula to be used for deciding the total bonus to be paid in a given year.

Total Quality Control (TQC): It is a management process based on the premise that quality costs are minimized with zero defects. The reduction of failure costs due to improved quality outweighs additional prevention and appraisal costs.

Total Quality Management (TQM): TQM is a management concept that directs the collective efforts of all employees and officers towards satisfying customer expectations by continuously improving the operations management processes and products.

Transaction Exposure: This exposure indicates the exchange rate exposure that a multinational company has in its cross-border transactions when the settlement of transactions is made at a future date.

Transfer Price: A transfer price is defined as the price that is assumed to have been charged by one department of a company for products and services it provides to another department of the same company, in order to calculate each department's profit and loss separately.

Translation Exposure: The erosion or appreciation in the value of earnings, assets and liabilities is referred to as Translation exposure.

Value Chain Analysis: Value chain analysis is a tool of strategic analysis that can be used to identify areas in which value can be enhanced for customers or costs can be reduced. It helps an organization to gain competitive advantage.

Variable Costs or Marginal Costs: Variable or marginal costs are the costs that tend to be a constant amount per unit. For example, cost of direct materials, direct labour, direct expenses. Variable costs are considered as product costs.

Variance: The deviation of actual from standard is called 'variance'. When actual cost is less than the standard cost, it is known as 'favourable variance'. When actual cost is more than the standard costs, it is known as 'unfavourable or adverse variance'.

Zero-Based Budgeting (ZBB): It refers to the 'nil' budget as the starting point. This budget starts with the premise that the budget for the next period is 'zero' so long as the demand for a function, process, project or activity is not justified for each rupee. The assumption of the top management is that without such justification no spending will be allowed.

Bibliography

Auditing and Assurance, Institute of Chartered Accountants of India (ICAI), New Delhi,

Agarwal, S., *Corporate Governance and Audit Committee, Chartered Secretary*, October 2003.

Allen, W.T., "Redefining the Role of Outside Directors", Monks, R.A.G., and Minow, N., Eds., *Corporate Governance*, Blackwell Publishers, Massachusetts, USA, 1995.

Allies, Michael, and Dater, Srikant, "Strategic Transfer Pricing", *Management Science*, April 1998.

Anthony, Robert N. and Govindrajan, Vijay, *Management Control System*, Irwin Publications, Washington, DC, 1995.

Apte, Prakash G., *International Financial Management*, Tata McGraw-Hill, New Delhi, 2006.

Atkinson, Anthony A., "Organization Control Systems for the Nineties", *CMA Magazine*, June 1992.

Baetge, J. and Thiele, S., "Disclosure and Auditing as Affecting Corporate Governance," Hopt, K.J., Kanda, H., Roe, M.J., Wymeersch, E., and Prigge, S. (Eds.), *Comparative Corporate Governance: The state of the art and emerging research*, (*Part II*), Oxford University Press, New York, 1998.

Banerjee, B., *Regulation of Corporate Accounting & Reporting in India*, The World Press, Kolkata, 2002.

Banerjee, B., *Financial Policy and Management Accounting*, Prentice-Hall of India, New Delhi, 2005.

Banerjee, B., *Cost Accounting*, The World Press, Kolkata, 1997.

Bartol, Kathryn, M. and Martin, C. David., *Management* Irwin, McGraw-Hill, New York, 1998.

Basel Committee Publications.

Basu, S.P. and Das, M., *Cost and Management Accounting,* Rabindra Library, Kolkata, 2005.

Bhattacharyya, S.K., "Management Control Systems and Conflicts—A Framework for Analysis and Resolution", *International Studies of Management & Organization,* Winter 1973–74.

Blocker, J. Edward, Chen, H. Kung, and Lin, W. Thomas., *Cost Management: A Strategic Emphasis,* McGraw-Hill, New York, 1999.

Burns, William J. Jr. and McFarlan, F. Warren, "Information Technology Puts Power in Control Systems", *Harvard Business Review*, 65(5) September/October, 1987.

Chandra, Prasanna, *Financial Management: Theory and Practice,* Tata McGraw-Hill, New Delhi, 2001.

Chandra, Prasanna, *Projects Planning, Analysis, Selection, Financing, Implementation, and Review*, Tata McGraw-Hill, New Delhi, 2006.

Chandratre, K.R., "Corporate Governance vis-a-vis The Listing Agreement–II", *Chartered Secretary*, October 2003.

Cross, Rob, and Majikes, Matthew, "Activity-based Costing in Commercial Lending: The Case of Signet Bank", *Commercial Lending Review*, 12(4).

Das, S.C., "Ethics in Governance Practices in Corporates–Some issues and implications," *The Management Accountant*, April 2006.

Das, S.C., *Corporate Governance in India: An Evaluation*, Prentice-Hall of India, New Delhi, 2008.

Das, S.C., *Corporate Governance: Codes, Systems, Standards and Practices*, PHI Learning, New Delhi, 2009.

Eisenhardt, Kathleen M., "Agency Theory: An Assessment and Review", *Academy of Management Review*, vol. 14, 1994.

"Environment Audit", Institute of Cost & Works Accountants of India, 1999.

Fernando, A.C., *Corporate Governance: Principles, Policies and Practices*, Dorling Kindersley (India), Delhi, 2006.

Fisher, Joseph G., "Contingency Theory, Management Control Systems and Firm Outcomes: Past Results and Future Direction", *Behavioral Research in Accounting*, (Supplement), 10, 1998.

Fowler, Alan, "Feedback and Feedforward as Systemic Frameworks for Operations Control", *International Journal of Operations & Production Management*, 19(2) 1999.

Franks, J. and Mayer, C. "Corporate Ownership and Control in the UK, Germany and France", Chew, D.H. (Ed.), *Studies in International Corporate Finance and Governance Systems—A Comparison of the US, Japan and Europe*, Oxford University Press, New York, 1997.

Gerhart, Barry and Milkovich, George T., "Organizational Differences in Managerial Compensation and Financial Performance", *Academy of Management Journal*, 13(4) 1990.

Hart, O., "Mechanisms for Controlling Management—Some theories and implications", Keasy, K., Thomsom, S., and Wright, M. (Eds.), *Corporate Governance*, Edward Elgar Cheltanham, UK, 1999.

Jackson, John B.H., "Board Structures", Midgley, K. (Ed.), *Management Accountability and Corporate Governance*, Macmillan, London, 1982.

Jaworski, Bernard J., "Towards a Theory of Marketing Control: Environmental Context, Control Types and Consequences", *Journal of Marketing*, 52, July 1998.

Kald, Magnus, Nilsson, Fredrik, and Rapp, Birger, "On Strategy and Management Control: The Importance of Classifying the Strategy of the Business", *British Journal of Management*, 11(3) September 2000.

Kaplan, R. and Atkinson., *Advanced Management Accounting*, PHI Learning, Delhi, 2007.

Kerin, R.A., Mahajan, V., and Varadarajan, P.R., *Strategic Market Planning*, Allyn & Bacom, Boston, 1990.

Lebas, Michel and Weigenstein, Jane, "Management Control: The Roles of Rules, Markets and Culture", *Journal of Management Studies*, May 1986.

Maciarello, Joshep A. and Kirby, J. Calvin, *Management Control Systems*, Prentice-Hall of India, New Delhi, 1997.

Macintosh, Norman and Scapens, Robert, "Management Accounting and Control Systems: A Structuration Theory Analysis", *Journal of Management Accounting Research*, 3, Fall 91.

Malina, Mary A. and Selto, Frank H., "Communicating and Controlling Strategy: An Empirical Study of the Effectiveness of the Balanced Scorecard", *Journal of Management Accounting Research*, 2001.

Mamoria, C.B., *Personnel Management*, Himalaya Publishing, 1994.

Marsh, A. and Rosewell, R., "A Question of Disclosure," Midgley, K. (Ed.), *Management Accountability and Corporate Governance*, Macmillan Press, London, 1982.

Merchant, Kenneth A., *Modern Management Control Systems: Text and Cases*, Prentice-Hall, New Jersey, 1997.

Meredith, Jack R. and Mantel, Samuel J. Jr., *Project Management—A Managerial Approach*, John Wiley & Sons, New Jersey, 2000.

Midgley, Kenneth, "To Whom Should the Board be Accountable and for What?" Midgley, K. (Ed.), *Management Accountability and Corporate Governance*, Macmillan Press, London, 1982.

Myer, John N., *Financial Statement Analysis*, Prentice-Hall of India, New Delhi.

"Operations Management and Control", The Institute of Cost & Works Accountants of India, 1996.

Pandey, I.M., *Financial Management*, Vikas Publishing, Noida, UP, 2003.

Pandey, T.N., "Ethics in Corporate Governance", *Chartered Secretary*, January 2004.

Pass, Christopher, "Transfer Pricing in Multinational Companies", *Management Accounting: Magazine for Chartered Management Accountants*, 72(8), September 1994.

Paul, Samual, *Managing Development Program*, West View Press, Colorado, 1992.

"Principles of Management Control Systems", ICFAI Center for Management Research, Hyderabad, 2006.

"Project Management and Control", The Institute of Cost & Works Accountants of India, 1996.

Raj, Veliyath and Hermanson, Heather M., "Organizational Control Systems: Matching Controls with Organizational Levels", *Review of Business*, 18(2) Winter 97.

Ramanathan, Kavasseri, "A Proposed Framework for Designing Management Control Systems in Not-for-profit Organizations", *Financial Accountability of Management*, Summer 1995.

"Revised Clause 49 of The Listing Agreement by SEBI", *Chartered Secretary*, November 2004.

Robbins, Stephen P., *Organizational Behaviour*, Prentice-Hall of India, New Delhi, 1999.

Shank, John K., "Strategic Cost Management: New Wine, or Just New Bottles", *Journal of Management Accounting and Research*, Fall 1989.

Sharma, Subhash, *Management Control Systems, Text and Cases*, Tata McGraw-Hill, New Delhi, 1997.

Snavely, Kay B. and Snavely, William B., "Communicating Control: Formal and Informal Sources and Processes", *Academy of Management Proceedings*, 1990.

"Strategic Management and Marketing", The Institute of Cost & Works Accountants of India, 2005.

Sundararaman, S., "Accountability—The Global View", *The Chartered Accountant*, August 2000.

Taxmann's Companies Act As Amended by Companies (Amendment) Act 2000, *Taxmann Allied Services*, New Delhi, 2001.

TaxMann's SEBI Manual, 2005.

Teall, Howard D., "Winning with Strategic Management Control Systems", *CMA Magazine*, 66(2), March 1992.

Tricker, Bob, "The Independent Director" Midgley, K. (Ed.), *Management Accountability and Corporate Governance*, Macmillan Press, London, 1982.

Vancil, Richard F., "What Kind of Management Control Do You Need?", *Harvard Business Review*, 51, March/April 1973.

Vancil, Richard F., *Decentralization: Managerial Ambiguity by Design*, Dow Jones-Irwin, Homewood Illinios, 1979.

Vernon, Raymond and Wells, Jr. Louis T., *Manager in the International Economy*, Prentice-Hall of India, New Delhi, 1982.

Wichmann, Henry Jr., et al., "Key Variables as a Management Tool", *CMA Magazine*, March 1990.

Wysocili, Robert. K, Beck Jr. Robert, and Crane David B., *Effective Project Management*, John Wiley & Sons, New Jersey, 2000.

Yavitz, Boris and Newman, William H., *Strategy in Action: The Execution, Politics and Payoff of Business Planning*, The Free Press, New York, 1982.

www.sebi.com

Index